WALKING THE LAND,
FEEDING THE FIRE

Walking the Land, Feeding the Fire

Knowledge and Stewardship among the Tłįchǫ Dene

ALLICE LEGAT

FOREWORD BY JOANNE BARNABY

FIRST PEOPLES

New Directions in Indigenous Studies

The University of Arizona Press   Tucson

THE UNIVERSITY OF
ARIZONA PRESS

www.uapress.arizona.edu

Library of Congress Cataloging-in-Publication Data

Legat, Allice.
  Walking the land, feeding the fire : knowledge and stewardship among the Tlicho Dene
/ Allice Legat ; foreword by Joanne Barnaby.
    p. cm.
  Includes bibliographical references and index.
  ISBN 978-0-8165-3009-0 (cloth : alk. paper) 1. Dogrib Indians—Northwest
Territories—Gamètì—History. 2. Dogrib Indians—Northwest Territories—Gamètì—
Folklore. 3. Dogrib Indians—Northwest Territories—Gamètì—Social life and customs.
I. Title.
  E99.T4L44 2012
  398.209719'2–dc23
                                                                    2011048711

Publication of this book is made possible in part by the proceeds of a permanent
endowment created with the assistance of a Challenge Grant from the National
Endowment for the Humanities, a federal agency.

♻

Manufactured in the United States of America on acid-free, archival-quality paper
containing a minimum of 30% post-consumer waste and processed chlorine free.

17 16 15 14 13 12   6 5 4 3 2 1

To the memory of Jimmy Martin, selected by the Regional Elders Committee as their *k'àowo*—traditional leader—because he continues to be considered knowledgeable, kind, fair, thoughtful, yet firm while guiding others in the "right way." Jimmy was always committed to ensuring his descendants would have stories to think with. This commitment was so powerful that during his last few days of life he asked me to continue finding ways to assist the elders in their work to share their way and to support Tłı̨chǫ speakers in learning and documenting oral narratives. He wanted Tłı̨chǫ to work together to learn and experience their land. He loved the Tłı̨chǫ way so much that he wanted their descendents to have the ancestors' stories to think with in Tłı̨chǫ. He wanted young people to know the Tłı̨chǫ way. This book is one small part of doing what he asked. I hope it will spur young people to listen to and learn the stories and to experience their truth while traveling Tłı̨chǫ nèèk'e.

Jimmy Martin outside his home in Behchokǫ̀, 2001.
(Photograph from Tessa Macintosh Photography)

Our stories help us survive.
—MADELAINE CHOCOLATE, 2003

Contents

Illustrations

Maps

Foreword

This publication is long overdue—at least, giving access to the important insights it contains is overdue. I am a bit biased. I have developed a deep friendship with its author, a relationship that had a very tumultuous beginning. In 1986, I was in the early stages of setting up the Dene Cultural Institute, with marching orders from the Dene chiefs and huge expectations from our communities, which were raised significantly because a well-intentioned Canadian premier had made noises about the importance of aboriginal culture and suggested significant financial resources would be available. Of course, that was not to be.

While slugging through a comprehensive planning process with twenty-seven communities in a basement with no light or air in downtown Yellowknife and trying to get our people to understand that it would take time to do $25 million worth of work with only $250,000 annually, I met Allice Legat at a traditional-knowledge working group meeting. Here was this tall, energetic white woman, excited about her new job with the Northern Heritage Society and enthusiastic about working together and living happily ever after. I reacted, big time. I was angry and at an age when I was a bit racist, having learned well from my oppressors. Although I can't remember exactly what I said in the meeting, I was thinking that I was not interested in supporting a white Yellowknife organization that would be competing for meager resources for cultural development. I left the meeting without resolving anything and certainly in no frame of mind to "cooperate." Sometime shortly thereafter Allice showed up in my basement office and said, "Why is it that you hate me?" I simply replied, "Because you are so white." She said, "Oh, OK," and left. Well, that threw me off and made me stop and take a good look at her—and at myself. I do know that is when I became open to her and from then on slowly got to know her. Four years later I recommended her for a term position teaching Native studies with Arctic College, and five years later I hired her to work on one of the many traditional-knowledge projects we were developing.

It became clear early in our working relationship that Allice was different. Within a relatively short period of time of working with Dene elders, she went beyond taking the information and framing it according to her own Euro-Canadian cultural way of thinking. She recognized quickly the importance of relationships—all kinds of relationships—as foundational to a distinct way of knowing and the Dene worldview. Relationships between humans and other life forms and the humility associated with knowing that we humans are inferior in so many ways to others who have no confusion about their place in the world or their responsibilities. Relationships with the spirits, which are just as important, if not more so, than relationships with those who have a physical form. Relationships between people and the understanding that everyone is here for a reason and has a role to play with respect to the circumstances in which he or she born.

Allice was able to "hear" beyond the literal translation of words and to interpret the knowledge and underlying concepts that elude so many. She was open to being challenged and challenging others (as she did with me), and in being so she learned a great deal. The fact that the elders she worked with teased her, "found her a husband," showed patience and respect for her, took her on the land, and shared sacred secrets with her was strong evidence in my mind that they knew she was "getting it." They also remained committed to working with her through their own poor health, and she was at the side of many when they passed on.

Upon reading Allice's manuscript, I remember saying to her that she indeed "got it." And I believe that this book will be the beginning of a new era of understanding the unique insights and understandings available through traditional knowledge. Her approach to her work—training local researchers and sharing full credit with them, carefully verifying with elders not only the information obtained from such research, but the analysis of it, and developing recommendations for moving forward and building on the traditional knowledge acquired—provides a powerful methodology that others would be wise to use.

I am hopeful that this book will help put into proper context the spiritual nature of some traditional knowledge and open the minds and hearts of those who are afraid of such insights.

Joanne Barnaby

Acknowledgments

A considerable number of people have helped me—from the beginning, when I started my research, to the end as I put together this book. I have the deepest respect for the elders I came to know. They are among the most intelligent and scholarly people I have met. It was a great privilege to hear their stories and to travel with them through Tłįchǫ nèèk'e; the depth of their love for Tłįchǫ nèèk'e is always apparent.

I thank Gamètì elders Mary Apple, Madelaine Arrowmaker, Àąwąą, David Chocolate, Elizabeth Chocolate, Madelaine Drybone, Paul Drybone, Andrew Gon, Elizabeth Gon, Pierre Gon, Angelique Mantla, Bella Mantla, Pierre Mantla Jr., Pierre Mantla Sr., Marie Mantla, Harry Mantla, Joe Mantla, Rosalie Mantla, Laiza Mantla, Alphonse Quitte, Elizabeth Quitte, Jane Quitte, Marie Quitte, Amen Tailbone, Rosalie Tailbone, Elise Simpson, Harry Simpson, Jean Wetrade, Paul Wetrade, Rosalie Wetrade, Romie Wetrade, Jimmy Wogary, Bella Zoe, Marie Zoe, and Phillip Zoe.

I am deeply indebted to Behchokǫ̀ elders Elizabeth Chocolate, Rosalie Drybones, Johnny Eyakfwo, Sammy Football, Laiza Germaine, Laiza Koyina, Eddie Lafferty, Matton Mantla, Jimmy Martin, Joe Suzi Mackenzie, Robert Mackenzie, Moise Martin, Elizabeth Michel, Joe Migwi, and Adele Wedawin; to Wekweètì elders Madelaine Judas, Margaret Lafferty, Alexie Arrowmaker, and Louis Whane; as well as to Whatì elders Albert Wedawin, Mary Adele Moosenose, Pierre Beaverhoe, and Dora Nitsiza.

I am most indebted to Jimmy Martin, whom the elders selected to be *k'àowo*, leader, of the Tłįchǫ Regional Elders Committee. He was always honest, straightforward, and clear when giving direction. I am thankful for Adele Wedawin, who had a story and positive words to guide us. Her words helped me through difficult situations more than once. I am deeply honored to have worked with and for Andrew Gon, Jean Wetrade, Marie Zoe, and Madelaine Drybone, who asked me not to write anything until they gave me permission. They wanted me first to listen to and to experience the land with Tłįchǫ and share with the researchers of their choice what I had learned in university. They eventually gave me permission to write. Most of these elders are now with their ancestors. Nevertheless, I can feel them nudging me to continue.

I am extremely grateful to my friends and coworkers, with whom I spent most days between 1993 and 2002 and with whom I worked and visited more sporadically as I was away at university from 2002 to 2005. My interactions were most consistent with Therese Zoe, Louis Zoe, Madelaine Chocolate, Rita Blackduck, and Sally Anne Zoe from Gamètì, as well as with Bobby Gon, Georgina Chocolate, Violet Camsell-Blondin, and John B. Zoe in Behchokǫ̀. They have heard many more stories from elders in Tłįchǫ than I ever will. I came to understand the stories and many of the Tłįchǫ concepts through discussions with them.

Since writing this manuscript, I have had the pleasure of working with more elders and the pleasure of discussing issues in depth with Rita Wetrade (nee Blackduck) in Gamètì, Camilla Nitsiza in Whatì, Moise Rabesca in Behchokǫ̀, and Joseph Judas in Wekweètì.

Between 1993 and 2002, much of my work with the Tłįchǫ was made possible through grants and contributions to the Arctic Institute of North America, the Dene Cultural Institute, and the Dogrib Treaty 11 Council. Many of these grants and contributions came from the Government of Canada's Social Development Program, Royal Commission on Aboriginal Peoples, Environmental Assessment Review Panel, Arctic Environmental Strategy, the Cumulative Impact Monitoring Program, Northwest Territories Protected Area Strategy, and the Social Sciences and Humanities Research Council. Funding was also secured from the Government of the Northwest Territories' Department of Renewable Resources; Department of Education, Culture, and Employment; and Ministry of Aboriginal Affairs. I am also thankful for the private funding from the Walter and Duncan Gordon Foundation, the West Kitikmeot Slave Study Society, and BHP.

A version of chapter 7, "Walking Stories; Leaving Footprints," was first published in *Ways of Walking: Ethnography and Practice on Foot*, edited by Tim Ingold and Jo Lee Vergunst, 35–49 (Aldershot, UK: Ashgate, 2008).

I am full of gratitude for those people who shared their ideas, commented on my work, and provided venues in which I could share my work and gain feedback: David Anderson, Joanne Barnaby, Denise Brown, Georgina Chocolate, Madelaine Chocolate, Debbie DeLancey, Jim Edmondson, Harvey Feit, Julia Harrison, Tim Ingold, Mary McCreadie, Leslie Saxon, Lee Selleck, Jacob Shank, Adrian Tanner, and Rob Wishart. I am thankful to Jim Stauffer, who assisted me with the Dene fonts; Mark Fenwick, who helped with the maps; and Tessa Macintosh, who assisted with the photographs. I am especially grateful to Georgina and Madelaine, who read drafts of what I have written here and explained its contents to key elders.

I owe it to the Tłı̨chǫ elders with whom I worked to express in writing the little bit I have come to understand through their patience and humor. And what I do and do not understand will, I hope, assist their grandchildren in the continuing endeavor to share who they, the Tłı̨chǫ, are.

List of Acronyms

BHP   *Broken Hill Proprietary Company Ltd.*
        (BHP Billiton after 2001)

GNWT   *Government of the Northwest Territories*

NWT   *Northwest Territories*

PAR   *participatory action research*

Tłı̨chǫ Pronunciation Key

Tłı̨chǫ has four vowels—*a, e, i, o*—and four kinds of vowels: plain, nasal, low tone, and nasal low tone. The nasal vowels are: *ą, ę, į, ǫ*; the low-tone vowels: *à, è, ì, ò*; the nasal low-tone vowels: *ą̀, ę̀, į̀, ǫ̀*. The nasal sound is made when air flows through the nose and the mouth; for the low-tone vowels, the voice is deeper, and the air flows through the mouth; for nasal low-tone vowel sounds, the voice is deeper, and the air flows through the nose and mouth. The sounds of most Tłı̨chǫ consonants are similar to the sounds made by consonants in English. The list given here consists of those sounds that require explanation and has been adapted from the Tłı̨chǫ dictionary (Dogrib Divisional Board of Education 1996, i–v). The arrangement of items follows the arrangement in the Tłı̨chǫ dictionary.

?	the "click" sound heard in the expression "ah-ah" or "oh-oh"
ą	similar to the sound in *w<u>an</u>t*
ch	<u>ch</u>air; some dialects sound more like *we<u>ts</u>uit*
ch'	same as <u>ch</u>, but with the "click" sound as part of it; an ejective <u>ch</u>
dl	similar to *<u>gl</u>ue*; at times like *ba<u>dl</u>y*
dz	similar to *a<u>dz</u>e*
e	usually like *s<u>e</u>t*, but after <u>w</u> it is similar to *w<u>oo</u>d*
ę	similar to *s<u>en</u>t*
gh	no similar sound in English; similar to the <u>r</u> sound in the French *rouge*.
gw	similar to *lang<u>ua</u>ge*

ı   same as *skı̲*

ı̨   similar to the sound in *me̲a̲ns*

j   can be as in *je̲t* or *adze̲*, depending on the dialects

k   *ki̲t*; but in some words it is pronounced like x̲ or h̲

k'   same as k̲, but with the "click" sound as part of it; an ejective k̲

kw   same as *qui̲t*

kw'   same as kw̲, but with the "click" sound as part of it; an ejective kw̲

ł   breathy l̲, similar to *fli̲p* or *sli̲p*

o   like *go̲*; some pronounce it like *go̲o̲*

ǫ   similar to the sound in *do̲n't*

t'   same as t̲, but with the "click" sound as part of it; an ejective t̲

tł   similar to *se̲ttle̲* or in some cases more like *clu̲e*

tł'   similar to *tł̲*, but with the "click" sound as part of it; an ejective *tł̲* but with the "click" sound as part of it

ts   like *ca̲ts̲*

ts'   same as ts̲ but with the "click" sound as part of it; an ejective ts̲

wh   breathy wh̲ as in *wh̲en*; wh̲ with a following e̲ sounds like *whirr*

x   no similar sound in English; sounds like a raspy h̲ and similar to the German ch̲ as in *Bach*

zh   similar to *plea̲s̲ure*, but in some dialects sounds more like *plea̲s̲e̲*

WALKING THE LAND,
FEEDING THE FIRE

Introduction

Understanding a Little Bit

Figure I.1. Tłįchǫ prayer song at the 1984 Papal Grounds in Fort Simpson, NWT. Nick Black in foreground.
(Photograph from Tessa Macintosh Photography)

The drive along the 110-kilometer gravel highway to Behchokǫ̀ was usually rough as the vehicle hit pothole after pothole, but in Joanne Barnaby's 1986 Grand Marquis we floated. Joanne, executive director of the Dene Cultural Institute, was telling me about her trip to Europe with her mother. She explained that in looking at all the heritage sites and considering the age of the castles, museums, and universities in Europe, she had come to understand why most Euro-Canadians have such a strong attachment to material culture rather than to "stories that come from the land." She went on to say that she now had a better understanding of why people with European ancestry like to build on and control the land rather than allow the land to teach through giving.

In reflecting on Joanne's comment, I am struck by the consistency with which I have heard other Dene in northern Canada make similar statements: "Our knowledge is from the land"; "Our stories are from the land"; "We are from the land." I have also heard Tłįchǫ painstakingly explain the importance of what they know from the past and how it is intertwined with the present. As a person who has made the North my home, I wanted to understand these statements. This book considers what it means to be knowledgeable if you say you are from the land.

I am also struck by the similarity between Joanne's observations and Tim Ingold's philosophical contrast between building and dwelling perspectives, as set out in his book *The Perception of the Environment* (2000). Ingold's concept of "dwelling" is consistent with the Tłįchǫ Dene's perception that *dè*—translated as "land, ground, dirt, earth" (Dogrib Divisional Board of Education 1996, 18)—is a living entity and is in constant flux as a result of the lives and interactions of all beings—including humans. I expand on these perspectives as they apply to the interplay between knowledge, storytelling, and place.

This work considers the period between 1993 and August 2005, when the Land Claims and Self-Government Agreement between the Tłįchǫ, the Government of the Northwest Territories (GNWT), and the Government of Canada—the "Tłįchǫ Agreement"—became effective.

Between 1993 and 2002, I had the good fortune to work closely with a number of Tłįchǫ, ranging in age from early twenties to midnineties. They were engaged in learning and recording stories that the elders considered important for current and future generations. The elders wanted younger Tłįchǫ to have the narratives that originated in the past to think through current issues. The elders were and continue to be very committed to the ongoing struggle to find ways to share their experiences and resulting knowledge with their children and grandchildren as well as with nonnatives who spend time working with them.

The Tłįchǫ individuals I came to know are abstract thinkers as well as humorous, hardworking people who love to tease. They find it distasteful for people to discuss or show how busy they are. For them, the outcome tells if a person is knowledgeable and hardworking, not the fact that he or she is visibly rushing to accomplish something. Tłįchǫ often discuss and evaluate aspects of an individual's character. This pastime has particular importance given that people choose to follow skillful and knowledge-able individuals when engaged in tasks as varied as negotiating land-claim agreements, hunting and trapping, leading canoe trips to the tundra, picking berries, and collecting rotting spruce wood for smoking hides.

I have heard Tłı̨chǫ of all ages defend the rights of others, including non-Tłı̨chǫ, to think and to go about their business in a way that is appropriate for them. Nevertheless, they "talk" about various aspects of a person's character as well as cultural characteristics such as those exhibited by the Chipewyan or Kweèt'ı̨ı̨ (whites). Most Tłı̨chǫ use certain terms to describe characteristics or the type of work one does or where one lives. Take, for example, the term *Kweèt'ı̨ı̨*, which I use rather than *whites* or *English-speaking Euro-Canadians*. When discussing past occurrences, elders explain Kweèt'ı̨ı̨ as "those who like to live in stone houses," probably an early reference to the newcomers living at Prince of Wales Fort Hudson's Bay (Helm and Gillespie 1981, 14), first established in 1689 (Parks Canada 2004; Payne 1979). The term has come to mean — to the younger generation — "people who like to steal our rocks," referring to the mining industry's exploration and development within Tłı̨chǫ nèèk'e, the place where Tłı̨chǫ belong. During meetings when interpretation must be done quickly, the term *Kweèt'ı̨ı̨* is translated as "whites."

I use the term *talk* to refer to a type of discussion in which characteristics are discussed. Talk about characteristics is often combined with stories, but not always. These verbal caricatures vary from the serious to the more light-hearted and demonstrate a deep understanding of Kweèt'ı̨ı̨ and, most important, of what Tłı̨chǫ are not. Although teasing and joking are regular occurrences among Tłı̨chǫ, I have rarely observed anything like the Western Apache joking imitations that Keith Basso describes in *Portraits of "the Whiteman"* (1979). Sir John Richardson noted in the mid–nineteenth century that both young and old Tłı̨chǫ enjoy joking and are "great mimics, and readily ape the peculiarities of any white man; and many of the young men have caught the tunes of the Canadian voyagers, and hum them correctly" (1851, 13).

The majority of Tłı̨chǫ speak Tłı̨chǫ as their first language. It is part of a widespread language family known as "Athapaskan" and spoken throughout the western subarctic, with pockets outside the subarctic in British Columbia, Alberta, New Mexico, Colorado, Utah, Oklahoma, Texas, and Arizona. The Athapaskan languages spoken in the Northwest Territories (NWT) — Gwich'in, North and South Slavey, Tłı̨chǫ and Chipewyan — are official, as are French and English (Indo-European language family), Cree (Algonkian language family), and Inuvialuktun, Inuktitut, and

Inuinnaqtun (Inuit language family). Interactions with non-Tłı̨chǫ are reflected in additions to the language. As Vital Thomas explained to June Helm while she was in Behchokǫ̀, "We can use some Chip [Chipewyan] words. They saw the schooners before we did, so we call the schooner *ts'imbà ts'i*, 'sail boat.' The York boat is *detsin ts'i*, 'wood boat' and steamboat is *kon ts'i*, 'fire boat'" (Helm 2000, 146).

Similarly, the Tłı̨chǫ term *masì*, "thank you," seems to be derived from the French *merci*. *Masì* can mean to "be thankful" or to "be well" and is said when "greeting people and saying goodbye" (Dogrib Divisional Board of Education 1996, 70). The Chipewyan had contact with Europeans earlier than the Tłı̨chǫ, so that the Chipewyan word *marsi* may be a link in the chain between *merci* and *masì*. However, Leslie Saxon, a linguist who specializes in Dene language, in particular Tłı̨chǫ, cautions against assuming that the Tłı̨chǫ word comes from the Chipewyan word because it is difficult to determine the root for *masì*. All we can be sure of is that the Chipewyan word is phonetically closer to the French word, with its *r* (Leslie Saxon, personal communication, 12 July 2006).

Sir John Franklin wrote that the term "Thlingcha or Dog-ribs" came from the Cree (1823, 290). Tłı̨chǫ stopped using the English name "Dogrib" as their official name in August 2005, when the Tłı̨chǫ Agreement became effective. A senior elder, Madelaine Drybone, told Madelaine Chocolate that before the coming of the Europeans, the Tłı̨chǫ called themselves "K'ets'et'i." Madelaine Chocolate has discussed this term with her mother, Elizabeth Chocolate, and her auntie Elizabeth Mackenzie, who was translator for and a good friend of June Helm. They agree with Madelaine Drybone but do not know what the name "K'ets'et'i" means (Madelaine Chocolate, personal communication, 2000).

Discussion on the oldest and most appropriate term to use in a current context is consistent with the extent to which Tłı̨chǫ discuss concepts and "what things are called." I have been present when family members—in particular husbands and wives who speak different dialects—ask each other what they call something and then have a lengthy discussion on associated concepts. It was through these discussions about how to explain and what to call something in English and Tłı̨chǫ that I became aware that Tłı̨chǫ rarely take anything for granted.

They place emphasis on knowing "two ways," as advised by Grand Chief Jimmy Bruneau, whether this means understanding the concepts and pronunciations of two dialects or understanding two knowledge systems—Tłı̨chǫ and Kweèt'ı̨. This emphasis led me to understand the importance they place on knowledge, including how Kweèt'ı̨ think when

Figure I.2. Elizabeth Chocolate (Gamètì) and Bella Zoe scraping hides at fall camp, Deèzàatì, 1999. Using everything to ensure the spirit of the caribou stays strong and returns. (Photograph by the author)

engaged in social and political relationships. This intellectual approach to understanding is more than likely the reason why Tłı̨chǫ elders and leaders, when deciding how research should be conducted in their communities, favor the participatory action research (PAR) method wherein social scientists participate with community members to understand an issue through research and support the community in its effort to find a solution and to take action.

The communities' request to use the PAR process to document their knowledge provided me, without my knowing, an opportunity to explore a paradox that was a source of tension for me. Both the leaders and elders had asked me to share my research skills with Tłı̨chǫ, including the process of documentation—journaling, taping, translating, and transcribing oral tradition. This process had troubled me over the years. My concerns were heightened when we attempted to tie fragmented stories to particular locations on maps through databases developed from geographic information systems. The process seemed to me to have the potential to freeze bits and pieces of written translated transcription, as if that were all there is to the narratives. This concern was dispelled, however, as I began to realize and marvel at how the elders see the research process and the documentation of their knowledge as a way to ensure that the stories and land-based experiences are part of young people's current reality (see Cruikshank 1998, xiii–xiv)—one more way to ensure that oral narratives are part of social practice in the future.

The commitment to community-led research did at times cause conflicts with funding agencies. "Getting it right," although worthwhile, can be time consuming. In 2000, the analytical and financial reports for two such projects—studying place-names and caribou—were late. Final funding would not be released until each report was submitted, peer reviewed, and signed off. I was worried about deadlines tied to funding and how to pay wages. While we verified the contents of the caribou report with the Regional Elders Committee, I was trying to relax but felt hurried and tense when the *k'àowo* for the Tłı̨chǫ Knowledge Program, Jimmy Martin, stopped all discussion and said, "If you get ahead of us, we all will be in trouble." The elders then teased me and others; we had a small bite to eat, shared a few stories, and returned to the work of verifying and clarifying ideas and concepts that were being explained in English.

By calling a temporary halt to our work, Jimmy stressed that he and the other elders wanted it done the right way and would take all the time they needed to do so. He continued, "They said these were our projects, so we will do it right." It was in situations like this that I felt very fortunate to be involved with a group of people in their eighties and nineties who realized the importance of giving the narratives they chose and who felt the unhurried need to pass on their knowledge and insights to their descendants, who can use them to think with.

I was changed by these occurrences. I began thinking of PAR as a philosophical approach in which research is conducted with groups of people who draw on the skills of academics to achieve their own goals. Community members understand the issues and have ideas about solutions; they do not need social scientists for that. PAR is more than the right approach; it is the right action because it provides an avenue for industry and government personnel to hear them and for their children and grandchildren to work with them and to hear oral narratives that influence the present.

Being involved in a PAR process, I was given an opportunity to see how attitudes, perspectives, and relationships played out while people continued traditional activities as they strategically sought to influence current relationships and to solve current problems. In all aspects of Tłı̨chǫ life, the importance of being knowledgeable came through. Due to my involvement with the Tłı̨chǫ elders, I was able to see elders give advice to men and women who pursued "bush" activities as well as to those who were negotiating with government and industry. I was able to sit in on various discussions and meetings. I was often in homes or camps of elders or friends where hunters, trappers, and fishers continually came and went. At times, I sat with women "making dry meat" or sewing clothing and footwear or talking over tea or coffee. In all these situations, people exchanged information through telling stories of recent experiences that included hunting, meetings, and travels to other parts of the world. At other times, we explored in depth the names of plants, places, and vegetation communities while walking in the bush and on the tundra and while staying in spring, summer, and fall camps. People exchanged all sorts of information with each other and voiced a variety of concerns while drawing on stories of the past to understand their expediencies in the present. The knowledge people share through oral traditions and how knowledge and interpretation of the past inform present decision making is tied to knowledge systems. Yet, information on how one becomes and is seen to be knowledgeable is relatively scant in the anthropological literature. In addressing my question on what it means to be knowledgeable if you say you are from the land, I frequently turned to Fred Myers for clarity on place, identity, and knowing and to Eduardo Viveiros de Castro on observing from the perspective of the other.

Although I grew to understand a little bit of the language, Rita Blackduck, Violet Camsell-Blondin, Georgina Chocolate, Madelaine Chocolate, Georgina Franki, Bobby Gon, Gabrielle Mackenzie-Scott, Charlie Tailbone, John B. Zoe, Sally Anne Zoe, and Therese Zoe took time to explain things to me. They explained what something meant, who was related to whom, who was traveling where, someone or other's characteristics, and how they themselves or others had received their nicknames. I am very thankful for these friendships and conversations.

The experience of becoming knowledgeable is integrated with all aspects of dwelling within dè. I have attempted to show this relationship by structuring the book according to how I observed the unfolding of becoming and being knowledgeable. Jimmy Martin, an elder known for his stories that travelers use, once said to us while at a fall camp, "It is good to follow the stories." For this reason, I begin with "Janiì's Story; Moise's Experience," chapter 1, which sets the scene for the book and reinforces the relationship between story and experience. It follows a story an elder heard seventy years earlier. Through this story, a number of issues come to light, such as "knowing more than one way," how people remember, and how the story grows out from where and when it originated.

Chapter 2, "Learning Stories," sets the context in which I heard and remembered a few of the stories in the first three years of my interactions with the Tłıchǫ, when the elders requested that I not write anything, but only listen, learn, and remember. When listening and not writing, I considered how most Tłıchǫ learn the stories by hearing them in various situations from the time they are babies. Listening to oral narratives on a regular basis provides one with a perspective to experience the dè, a perspective that includes knowing the temporal origins of these narratives.

Chapter 3, "Dwelling within Dè and Tłıchǫ nèèk'e," places the Tłıchǫ and other beings within the dè. It emphasizes how the unpredictability of entities associated with the ebb and flow of seasonality brings a need to know and to show respect to other beings, to maintain harmony. I discuss how being knowledgeable demonstrates respect toward other-than-human beings. Those who show gratitude are successful, can share, and are followed.

Chapter 4, "Experiencing Kweèt'ıı̀: Traders, Miners, and Bureaucrats," and chapter 5, "Experiencing Kweèt'ıı̀: Collaborating and Taking Action," provide an overview of Tłıchǫ memories of events and interactions with Kweèt'ıı̀ since the 1700s. I show how the personal autonomy that is so important to becoming knowledgeable is increasingly at risk and how Tłıchǫ continually think about how to maintain harmony with all beings—including Kweèt'ıı̀. Chapter 4 establishes the context resulting from the arrival of and interactions and relations with explorers looking for resources and government personnel responsible for public policy and legislation that affected the Dene's rights as well as their individual and collective self-determination. I provide a brief overview of these relations and reactions. Chapter 5 is also an historical overview, but with a focus on relations between Tłıchǫ and Kweèt'ıı̀ who are prepared to listen and learn something of the land and the Dene who belong there. In this chapter, I consider the participatory and collaborative research that is similar to Dene philosophy as well as the methods that the Dene people request and that several of us Kweèt'ıı̀ have worked with.

Chapter 6, "'Following Those Who Know," describes a situation in which tension is associated with the interplay among being knowledgeable, leadership, and followership. I focus on how the use of stories helps to maintain harmony and demonstrates consistency in the Dene approach to solving problems.

Chapter 7, "Walking Stories; Leaving Footprints," returns to the relationship between story and experience. It shows how occurrences grow out from their original place through the telling and retelling of stories along the trails and how individuals are drawn back to significant locations through their endeavor to follow the footsteps of their knowledgeable predecessors. It is here that the tension between hearing the story and questing to be knowledgeable becomes apparent.

In the final chapter, "The Centrality of Knowledge," I accept Fredrik Barth's (2002) challenge to help bring to bear an anthropological framework that stresses the centrality of knowledge.

In writing, I draw on my own recollections and experience with Tłıchǫ in Tłıchǫ communities and Yellowknife, in the bush, and on the tundra. I quote from personal communications with individuals and from stories I learned along the way. At times, I quote from reports I wrote in conjunction with these colleagues. I wish to convey both facts and feelings, for two reasons. First, I was asked several times if I was thinking with my heart or my mind. The elders who oversaw the projects used their hearts and minds to think with and to listen to others. This ability was conveyed in very philosophical, thoughtful, and rational ideas on epistemological and ontological matters. I feel very fortunate, indeed, to have worked with such individuals; they are among the most intelligent and considerate people I have ever spent time with. Second, the Tłıchǫ people I know do not deny that feelings are involved in interpreting their surroundings and behavior. Thus, for me to write without feeling would be to tell only part of my story with them.

My aim is to describe accurately and sensitively what I observed. I noticed that every researcher who has worked with the Dene has a slightly different interpretation of similar experiences. I believe this variation has to do with the perspective we receive through story and the respect that the Dene have for personal autonomy—including ours as researchers—and for our own interpretations. I chose to concentrate on the Tłıchǫ love of learning, their perspective on dwelling as part of the place where they belong and deeply love, and their respect for the intellect of all entities, with whom they desire harmonious relationships.

Out of respect for the Tłıchǫ, throughout the text I have used their names for places, especially for the Tłıchǫ regions within Tłıchǫ nèèk'e. These regions can be found on map 3, along with the limit of Tłıchǫ Lands (as defined by the Tłıchǫ Agreement) since the land-claim settlement of 2005. As a result of working with the linguist Dr. Leslie Saxon of the University of Victoria and Tłıchǫ language specialists on a place-names project, I follow the spellings found in the place-names report (Dogrib Treaty 11 Council 2002). Map 1 shows the locations of Tłįchǫ communities, Yellowknife, Mǫwhì Gogha Dè Nįįtł'èè, and the extent of the trail system throughout Tłįchǫ nèèk'e. And map 2 shows two important trails systems and several of the place-names used in this book. In several chapters, I refer to places outside Tłįchǫ nèèk'e. In these cases, I use official government names; some are in English, and others in the aboriginal language of the place.

When referring to individuals and their titles, I use a mix of Tłįchǫ and English. I use the Tłįchǫ term when referring to a position of leadership, given by followers and based on traditional ideals of a person's being "an authority" on a topic or of a skill. I use English terms for those positions established under the Indian Act first enacted in 1876, with the current act being passed in 1951, where an individual is "in authority" after an election. For individual names, I use English unless I know only the person's Tłįchǫ name. I use the name "Mǫwhì" because Tłįchǫ themselves use it. When referring to individuals in English, I initially use their full name and then only their first name, as I have heard in the community. I do not use pseudonyms because among Tłįchǫ people it is appropriate and respectful to give credit to those whose "words" you use.

Throughout this book, I write the oral narratives that I heard and came to understand. In each case, I explain the context in which I heard the story and who told the story because that is the "right way" for Tłįchǫ to situate one's experiences. Most of these narratives are encompassed within one chapter because together they paraphrase many Tłįchǫ occurrences since the "world was new." Nevertheless, I do use the stories I have heard throughout this book because they are meaningful to grounding the context of this ethnography.

Georgina Chocolate in Behchokǫ̀ and Madelaine Chocolate in Gamètì read drafts of what I wrote and interpreted it to key elders. As I expected, my interpretation of my experience with them was addressed through dialogue and story. No one told me directly if I was right or wrong, but they shared their experiences in similar situations, which were usually tied to other stories of the more distant past. Listening and discussing topics initiated by those I was visiting usually helped me to address my questions and to clear up any confusion or concerns. Of course, I seem to have a never-ending list of questions.

CHAPTER ONE

Janıı's Story;
Moise's Experience

A constant theme for discussion and action among the Tłıchǫ elders is their insistence that stories and knowledge that come from the past are important for the present and for the future. For them, both stories and experience will ensure Tłıchǫ survival, while maintaining Tłıchǫ character and protecting the dè during the never-ending negotiations with government and industry. Anthropologists generally accept that northern Dene narratives contain knowledge of considerable time depth. June Helm was among the first researchers to match the written records of explorers and historians to occurrences remembered in oral narratives and has argued that Tłıchǫ recall events that occurred long before the coming of Kweèt'ıı̀ (1981a, 296). Studies such as those made by Jean-Guy Goulet (1998) and Robert Jarvenpa (1998) have shown that Dene knowledge is primarily experiential. It is also generally accepted that oral narratives are told with the intended purpose of improving other people's current behavior (Basso 1984a, 1996, 3–35; Cruikshank 1989), with most scholars emphasizing the relevance of context (Basso 1984a, 1996, 3–35; Ridington 1988; Sarris 1993; Vansina 2006). I build on these anthropological understandings by addressing the question of why remembering the past is so important to the Tłıchǫ elders, especially when it entails action and experience with others.

Closely tied to this question is why Tłıchǫ elders, on the one hand, accept knowledge originating from the dominant society as important, as prescribed by Grand Chief Jimmy Bruneau in the 1960s, and yet, on the other hand, reject it. In addressing these questions in this chapter, I

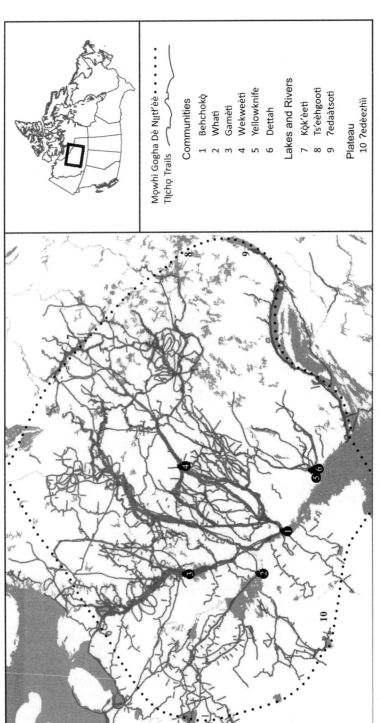

Map 1 Ancestor trails as documented by Tłįchǫ researchers during the Dene-Métis Mapping Project in the 1970s. Mǫwhì Gogha Dè Nıįtł'èè as in the Tłįchǫ Agreement. Both show the extent of Tłįchǫ nèèk'e. Mǫwhì Gogha Dè Nıįtł'èè was documented by elders present at the 1921 Treaty 11 signing when "Mǫwhì drew in the minds of those present" the outer boundaries of Tłįchǫ nèèk'e. (Base map courtesy of Mark Fenwick, Land Protection Department, Tłįchǫ Government)

Mǫwhì Gogha Dè Nıįtł'èè ••••••••
Tłįchǫ Trails ～～～

Communities
1   Behchokǫ̀
2   Whatì
3   Gamètì
4   Wekweètì
5   Yellowknife
6   Dettah

Lakes and Rivers
7   Kǫ̀k'èetì
8   Ts'èèhgootì
9   ʔedaàtsotì

Plateau
10 ʔedèezhìi

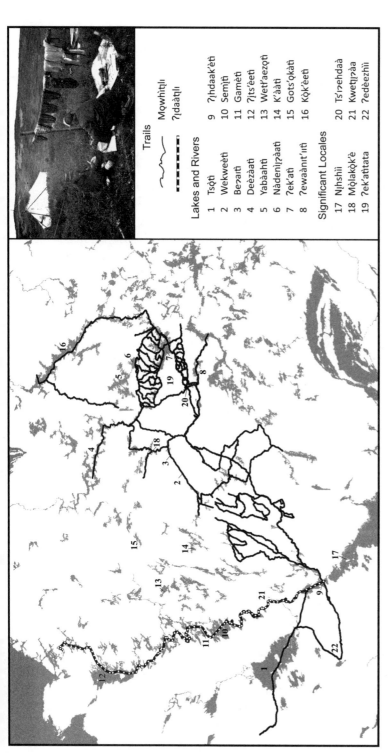

Trails

~~~~ Mǫwhìtłį

‑ ‑ ‑ ʔįdaàtłį

Lakes and Rivers

1   Tsǫ̀tì
2   Wekweètì
3   Beʔàatì
4   Deèʒàati
5   Yabàahtì
6   Nàdeniįʒàati
7   ʔekʼati
8   ʔewaànntʼiti
9   ʔįhdaakʼètì
10 Semǫ̀tì
11 Gamètì
12 ʔįtsʼèetì
13 Wetʰaezǫtì
14 Kʼàatì
15 Gotsʼǫkàtì
16 Kǫ̀kʼèetì
20 Tsʰ ɪʔehdaà
21 Kwetįʔàa
22 ʔedèezhìì

Significant Locales

17 Nįhshii
18 Mǫlakǫ̀kʼè
19 ʔekʼàttata

Map 2 Mǫwhìtłį, ʔįdaàtłį, and places referred to in this book. Mǫwhìtłį is a trail system the elders requested be protected under the NWT Protected Areas Strategy, and ʔįdaàtłį is between Sahti and Tıdeè. Mǫwhìtłį was documented by Tłįchǫ researchers under the guidance of the Tłįchǫ Regional Elders Committee in 1999; and ʔįdaàtłį was documented by John B. Zoe and Tom Andrews over several years under the guidance of elder Harry Simpson. Photograph of Harry Kodzin and Alphonse Quitte at 1999 fall hunting camp on Deèʒàati by the author. (Base map courtesy of Mark Fenwick, Land Protection Department, Tłįchǫ Government)

exemplify how personal truths and knowledge are acquired, and in the following chapter I consider more closely the relevance of context in gaining a particular perspective. The questions here are about the relationship between oral narratives, experience, and knowing something as well as about what this relationship has to do with rejecting or accepting Kweèt'ıı̀ knowledge.

Here, I use a story told by Moise Martin—who was in his nineties at the time I heard it—to show why the elders put so much emphasis on the importance of stories and experience from the past in interpreting the present and in preparing people for the future. I explore how memory of the past becomes part of present knowledge through action and experience with others. It is the constant bringing forward of information and the reestablishment of knowledge that comes from the past through current experience that provide the Tłıchǫ with personal truths.

Moise Martin Telling Janıı's Story

Responding to the concern that young people have limited opportunities to live the Dene way, Tłıchǫ leaders—along with the Dene Cultural Institute, the Dene Nation, and the Chipewyan, Yellowknives, Slavey, and Gwich'in leaders through land-use and heritage programs—have put pressure on industry and government to include Dene knowledge in baseline studies, environmental assessment, and monitoring projects. While working on such projects, the elders are able to tell stories when and how they choose, and younger people can listen, learn, experience, and document the elders' narratives at the same time that they become wage earners within the dominant Canadian society.

In 1999, the Tłıchǫ Knowledge Program research team was asked to carry out a project on the elders' understanding of biodiversity, which was translated as relationships within the dè. Moise Martin and Georgina Chocolate were verifying Tłıchǫ names for vegetation communities as part of the process of documenting biodiversity in areas of the tundra where Tłıchǫ hunt, fish, and trap (Chocolate et al. 2000). Georgina was showing Moise pictures and asking him if he agreed with the terms she was using to describe the vegetation in communities. He looked carefully at several pictures and then said, "You know. You were there. It is all here. Why are you asking me?" In listening to this exchange between Georgina and Moise, I realized that because we were the ones who had taken the pictures, and we had visited and experienced the places where these vegetation communities were found, we should know; we should not have to keep asking. Georgina explained to him that she would like to document the relations within the ʔek'atì area, where one diamond mine was producing and another was under construction so that the land, water, plants, and animals that reside there might have a better chance of being protected, and she wanted to be sure she was using the correct terms. Moise answered by telling Georgina Janıì's story.

We were staying at Mòlakòk'è near Wekweètì, when these elders said, "Let's go farther north—let's go trapping for white foxes." That's why we went toward the tundra. There were five of us—my uncle ʔadıı, Dzèmadzìı, and Gotsè and his younger brother, Janıì, and myself. We headed toward Deèzàatì, where there was a small valley with trees and a stream to pack up some firewood to take with us. We did this because the elders told us that along Nàdenı̨̀ʔàatì there is no wood, but it was a good place because there are many eskers for fox dens.

"Let's go and take a look over there," they said.

We traveled with two dog teams for two nights before we finally arrived at Nàdenı̨̀ʔàatì. We saw lots of caribou tracks and a few caribou. We set up camp and then split up to set the traps. Janıì said he was going to set traps along the esker that runs along the south side of Nàdenı̨̀ʔàatì. He hoped to see some caribou out there, so he set out. Three of us set out to the other side of Yabàahtì. And Dzèmadzìı went toward ʔek'atì.

When we got back to the camp that evening, we all had shot caribou and had set traps with some of the caribou meat.

Gotsè's younger brother Janıì said, "When I was walking on top of Nàdenı̨̀ʔàatì's esker to look for caribou, I think I saw a burial. It looks like a burial. I saw some rocks on sand, and it looks like a burial. It looked unusual; there shouldn't be any rocks like that there," he said.

The elders told him to look at it again and to look for whether rock tripe was on the rocks and to look at how the rocks were placed. Later, when he checked his traps, he took a look, and when he returned, he said, "Sure enough, that is a burial. There are rocks lying on the sand, and the rocks have rock tripe on them. There are rocks, and they are placed like a burial. There is a rock in each of the four corners and one at the heart. Sure enough, it must be a burial," Janıì said when he returned.

But now there is a mine near Nàdenı̨̀ʔàatì. Last year I flew to the mine by plane. Bobby Gon and I spent three days looking at caribou around the mine—I spent two nights at the BHP [Broken Hill

Proprietary] mine site and one night at ʔek'adìi where Diavik Diamonds is constructing a mine.

I'm concerned about these young men today. They have never lived off what Tłįchǫ nèèk'e provides. But us, the older elders, we have. I am talking about how we worked and struggled by dog team to the tundra. That is how we know; that is what we are talking about. The burial is between BHP buildings and Nàdenìįʔàatì. Someone placed those rocks on the sand so we would know there is a burial there.

As Moise told the story, he set the scene: he told of the relationships between both places and people, and he laid out the specific context in which he had learned about the burial. Moise was clear that he knew the story but had never seen the burial. In telling the story, he wove his knowledge of the landscape together with the information of the burial he heard in Janìi's story. And in so doing, he told us of the relationships, past and present, between people, animals, plants, and place and how trails connect them. He trusted Georgina to know enough to understand his story, including that when and how the knowledge originated are as important as the knowledge itself (cf. Basso 1996, 34).

Acquiring, using, and sharing one's knowledge through story as well as acting on that knowledge are vital to the continued existence of the dè. Moise's story of Nàdenìįʔàatì was stimulated by Georgina, who wanted to document relationships with the dè as Tłįchǫ understand them. Moise knew Georgina understood concepts of the dè and so used those concepts to share a narrative of his experience while traveling to places where resources were acquired that would secure success as Moise and the others traveled farther into the tundra.

The story can be understood on several levels. On one level, Moise's story offered information about a burial site at Nàdenìįʔàatì. Moise provided BHP, which funded the project, with information on archaeological sites. For him, the ancestor's burial place was an important part of sharing information on relationships within the dè. Most people, including Kweèt'ìį, would appreciate that the site should be protected. Like the Dene Tha Slavey with whom Goulet (1998) worked, the Tłįchǫ often attempt to communicate and provide information in a form that Kweèt'ìį can understand. Julie Cruikshank has also discussed how different aspects of First Nations' stories in the Yukon reach various members of the audience—including Euro-Canadians—at the same time (1998, 138–59). Greg Sarris (1993) also shows the same for the Cache Creek Pomo in his description of Mabel McKay's discourse with a group of Stanford medical students. Here, Moise used Georgina and me to share information with the mining personnel.

On a completely different level, Moise was telling Georgina about people with whom they both have relationships and about the importance of maintaining relations with the ancestors, who continue to occupy the Tłıchǫ nèèk'e. Georgina did the same when she told me the story in English; she wove into the story her version of relations and how she remembered them. She made statements such as "I remember Gotsè. I saw him when I was a child. He was a big man. Eddie Weyallon is Gotsè's grandson; he must know this story."

On yet another level, Moise was telling Georgina the importance of respecting their place within the dè by paying attention to it and knowing it. He told of how the elders encouraged Janı̀ to return and walk the esker, looking carefully at the location to determine if what he saw was indeed a burial. On several occasions, I heard elders encourage young people to observe all that is around them, to pay attention to what stays the same, and to watch for change. If they observe something unexpected, then they are encouraged to pay more attention to their surroundings. The elders encouraged Janı̀ to return and observe the burial more closely.

The idea of paying attention to and knowing the dè is a common theme for the Tłıchǫ elders. During research on the use of caribou fences, Sally Anne Zoe asked several elders how their ancestors first learned about using the movement of cloth and sound to direct caribou to the snares. Romie Wetrade explained that "they observed the animals. They used their minds. That is the way they have survived on caribou" (personal communication, 6 March 1995). Romie's statement was actually a clarification of Amen Tailbone's question to Sally Anne Zoe a few days earlier, which came at the end of a story he told:

> In the summer some caribou wandered to where there was a point [of land]. It was a point where there was a short portage. . . . [W]e canoed and went ashore. . . . [The caribou] were about to go into the water so we walked towards them. . . . We noticed some caribou jackets, blankets and things like that were hanging; about six [items] that had straw sticking out of them and they appeared like they were people standing. Despite that, the caribou ran ashore. We shot at them so the caribou ran ashore. . . . The caribou ran in between them [the clothing] and that's how it was. I know for I saw it with my own eyes and that's what I am talking about. I don't talk with uncertainty. What do you make of the information anyway? (Legat et al. 1995, 12)

Amen Tailbone was encouraging Sally Anne to think about what happened, about why movement can be used to direct caribou during spring migration when the sun is reflecting off the snow and caribou are prone to snow blindness, but not during fall migration. In this way, individual experience both augments personal knowledge and contributes to the stories held by all Tłıchǫ; all individuals have the possibility of enhancing their knowledge as stories "go around." The stories account for personal experiences, which in turn are told and used by others—intertwining with other occurrences that are remembered through telling and listening to oral narratives—added to and changed, and start and stop depending on current conversations. Although some very old stories have a beginning and ending in the telling of them, all stories, including these old ones, are reaffirmed as truth through experience. When individuals share their personal experiences, knowledge from the past is brought forward to the present through story.

On yet another level, Moise addressed Georgina's request for information on biodiversity so that the environment could be protected. She had explained biodiversity to be the degree of variation of life forms within that area. In his oral narrative, Moise told of the relationships within a much larger region as knowledge necessary to survive when at Nàdenìį̀ʔàatì and ʔek'atì.

To know is to maintain proper respectful relationships with all that is part of the dè. As with other subarctic indigenous peoples, respect—of which knowledge is an important aspect—is key to any relationship between people, animals, and place and hence to people's capacity to maintain flexibility within changing environments (Berkes 2000; Nelson 1983). For the Tłıchǫ, being respectful, being knowledgeable, and having the skill to use all that is part of the dè are vital to the continual return of other-than-human beings. Only through respectful use will the other-than-human beings return to places where they interact with humans. It is not morally wrong to kill and use animals, but it is morally wrong to treat them disrespectfully. Moreover, not knowing is the basis for disrespect. To use in a disrespectful manner is fundamental to abuse. Rules are followed by treating beings with appropriate care and by using everything.

Being respectful signifies the ability to think. Individuals who are unable to think are referred to as "pitiful." To the elders, this means that individuals are unable to remember, acknowledge, and respect the past and those relationships learned through remembering the past. People like this are usually unable to care for themselves. "Pitiful" individuals do not acquire food easily or produce useful and beautiful goods. If an individual cannot provide, then it is a real indication that he or she does not know anything. The results of a person's activities are constantly discussed as an indication of their knowledge and ability, their level of intelligence, and therefore their level of respect.

Such discussion includes how many and what type of skins a trapper gets; the look and taste of a woman's dried meat or dried fish; the taste of a person's bannock; the skill evident in a person's drum making or sewing; the ability to share within one's home; and the marks young people acquire in school. If a young person produces in a way that manifests both Tłįchǫ and Kweèt'į̀ knowledge, then he or she is regarded as someone who will probably be followed in the future. By creating beautiful items and taking care when cutting meat and fish, human beings show that they appreciate and respect what other beings are providing for them. If a human being lacks knowledge of how to use and care for other beings in the dè, the resulting lack of respect may lead to the spirits' deciding not to contribute to human well-being.

As Moise exemplified throughout his narrative, one should not just do a task well; one must also know how to speak about it. For two years, the elder Jimmy Martin gently suggested that a video be made of butchering caribou. He wanted the movie to be used to teach young people the Tłįchǫ terms for the parts of the caribou. I have never heard Tłįchǫ discuss the process—such as how to cut up caribou in a respectful manner—if all the rules and laws are being followed. They do, however, discuss the process if the rules are not followed because they have grave concerns. They usually express their concerns through sharing stories that will encourage the listener to think.

As among most subarctic people, another aspect of this respect is having the skill and the ability to survive. Moise provided some practical information about harvesting and traveling when he told where he and the others got their wood prior to traveling to the area where they would be trapping for foxes (see Tanner 1979, 134, for a discussion of respect in subarctic societies).

Experiencing the Story

Most archaeologists working in the North use elders' oral narratives to find sites (cf. Nicholas and Andrews 1997). Having listened to Moise's story, Georgina was able to locate the site on a topographic map. To do this, she had to trust her knowledge of the terms and concepts Moise used in the story, trust her knowledge of how the various eskers in the area were named, and trust her skill and abilities with topographic maps. Moise knew Georgina. He knew that she had walked on the tundra with the elders and that she knew which esker he was talking about, even though there are several in the area. He placed the story within a context that Georgina could follow as he mapped it in his mind and hers, weaving relationships in speech that connected different parts of Tłıchǫ nèèk'e.

Elders often speak of the dè in ways such as, "Like our parents, the dè takes care of us; the dè provides us with everything." It is the dè that furnishes individuals with the experiences they need to grow and develop (Ingold 2000, 141). As Moise told this story to Georgina, he described the relationships and the activities of the men who hunted, fished, and trapped on the dè. To protect the site, the location was noted, and because Moise wished to visit the site and we wished to verify it for BHP, BHP provided a helicopter to enable us to follow Janıı's story.

Moise's knowledge was not of the burial itself. Rather, it lay in his ability to follow the trail as outlined in the story (cf. Ingold 2000, 132–52, and Tilley 1994 on the importance of landscape to remembering). We took him to the place where they had camped seventy years earlier and from there followed the story as he told it. Because his eyesight was failing, this process demanded that we watch carefully to find the trail through the story. Both Georgina and I needed to know the Tłıchǫ terminology and concepts he was using to describe the locations as we guided the pilot so that we could fly the story.

As Moise told us the story again, he remembered more details, urging Georgina and me to watch specifically for certain vegetation communities: *kwekàanǫ̀hkwǫ̀* (rocky area with moss), *ts'oo* (muskeg), *whagweè* (sandy area with particular vegetation), and *tł'ogaa* (type of grassy area). Moise repeated the part of the story that told of the burial. "It is located," he said, "between the ts'oo and the whagweè, where a little sandy hill was attached to the esker running along the shore of Nàdenìıʔàatì."

Moise again repeated parts of the story so that we would look for an odd cluster of rocks with rock tripe on them. He repeatedly stated how the rocks would be placed: they would not look like they belong because people had moved them; we would know that people had moved them because rocks with rock tripe do not exist on small sandy hills attached to eskers. By following the story, we found the burial site with little trouble, the past being validated as the relationships associated with the place were remembered and reestablished by our traveling there. We had started from where Moise and his companions had camped so long ago and then followed his story, as happened so often in the past when Tłįchǫ were traveling from one place to another (Andrews, Zoe, and Herter 1998).

Once we arrived at the burial site, the first thing Moise said was, "It's true," which was followed by Georgina's exclamation, "What a memory! It's here." Both of these statements marked the transformation of the re-membering of a story about the burial into knowledge of the burial. This happened for both Moise and Georgina. My own reaction, however, was slightly different. Based on my experience with the elders, who know in-tricate details of many places, I had considered the story to be true before we even arrived at the burial. Moise and Georgina were basing their ex-pectations on past experience but did not consider them "true" until they were confirmed by experience. At the moment Moise said "it's true," the story and the experience came together, and information became personal knowledge.

The area around a burial or grave is normally cleared to show respect for and reestablish relations with the ancestors. Once this is accomplished, a "picnic" is held, and the fire is fed for the ancestors. Because we were on a sandy hill attached to an esker in the tundra, the burial site did not need to be cleared. And the helicopter had to be returned at noon, leaving

Figure 1.1. Moise Martin and Georgina Chocolate at Nàdenìįʔàatì, spring 2000. Moise is explaining rock placement on the burial. (Photograph by the author)

insufficient time to make a fire, eat, and feed the fire. So Moise spoke to the ancestor through prayer, drawing a cross in the sand just below the rock over the heart. We all felt touched by the ancestor.

We had now seen and experienced what we had only heard previously; we all now had our own story to tell; each story would be different yet would add to the original story told by Janì. The past was now part of the present.

Moise's Story

On returning to Behchokǫ̀, Moise gave an account of his experience to other Tłı̨chǫ and officials from the West Kitikmeot Slave Study Society office, of which BHP was an active member. His new telling of the story wove in additional occurrences of how his contemporaries lived and survived. And in so doing, he added his recent experience at the esker running along the shore of Nàdenìįʔàatì to Janì's story from seventy years earlier. I retell this version here to show that stories that come from the past and tell of a particular place are not stagnant but instead are continually expanding and include new experiences that provide new relations while reestablishing relations with the past.

> Long ago our ancestors used to bury their people with four rocks on each corner of their grave, and at that time they put one rock on the heart. That's the sign for burial. I heard Janì tell a story. He described the place where he found the burial on Nàdenìįʔàatì's esker. I know where the head of the body is because of the rock that is put on the heart. Long ago all the graves were like that. When we see rocks covered with rock tripe on sand, we know someone put the rocks there—usually it is a burial.
>
> My uncle Mǫwhì said that our ancestors used to dig the graves with chı̨hkw'à. It is made out of wood, like a large wooden spoon. They also used it for dipping the grease from meat cooking on the fire. Long ago we never traveled anywhere without chı̨hkw'à because it is good to use for drinking caribou blood and grease, which makes you strong and healthy. My uncle Mǫwhì told me there are some gravesites around ʔek'atì, but I don't really know where. I know there should be lots all over.
>
> When I was about twenty years old, I traveled to Nàdenìįʔàatì for trapping. Just last year I went back to the same places by helicopter. The places sure look the same to me. After all these years, we went to Nàdenìįʔàatì, and we saw the burials.

When I was about twenty years old, this elder Gotsè's younger brother, Janìi, said he was going to the esker to look for caribou and to set traps. When we—Gotsè, Janìi, ?adii, Dzèmadzìi, and I—got back to camp, Janìi said, "I saw what looks like burials on an esker beside Nàdenìɂàatì. There are some rocks just like around a grave, and it looks like there is more than one grave. I know that rocks with rock tripe do not naturally appear on sand on any esker."

We knew someone put them there; we knew someone had put the rocks on the graves. I'm concerned about these young men today; they have never lived from the dè. But us, the older elders, have been on the dè; we have depended on the dè. I am talking about how we worked and struggled by dog team to the tundra. Now that is the truth. We are talking about what we have seen because we have been on the land. We are here in Behchokò, but we can still see how everything—plants, animals, water, and burials—used to look on the land. When I was young, people used caribou hair coats and hare fur around their wrist so the snow will not go in their mitts. We were not raised to use store-bought clothes.

I have been to BHP and Diavik in the plane. I have traveled just like the Kweèt'ìi. I don't think they can know all that much because they have never lived off the land and walked like we did. In Nàdenìɂàatì, on the same side as the burials, there are trout, whitefish, jackfish, and sucker.

Janìi was trapping around the esker on Nàdenìɂàatì. That's how he saw the gravesite. It was a little sandy hill on the esker where he spotted the rocks that look like a burial. He was walking right on top of the esker to look out for caribou when he spotted the burial. He knew because the stones around it should not have been on the little sandy hill, which is not a rocky place. That place is just above a sandy area with very little vegetation mixed with muskeg. I heard about this gravesite because I was with these four elders when we went trapping to Nàdenìɂàatì, back when I was about twenty years of age and Janìi told us the story. I can still remember it clearly.

Georgina, Allice, and I decided to take a trip to BHP. We were taken by helicopter to Nàdenìɂàatì, and sure enough we found the burials just the way Janìi described them.

It is the truth, we saw it ourselves.

There is not only one grave; it looks like two graves. One of them looks like a child's grave. That's why we elders talk about what we see; we don't make up stories from the air. We walked and we traveled by dog team, too. Long ago, we struggled to live, and what we saw we talk about—it is true, and that is good. But what you see from the air and what others tell you are unknown. What this older elder said about the burials is the truth.

Because I mentioned Janìı's story about the gravesite, Allice, Georgina and I, and the helicopter pilot went to Nàdenìıʔàatì to take a look. We found the gravesite where the elder had said it would be. We all were so happy to discover this gravesite. Allice was really happy, too. We said a few prayers on the grave. We talked to this person; we said to this person, maybe you are our elder, but whoever you are, please take care of Tłıchǫ nèèk'e, take care of our ancestors' knowledge, and help us to have a safe trip back home. We asked this person to let it all be well with us. That is the kind of message I give to the person buried there.

These are not the only burials; there are lots of others all over the tundra—even toward Yabàahtì and around ʔek'atì and Deèzàatì, too. That's where the Gamètì people traveled. We once traveled there by boat for caribou hunting; we came upon a gravesite. There was a fence around the gravesite, made out of poles. And Pierre Wedzin, who died in his nineties in 1999, said it was my younger brother's gravesite. We camped out there. Father Amourous was with us at the time. There were two other children's graves. So we had a mass on their graves.

That is how we know, we see it with our own eyes—that's called the truth. Just because one elder told us this story, we went out there, and we found the grave. We found what we went out there for. We did a good deed.

Long ago that's how we traveled to the tundra. We carried firewood on the dogsled; we used only snowshoes, walking after the dogs. That is how I had worked around the ʔek'atì area ever since I was a young lad. I traveled throughout the tundra until I got married and had children. That's where we have walked and what we have seen. That is the story we told, and it is the truth that is really good.[1]

Moise's story did not change; rather, it encompassed more of his relationships within the dè as he expanded his knowledge. For Moise and Georgina, Janìı's story became truth. Moise's story, like Janìı's, contains knowledge that comes from various times in the past. Telling stories about relationships within the dè evokes a memory of Yamǫǫ̀zaa,[2] who is acknowledged for teaching all beings the laws governing the placement of and relationships between other-than-human and human beings. Moise told of many relationships. He spoke of the type of fish available at

Figure 1.2. Moise Martin telling his experience of following Janiì's story to the burial site at Nàdenìį̀ʔàatì, 2000. His main audience were the sixty Tłı̨chǫ feasting and teaching young people hand games. Government officials were visiting Behchokǫ̀, so Moise asked James Rabesca (standing at the top of the steps) to translate. (Photograph by the author)

Nàdenìį̀ʔàatì and their place within the lake. He drew attention to the use and importance of spruce during his discussion of a large wooden spoon that is utilized in various situations and to the importance of the blood and grease of caribou and of the fur of the snowshoe and arctic hares for making cuffs.

Moise's reference to his uncle Mǫwhì immediately brings to mind not only the latter's reputation as a hard-working man who cared for others, but also his "stubborn character," which was the reason why he was chosen by the Tłı̨chǫ people to speak for them to the Federal Treaty Commission in 1921. Mǫwhì's name also brings to mind the promises made by the treaty commissioner, especially that everything would stay the same for the Tłı̨chǫ. The name evokes a number of moral obligations associated with knowing and therefore respecting everything that is part of the dè. Both Moise's and Janiì's stories stimulated thoughts of past experiences in which oral narratives telling of occurrences and happenings became present truths and personal knowledge.

In the telling, Moise emphasized the reestablishment of relationships with the ancestors, with the trappers with whom he traveled, with Georgina and me, and with the helicopter pilot. He also publicly shared his story and in so doing brought Janıì's experience to the present as a valid occurrence that can be used to protect the Tłıchǫ nèèk'e. By reestablishing relationships, the stories of the past also help create harmony in the present. Moise wove the past into his knowledge of the present by expressing his concern about the young who no longer walk places but rather "fly around in planes." He asked, "How can they know anything [experience truth] if they do not walk [observe while using] places and learn about them?"

The past, then, is imminent in the present rather than extinguished by the present, as is so often assumed by members of the dominant society. This difference between Tłıchǫ and Kweèt'ıì cultures is one of the reasons why the elders are concerned about the schooling of young people in Kweèt'ıì knowledge. This particular concern became a reality for Georgina during the summer of 2001, when she, I, and others were visiting Ts'ı?ehdaà, a significant place in the tundra due to its location on the lake known as "?ewaànıt'ııtì," the last stand of white spruce trees where in the past women, children, and older people stayed behind as the hunters and trappers went farther into the tundra around ?ek'atì.

While there, we visited a grave with a fence. Everyone present knew who was buried there and to whom that ancestor was related. The elders spoke through prayer to the ancestor. As we were leaving, walking on the lower part of an esker, Georgina came across a spot where the rocks were placed in a similar pattern to the rocks at the burials at Nàdenìı?àatì. When she showed the site to some of the younger men, they admitted they had never seen that configuration of rocks before. But Joe Suzi Mackenzie, an eighty-eight-year-old man who had lived in the area, and Pierre Beaverho and Harry Simpson, both sixty-year-old men who live in smaller Tłıchǫ communities, acknowledged it to be an old burial. Joe Suzi stated that it might be one of the ancestors they had been looking for years ago.

Both Pierre and Harry noted the wind that was coming up on the lake and that we were several hours from our camp. The group quickly concurred that we could not take even a few minutes to reestablish a relationship with the ancestor and that ancestors understand the wind.

Knowing Something; Showing Respect

Tłıchǫ elders with whom I have worked are concerned that Tłıchǫ knowledge and skills are being forgotten in favor of knowledge that originates elsewhere or that comes from non-Dene individuals who have not used the Tłıchǫ nèèk'e yet consider themselves capable of predicting the future. Although Tłıchǫ elders consistently refer to the possible problems their grandchildren may face in the future, they also make statements such as, "We cannot know what will happen in the future; we can only know the past" (personal communication, Adele Wedawin, September 1999). Others may give credit to an individual who knows through dreaming or visualizing the future, but the prophesier would never "brag" about having special abilities. As Henry Sharp notes from his time with the Chipewyan, one can understand what occurred in the past only from a position in the future (2001, 163–76) .

The elders maintain that learning the stories of the past allows you to be ready for the present and the future. They may base their plans on the stories and their own experience, but they would never claim to know what will happen. In discussing information they have heard at meetings about whether the process of diamond mining is clean or contaminating, the elders often tell stories about Rayrock Mine Ltd., located in Tłıchǫ nèèk'e just off the main trail known as "Ɂıdaàtłı." These stories emphasize how they were told that uranium mining was safe even though the hunters were seeing and reporting dead beaver whose fur was falling out as well as dead fish floating close to the mine.

These oral narratives also name people who worked at the mine and subsequently died of cancer (Legat et al. 1997). The elders want those younger than themselves to proceed with caution and to think about possibilities—because the dè is highly unpredictable and what happens in it can never be fully understood, except in retrospect through discussions with those who have experienced similar occurrences. Consideration of an event and of those occurring prior to and after it are revisited and discussed in various contexts for years after.

It is not that the elders want to ignore new knowledge that is being taught in their schools and that, due to industrial development, is affecting their lives; it is just that they think humans must have sufficient knowledge of the past. In fact, they also discuss new occurrences that are continually coming to light and that lead to new or renewed understanding. In acknowledging what comes from the past, they do not deny the importance of the knowledge that is continually being brought to the communities from the worlds of science and politics. However, they think that this new knowledge is not enough. Their concern is not to deny change, but to ensure the survival of Tłıchǫ nèèk'e and of all the beings with whom they have relations within the dè. Their concern, then, is for all things, including their children and grandchildren, the caribou, the water, the plants, the places, and the ancestors. They stress that just as the knowledge itself is important, so too is how it was gained and how "knowing something" shows respect for dè.

In talking about knowledge from the past, Tłıchǫ elders often use terms that indicate when and how that knowledge came about. In telling Janıı's story as well as his own, Moise explained that his story came from the time of his elders. Tłıchǫ elders' statements thus imply that because most people do not know the future, remembering the stories of the past may be a matter of survival for themselves and for the dè. They emphasize that the past, including the ancestors, who continue to walk the land, is as much a part of the present as industrial developments, government-run schools, and government legislation. They stress the importance of knowing a little and continually increasing one's knowledge for respecting and maintaining relationships with all that is part of the dè. Whereas knowing something signifies respect, bragging signifies ignorance and the inability to respect either other-than-human beings or human beings. It is, then, others who notice whether an individual knows something and is respectful.

These elders consider that stories told by individuals are a constant reminder of truth that comes from the past in a changing world. When a person goes to a place she has only heard about, such as where Yamǫǫzaa killed the wolverine, which is also a place capable of predicting how long one will live, she will say, "I have been there; it is true." Charlie Tailbone, a Tłıchǫ hunter and trapper, exemplifies this point in the comment he made when he visited Edinburgh Castle in Scotland. He said, "I have seen castles on TV, but I didn't know if it was true. Now I have seen it with my own two eyes—it is true!" (comment to the author, September 2002). Personal experiences gained through various means—including dreams, hunting, trapping, traveling, as well as attending meetings with government and industry—validate the occurrences as described in stories. These experiences are shared with close friends and relatives; stories are repeated so that the truth of occurrences told through oral narratives is reaffirmed at the same time that an individual's experience is augmented and shared.

Knowledge systems that are inclusive, such as the Tłıchǫ's, are open to new information, including that coming from formal academic or scientific sources; for the elders, learning the ways of other humans and other beings shows respect for these others and allows one to maintain personal autonomy. Only through knowing something of others can one gain and maintain relations. During the 1960s and 1970s, the Tłıchǫ fought for schools in each community with the hope that young people could learn both Kweèt'ıı knowledge and the knowledge of their ancestors so that every Tłıchǫ person would become "strong like two people."

The elders are concerned that the new information and skills being learned by their children and grandchildren now might be replacing the Tłıchǫ knowledge. It is this threat of total replacement that they think is dangerous and ultimately corrupting. These concerns are being expressed in a context in which their children and grandchildren are being taught Kweèt'ıı knowledge in the dominant school system and against the background of thirty years of land-claim and self-government negotiations. The pressure to sign a land-claim agreement and to conform to the Kweèt'ıı system of decision making has increased with the discovery of diamonds.

By 2000, several young Tłıchǫ men were of the opinion that knowing the stories or how to hunt caribou—even though caribou meat is consumed by 96.8 percent of the Tłıchǫ in Behchokǫ̀ (Tracy and Kramer 2000, 47)—would never provide them with the prestige that comes with a wage. According to Elisabeth Croll and David Parkin, this attitude, even when hunting and fishing are providing more food, is widely encountered in the developing world (1992, 11–13). But human behavior is varied, and by 2003 I noticed that several of the same young men were turning to trapping and hunting as a "better way." They claimed it was more "flexible" and that if they worked hard, they could achieve a level of financial security without working for companies whose actions cause air pollution that ultimately damages fish and caribou, which, according to them, is occurring more and more often these days.

These statements are reminiscent of Richard Slobodin's findings that Gwich'in in the late 1940s and early 1950s were able to participate in both the wage and foraging economy without being overwhelmed (1962, 84). Robert Wishart and Michael Asch have found that among the Dene this pattern has persisted (n.d., 12). Asch (in the 1970s and 1980s) and Wishart (in the 1990s and 2000s) have noted that even the move into permanent communities has not overwhelmed the foraging economy.

Most Tłıchǫ elders think that if young people do not work and travel within Tłıchǫ nèèk'e, they may lose their Tłıchǫ "character." This character is linked to the personal responsibility to listen, observe, and think about all that is occurring within the dè so that, when necessary, one can take action. They think that without this ability and its demonstration of respect for the dè, most beings dwelling therein will slowly disappear. At times, the elders may sound as if they are judging the young and blaming them while glorifying their own youth. However, I do not think this is the case. Rather, their concern is that young people have limited possibilities to experience and know the Tłı̨chǫ nèèk'e or the skill necessary to continue to do so and that this limitation prevents them from knowing their place as defined by Yamǫ̀ǫzaa. As among many other indigenous hunting and gathering peoples, what is important for Tłı̨chǫ is the continuity of the process of experiencing their home, not that their lives should be lived just like those of their ancestors (Ingold 2000, 147).

"Knowing Two Ways"

I asked earlier why, on the one hand, the elders accept Kweèt'ı̨̀ knowledge as important yet, on the other, reject it. I also asked what context, experience, and "true knowledge" have to do with the rejection or acceptance of Kweèt'ı̨̀ knowledge and with the significance of remembering stories of the past for the present. What is causing the elders to be so concerned, especially when they encourage young people to know Kweèt'ı̨̀ knowledge as well as their own?

The relationship between the story and experiencing the information in the story seems to lie at the crux of why elders both accept Kweèt'ı̨̀ knowledge and fear that it is taught to the exclusion of Tłı̨chǫ stories and experiencing the dè. In emphasizing the importance of knowing both ways, the elders often tell the story about the woman who discovered Kweèt'ı̨̀ (told in chapter 2). They claim she survived because she knew how to live on the land, and she is credited with having been the first to bring Kweèt'ı̨̀ knowledge of trapping and trading to Tłı̨chǫ and to some extent with making life easier for them.

Most Kweèt'ı̨̀ school systems are built on the assumption that knowledge can be removed from the context of its production (Gardner n.d.; Lave and Wenger 1991, 40), that it can be accumulated, and that each grade provides young people with a little more of it (Lave 1990). For the Tłı̨chǫ elders with whom I worked, knowledge cannot be removed from the context of its production because one becomes knowledgeable through action. One starts with the occurrences and happenings shared through stories and then converts the information in the story, through a personal experience, into one's own knowledge and skill. Thus, there can be no distinction between the acquisition and the application of knowledge. For Tłı̨chǫ, experience, skill, and knowledge are not separate. Knowledge is not—as with most Kweèt'ı̨̀ schooling—first acquired (in the abstract) and then applied (in concrete situations). For most Tłı̨chǫ, bringing information contained in stories to bear on the present can be accomplished only through experience. Knowledge and skill are simultaneously acquired and applied and are continually enhanced through this experience.

The Tłıchǫ elders seem to fear that what is being lost with the domination by Kweèt'ıı ways is the ability to be flexible, to accommodate change while still continuing to gain experience, to acquire skill and knowledge, and to establish and reestablish relations with beings inhabiting places throughout the dè. Without a continual flow of stories and experience, individuals do not have sufficient personal knowledge and skill to cope with an unpredictable dè. Maintaining the total web of relationships within the dè is vital to the elders both for the survival of the dè and for the continual rebirth of all that has spirit. If people are not able to relate stories to experience, then they lack the skill and knowledge to treat the dè properly and respectfully.

The Tłıchǫ elders attribute the disappearance of wildlife to industrial development and to a lack of respect, which inevitably causes destruction. The ability to be flexible is seen in individuals who have had a great deal of experience because they know that two situations are never the same. The elders want their children and grandchildren to be flexible enough to accommodate the unpredictable and change. They fear that if future generations do not experience for themselves the stories that originated in the past, they will not be able to validate occurrences that come from other people's experiences. Without proper knowledge and understanding of the dè, these generations will lack the skill to survive. Elders fear that they will only do what the Kweèt'ıı do: brag that they know without having the experience behind the knowledge.

The question remains: Why do the elders encourage individuals to know the Kweèt'ıı way? I can answer this question only by saying that the dè includes everything. Kweèt'ıı are part of the dè and interact within the taskscape, which, as described by Ingold (2000, 154), is created and re-created through a constant exchange of inhabitants, human and other-than-human beings, within the dè. The taskscape of Tłıchǫ nèèk'e, then, is the result of the giving and taking, through established relations, of all beings and entities that involve the tasks and skills of living. Because Kweèt'ıı are part of the dè, it is vital for the Tłıchǫ to hear stories told by Kweèt'ıı about their laws, rules, behavior, thinking, and beliefs, and it is equally important to experience these stories to have knowledge of Kweèt'ıı with whom one hopes to have reciprocal relations.

Those who follow the Kweèt'ıı way at the expense of destroying harmony within oneself or within the dè are repeatedly told stories. Elders I have met would agree with Asch (1997), who emphasizes how Dene have remained open to new ways, whereas Kweèt'ı̨ have remained closed, leading to the creation of government policies that are controlling and inflexible, designed to limit the ability to think for oneself. I know of no Tłı̨chǫ who would like their children or grandchildren to know so much Kweèt'ı̨ knowledge that they become Kweèt'ı̨ in mind and spirit. Rather than follow the way of the Kweèt'ı̨, one should think about the Kweèt'ı̨ way and the Kweèt'ı̨ character so that one can share stories with those with less experience of Kweèt'ı̨ and can share stories in a way that Kweèt'ı̨ may hear and start to understand the Dene way.

When Jimmy Bruneau spoke of "knowing two ways," he meant both the Kweèt'ı̨ and the Tłı̨chǫ ways. For Tłı̨chǫ, to know something of another human being or other-than-human beings is to show them respect. This was exemplified in the spring of 2002 when elders from all four Tłı̨chǫ Dene communities (Behchokǫ̀, Gamètì, Whatì, and Wekweètì) were meeting at the school in Whatì to share thoughts on what they wanted young people to know. The most senior of the elders I worked with have expressed their concern that since attendance of the schools began, women's knowledge is not being respected, and it is part of "knowing two ways." Robert Mackenzie, an elder from Behchokǫ̀, told the story of his first child: "My wife, my father, and I were staying on an island while fall fishing. My wife was pregnant with our first child. The temperature dropped, creating a thin layer of ice on the water. It was time for my wife to return to Behchokǫ̀ and have the baby, but we could not leave for fear that the ice would puncture our canvas canoe. My wife went into labor, and my father delivered the baby. My oldest daughter and wife would probably have died if my father didn't know women's knowledge." As moisture formed in his eyes, he continued, "Young men do not think they need women's stories or elders' stories, but you never know when you will need to think with them. My father not only had the narratives, he had women's knowledge. My daughter and wife may have died. We must tell our grandchildren so they can listen even if they think it isn't important — we should keep giving them our stories and keep recording our narratives for the future."

After Robert finished, the students who had wandered in to listen to the elders from the four communities sat in silence, just as the elders did. Then Albert Wedawin, a senior elder in his nineties who took care of the community drums, said light-heartedly that a hand game would determine which community "knew something."

The key to being knowledgeable is knowing the "truth" of the past through experience, not through the story itself. One cannot experience the past without the story. The original happening begins the process, with the telling and hearing of the story following. The stories are told and heard by others, and as a person experiences the story in everyday life, he tells the story, collapsing the past and present into his own personal truth.

CHAPTER TWO

Learning Stories

In May 1996, Madelaine Chocolate, Sally Anne Zoe, and I were visiting Romie Wetrade. We listened as the several elders who were present told of events. In winding their stories back through time, these elders emphasized information on when the event first occurred. Later I asked Romie if knowing when occurrences first happened is as important as knowing the place when they first occurred. He told us several narratives that emphasized the relationship between Tłıchǫ temporal and spatial relationships of places I had visited.

Romie confirmed that how, when, why, and where knowledge originated are as important to know as the knowledge itself. He did this by weaving several stories together, always specifying the temporal era in which each particular story originated. He did not tell the stories in temporal sequence but rather moved between times, tying them back to his life with the elders from whom he had first heard them. Temporality, then, is an aspect of the places where events and therefore stories reside.

This chapter has three intertwined purposes. The first is to write the stories of the past I heard being told on a regular basis in a variety of situations to individuals of all ages. It is from these stories that very young children first gain a perspective from which they can think about their relations with other humans and other-than-human beings. Second, in telling of events and happenings in association with the era whence each story originated, I can explain more clearly how they are brought forward for future generations. Third, in telling these stories, I can illuminate the

Figure 2.1. Roger Drybone with maternal grandmother, Madelaine Drybone, at a summer camp at Nı̨dzı̨kaà on the lake Semı̀tì, 1998. (Photograph by the author)

tensions between story and experience, between older and younger generations, between not knowing and knowing, and between leader and follower. These stories are the Tłı̨chǫ interpretations and, as such, are crucial to the ways knowledge is used to solve problems and maintain harmony in the present.

Young children hear the stories on a regular basis from their grandparents, from their parents, and from other members of the community when visiting. Variations on many of these stories are included in several works (Andrews and Zoe 1997; Andrews, Zoe, and Herter 1998; Blondin 1990, 1996, 1999; Gillespie 1970, 1981; Helm 1981a, 1994, 2000, 271–92; Helm and Gillespie 1981; Petitot 1976). When I first started working for the Tłı̨chǫ elders in the community of Gamètì in 1993, they requested that I not write, but listen. Harry Simpson, a man in his sixties, explained to the other elders that Kweèt'ı̨ learn by writing and that perhaps I should write down Tłı̨chǫ terms and names. I rarely did because writing interrupted my ability to listen, and the majority of the elders requested that I listen carefully to what they, the Tłı̨chǫ researchers, and the interpreters-translators were saying.

I did, however, note—immediately after each visit—which stories were being told and by whom. When appropriate, I also took photographs to assist my memory. As the elders directed, I learned through listening, observing, and experiencing rather than observing and writing fieldnotes. In following their direction, I spent most evenings contemplating my day, reviewing the stories I had heard, and fitting them to my surroundings. Sometimes I did this alone in my cabin; sometimes I shared my day with others.

I have attempted to write the stories given in this chapter as I heard others tell them. Thus, I include both the context in which I heard each narrative and who told it. These narratives are written as a chapter because they belong together. I heard them told in numerous situations and in several ways, just as other researchers have noted among the Dene (Basso 1984a, 1988, 1996; Cruikshank 1990b, 1998; de Laguna 1995; Moore and Wheelock 1990b; Ridington 1988, 1990). Tłįchǫ regularly share oral narratives. Telling and retelling provide individuals with a perspective to live their lives. Young people repeatedly hear these stories both in the community where they live and in the locales where the stories originated. The majority of young people had heard them on numerous occasions before visiting the locales where the events and happenings of the stories took place and where, as Thomas Andrews and John Zoe (1997) explain, the stories dwell.

Evidence certainly suggests that there is a long history of grandparents telling the stories to their grandchildren so the latter can use them in the future. As Madelaine Drybone said to Sally Anne Zoe and me, "The stories never die. We are still using the story. We live our lives like the stories. These stories are from my grandmothers, my grandfathers. I am talking with my grandparents' stories. Their words are very important because they will help you live in the future. Their words will help you to think for yourselves" (personal communication, 18 May 1994).

Three Yukon elders similarly told Julie Cruikshank (1990b) about living life like a story. This does not mean that one should live exactly as one's predecessors did. Rather, one should think about new situations, which may bring new behaviors and actions while "doing things the right way" (Ryan 1995).

As Keith Basso has described so eloquently (1996, 3–35), I have heard stories told when the storyteller is making a particular point about behavior. I have just as often heard the stories merely told. People tell stories around fires while cooking or smoking meat and fish; while sitting in their living rooms, in hotel rooms, and in vehicles when traveling the ice roads;

and while visiting. I have never heard stories while walking around a site; rather, it has been my experience that stories come just before and just after walking around a locale, when people are sitting comfortably around a fire, cooking, and after eating.

When walking around, the most knowledgeable person usually points out aspects of the surroundings. This musing includes mentions of anything from plants that can be used for medicine to the trails and dens of animals in the area to when birch trees were last used and who may have used them, smells—some of which indicate the passing of bears—rock chimneys that are left from disintegrated log cabins, and a good location for fish nets. The person might remark on the feeling of being watched by any of the entities who dwell in the location—including "bush men." This musing as well as the chitchat interspersed with storytelling and the stories that are told while engaged in tasks that allow listening and long oration—all engrave in the mind of the listener a perspective from which to understand Tłįchǫ cosmology. Oral narratives are always best learned from elders who have experienced them all their lives.

Figure 2.2. Paul Wetrade preparing a birch pole for Laiza Mantla to use to work on her caribou hide at summer camp at K'ǫ̀hkw'ą̀ǫkaà on the lake Gamètì, 1994. (Photograph by the author)

Writing the Stories

The stories set out here are those that I remember and that are relevant to my discussion in this book. They demonstrate the perception of the dè that the Tłchǫ elders want to leave with their grandchildren, with the individuals they selected to work with them, and with me. I heard all the stories more than once. I heard them initially in Gamètì and later in Behchokǫ̀, Whatì, and Wekweètì. A list of elders with whom I worked most closely and whose stories I therefore heard can be found in the acknowledgments. Because the stories were always told in Tłchǫ, I came to understand the stories and many of the concepts from many individuals, but it was Therese Zoe, Madelaine Chocolate, Rita Blackduck, and Sally Anne Zoe in Gamètì as well as Georgina Chocolate and Bobby Gon in Behchokǫ̀ who discussed in depth with me the issues raised by the stories.

As stated earlier, for Tłchǫ, knowing when a story originated as well as where it originated is an important aspect of being considered knowledgeable by others. There are four time periods. The first three are *gowoo*, "the time when all beings were the same"; *whaèhdǫǫ̀*, "the time of Yamǫ̀ǫzaa when all was in harmony and places were named so people could travel safely";[1] and *gotso*, "the time of predecessors whom one's elders knew." Individuals should know that each of these first three periods is associated with a powerful leader who came to know what "laws" need to be followed to establish harmonious relations out of the chaos. One day when sitting around the office, Paul Wetrade explained to Sally Anne Zoe and me that *gotso nàowoò* is "the knowledge of my father's father's father or Sally Anne's father's father's father's father or her mother's mother's mother's mother."

When elders are telling stories, they will say, "I am telling a story of a story." The knowledge originating from this period is passed to individuals through stories told by their relatives, such as "mothers, fathers, uncles, aunts, grandmothers, grandfathers, people who are like us; all our elders because we regard them as relatives," as Paul put it. When comparing gotso knowledge, agreements, and laws with those that originated from the whaèhdǫǫ̀ era, Paul said on 9 July 1994, "Our elders lived, and we have been raised on gotso knowledge."

The fourth era, *dìı*, is "the time of one's own memories," corresponding to the lifetime of the current generation of elders.

In writing these narratives, I try to refer to the time of the original happening. Doing so is often difficult because in experiencing the story, one draws the reality of the narrative to the present. Occurrences, then, cannot be bounded by a beginning or an end. Stories reflect the reality of occurrences originating in the past, yet individuals listening to narratives may hear them differently, depending on when they heard them. For this reason I provide the context in which I heard the story. For the Tłı̨chǫ, all oral narratives relate real-life experiences, regardless of whether the protagonists are humans or other-than-human beings, regardless of whether everyone has experienced it, and regardless of whether the occurrence happened while dreaming or while awake.

Remembering and Writing the Stories

On 18 May 1994, Sally Anne Zoe and I walked over to Madelaine and Paul Drybone's home. Sally's mom had asked us to deliver some caribou meat to them. When we arrived, we could see Madelaine Drybone, a woman in her late eighties, pulling her fish net through a hole in the ice that her grandson, Roger, kept open for her. Most community members, not just Madelaine's extended family, watched out for her. The day was warm, and Madelaine liked to work. When she finished, we stoked the fire and sat together with our tea. Madelaine, like other elders in Gamètì, wanted us to understand traditional governance, and I wanted to understand where social rules came from. As we drank tea, Madelaine told us the story of Muskrat.

What I say is all true.

During the time when all beings were the same, there was only water. Everyone was looking for the ground. Beaver and Otter dived in the water to look, but they could not find any earth. Loon dived and looked but surfaced exhausted, finding nothing. They kept working together, continually taking turns. They cooperated and searched the water together. Muskrat, who could dive deeper, simply floated. Muskrat let the others try first. Muskrat knew it was important for everyone to try and to work together.

When they could not find anything, Muskrat said, "I can dive deeper, and I can stay underwater longer. Perhaps I can find something. I will dive."

Muskrat dived repeatedly. When Muskrat surfaced, the k'àowo would check for evidence of earth, and then Muskrat would try again. Finally, Muskrat surfaced and said, "I hit something!"

The k'àowo looked between Muskrat's toes and found moss. The k'àowo put it down, and everyone ran around and around on the moss. They ran around and around. Fox ran around longer, and as Fox did, the ground became bigger and bigger. Finally, the ground was big enough for everyone. For this reason, Muskrat is known as "k'àowo of the ground."

I never heard Madeleine tell the whole story in my presence again. She did, however, continue to refer to Muskrat—especially when she listened to territorial and federal bureaucrats talking about policy and legislation that govern land and resource use. On several occasions, I heard her simply say, "They think they are the boss of the land, but really Muskrat found the ground. Muskrat is boss of the land." Madelaine often used the Muskrat narrative to set the framework for larger political discussions associated with land claims and government undertakings, such as the Federal Environmental Assessment Review held in February 1996 for BHP's proposed Ekati Mine. I was reminded of Madelaine Drybone's approach while reading Cruikshank's comment about how Angela Sidney, of Tagish and Tlingit ancestry, first ensured that Cruikshank understood the narrative and then made regular mention of it in their conversation to connect events that would otherwise seem unrelated (1998, 28).

Madelaine Drybone was constantly weaving together events in life. For her—as for all Tłı̨chǫ I met—one participates in life rather than viewing it from the outside.[2] Immediately after Jean Wetrade sang a prayer song at the beginning of the first land-claim negotiating session in January 1994, Madelaine turned to Rita Blackduck, Sally Anne Zoe, and me and said with a smile, "Those guys [the federal and territorial negotiating team] should have a hand game with the Tłı̨chǫ negotiators; then we would know who should speak for the land and the animals."

Disagreements are often solved through competitions if harmony cannot be established through various forms of discourse. As many elders explained, it is often difficult to know who is strongest and most intelligent[3] and therefore to know who should be k'àowo. Madeleine's playful comment reminded me of Pierre Mantla Sr., an older elder, who told a story on 4 August 1993 that set me thinking about the importance of competition in solving disagreements. Before telling the story, Pierre Sr. explained that he had heard it from his grandmother.

This story comes from the time when there was harmony, but it was always cold, and there was never any spring or summer, only winter. Bear and Squirrel could not agree. Squirrel and Bear were different. Squirrel often thought about why it was so cold and suggested they all sleep on it. That night everyone slept on that question. In the morning, when all the other people got up, Squirrel was still sleeping, so they kept the fire going. It is never good to wake a person who is dreaming, and they knew he was dreaming. When dreaming, Squirrel saw light beyond the snow. When he got up, he stood very close to the fire and that is why his back is dark.

Squirrel said, "I dreamt that beyond the snow there is sun, it is summer, and it is warm. That is what I dreamed."

He suggested that they go to the light. Bear and Squirrel discussed it for a long time but did not come to an agreement. Squirrel suggested that they have a race around the island and whoever lost would have to listen to the winner. They started their race. Squirrel was fast, running up and over the trees. Bear was slower, sauntering around the island, sleeping and resting. Squirrel arrived first and was running up and down a tree and chattering—as squirrels do—when Bear finally arrived. Bear agreed to listen to Squirrel, and they then worked together to get the light. Squirrel made life easier and is remembered as being responsible for bringing light and warmth to all beings.

It is said that Yamǫǫ̀zaa and his brother, Yamǫǫ̀gaà, wrestled to determine which of them was older and therefore the most powerful. Although they wrestled for days, neither could beat the other, so they decided that each would go his own way. Yamǫǫ̀zaa travels toward the sunrise, and his brother, Yamǫǫ̀gaà, travels toward the sunset.

Jean Wetrade, younger brother to Madelaine Drybone, older brother to Paul and Romie Wetrade, and k'àowo for the elders until his death in April 1994, encouraged the telling and retelling of the story of Yamǫǫ̀zaa. Jean encouraged all the elders to tell this story and to be audiotaped for the future. All those I heard tell the Yamǫǫ̀zaa stories give credit to their grandparents for telling them the stories. I have never met a Tłįchǫ who does not know Yamǫǫ̀zaa and his brother, Yamǫǫ̀gaà, as having been responsible for the setting down of social rules for all beings to live by.

It is said that during the time when all beings were the same, great birds were swooping down, picking up and eating people. Everyone was afraid as there was indiscriminate killing—there were no rules. They were starving, yet they were unable to get to the food. At first, they moved away from the lakeshore and lived in the trees, but the birds hunted the people among the trees. Because all beings were the same, some could switch back and forth at will, but they could not change into just any other being. They all could not become big birds. Sometimes they wished they could be something other than what they were so they could protect themselves from the big birds, but they were helpless. They tried to feed and protect each other, but no matter what they tried, they could not find a way. The birds were too smart.

It is said, after a long time Yamǫ̀zaa and his brother, Yamǫ̀gaà, came along. They were physically and intellectually very powerful, knowing how to draw on the ʔık'ǫ̀ [medicine power]. They listened carefully to what the people had to say, and they realized there was only chaos within the dè. They knew a lot about the dè because they had listened to and traveled with their grandfather. The people told them what was happening with the big birds. The brothers listened, asking questions and then thinking about the problem. They discussed and decided how to put an end to the indiscriminate killing. They used all their knowledge, their intelligence, and their skills on the birds. They caught the birds and told them that from now on they were not to eat any person who walked on the ground. They were to eat the fish in the lake and some of the smaller beings that lived in the ground. Not only

Figure 2.3. Barren-ground caribou wintering in boreal forest.
(Photograph from Tessa Macintosh Photography)

did Yamǫ̀zaa and his brother tell the big birds and fish about their special relationship and the rules they were to live by, but they traveled the
dè giving laws to all beings, telling them how to live together. Yamǫ̀zaa
and his brother were the first and greatest *yahbahti* [a powerful and
highly intelligent regional leader with considerable access to ʔ̜k'ǫ̀] as
they took care of everyone within the dè.

Sally Anne Zoe, Rita Blackduck, and I heard a portion of this story from
Jean Wetrade during the spring migration in 1994. We were discussing
traditional governance with several elders in Gamètì. The topic changed
to caribou in the afternoon because several hundred caribou were close
by, and most hunters had already left on their skidoos. The oral narratives
continued to focus on k'àowo but shifted from the k'àowo's responsibility
toward the community to those specific k'àowo who had the ability to
dream of caribou and call caribou to them. It was after several of these
stories that Jean Wetrade told how Yamǫ̀zaa and his brother, Yamǫ̀gaà,
came from between the cleft hoof of the caribou, which, he explained, is
why they were very tiny when their grandfather found them crying under
the tree—because they did not have parents. They did not have human
parents; the two yahbahti who provided all beings with their knowledge of
social relations came from caribou. And, as Jean said,

Yamǫ̀zaa and his brother were great yahbahti because they came from
the caribou. As babies, they were yellow and very tiny as they came
from the space in the caribou cleft hoof. After they were born, they
sat under a birch tree, holding each other and crying for the mother
and father they did not have. No one was there to name them, so they
named each other. They were really weeping when an old man came
along and found them. He raised them as his own. He became their
grandfather, and so they traveled with him, and he taught them about
the dè. When they became adults, they decided they knew enough and
no longer needed their grandfather, so they put hot rocks in his head. It
is said, you can still see the crack in his head at Kweedoò.

It is said, after the brothers became more knowledgeable than their
grandfather and killed him, they helped everyone, just as their grandfather had helped them. They created clear laws that, if followed, made
life easier.

It is said, although this was the start of social organization, there was
still tension because people did not know where they belonged. So some
killing continued. Even Yamǫ̀zaa and his brother had no idea of their

place. They discussed this problem, trying to determine who was the oldest and therefore the most powerful. They decided to wrestle. They ran at each other, fighting for several days, but neither could harm the other. They were equal; neither was stronger. They were unable to tell who was the oldest. They had no way of knowing. Because neither was able to overpower the other, they shook hands, and each went his own way. Yamǫ̀zaa went toward the rising sun, and his brother went toward the setting sun.

Both brothers traveled the earth. Each had his own place, and as the brothers encountered other beings, they told those beings to remain where they were, told them who they were, and gave them their own language. Beings were no longer the same. Each being was unique. Yamǫ̀zaa and Yamǫ̀gaà told them the laws so their lives would be easier.

Yamǫ̀zaa, who traveled in this area, said, "This is what you are here to do. This is how other beings can use you and how they will respect and use you properly if they know you. This is who you are and where you will stay."

It is said, the brothers did this so that everything—humans, plants, animals, stars—would have their own place within the dè and there would be less fighting and less chaos. The brothers are responsible for languages and cultures. They taught humans what they could use and how to show respect. They taught the animals the laws and where they should make themselves available to humans and other animals. Yamǫ̀zaa is the one who said that berries must not be taken away from their place, that they must be used where they grow. Because Yamǫ̀zaa made the laws clear, everyone knew when the laws were broken. There was less starvation, and people lived well for a long time.

Yamǫ̀zaa is the reason that only some individuals can become other beings. It is these individuals who can truly know another being and teach others to live well within the dè. Yamǫ̀zaa is responsible for the different knowledge and cultures, social relationships, and attachments to the places where beings belong. It is said, Yamǫ̀zaa did this so that all people and animals would have their own place in the world and there would be less fighting. There would be less fighting because each being would have different knowledge of the dè and in sharing that knowledge can help others rather than fight.

Yamǫ̀zaa wanted order within the dè. There had been too much conflict, and the people did not know how to act or who they were. It was Yamǫ̀zaa who told the people and animals where they should live and what they could use. Yamǫ̀zaa was a great yahbahti. He is responsible for order in the dè and responsible for the laws and knowledge for cooperating in order to coexist. All beings know these laws and knowledge; animals know when to make themselves available to humans, and humans know how to treat what they use within the dè. Because the laws are clear, everyone knows when laws are broken. Before the brothers gave all beings laws, all beings were the same; they all were like people. Yamǫ̀zaa is the reason only some beings can still change into something else.

In spite of the social rules' being clear, some individuals forget the laws sometimes. Even Yamǫ̀zaa sometimes neglected the laws he taught others, or at least he forgot that when an agreement is made, it is to be honored. It is said that this often happens when people are in a hurry and forget to respect others and honor what is required.

At a feast for the elders held at Jean Wetrade's home on 28 February 1993, Andrew Gon emphasized the importance of respecting one's followers and what can happen if the needs of followers are neglected. All of us sat on the floor, each person with his or her own plate and cutlery placed on a tea towel in front of him or her. Jean's son served us until all the food that had been contributed was served. A short prayer was said, and only after the stories and discussion were finished did we eat. The elders discussed the breakdown of the Dene-Métis Secretariat that had been negotiating the Dene-Métis land claim. They were worried that their elected leaders would have to rush to finish their regional claim to counter the land being staked due to the diamond rush. They wanted all four Dene chiefs to "walk the places" of their elders. They wanted them to walk the places where their ancestors had left their footprints and to think about all the laws, social relationships, and agreements that had been made in the past. Therese Zoe interpreted some of these discussions for me. Andrew Gon said, "Anyone can forget how to act—especially if they get into a hurry, even Yamǫ̀zaa. We need to help those younger than us." He then went on to tell a story of Yamǫ̀zaa and Beaver.

It is said, Yamǫ̀zaa proposed marriage to Beaver, who answered, "No, I live in and by the water, whereas you wander the ground." Yamǫ̀zaa kept asking and finally convinced Beaver to marry him. Beaver said, "OK, if you want to live with me, you must cut logs and place them across all the water that we will cross." Beaver has ʔįk'ǫ̀ for water; therefore, if she were to touch it, she would have to live in water again.

For a long time, Yamǫ̀zaa did cut the logs, and Beaver crossed easily. They had a baby, and they all traveled together. They were a happy family. One day when they were traveling, Yamǫ̀zaa came to a small stream with lots of rocks. Yamǫǫ̀zaa thought to himself, "I will not put logs here; this stream will be easy for Beaver and our baby to cross." He crossed and went ahead. Beaver came to the stream and found there were no logs to cross. Once she touched the water, it took her back. She needed the logs to cross the open water, but Yamǫǫ̀zaa had not left logs for them. Their baby followed her mother into the water. Yamǫǫ̀zaa came back to the stream to look for Beaver, and when he saw Beaver was swimming away from him, Yamǫǫ̀zaa called for her to come back, but Beaver was carried away.

I remembered this story because I heard it shortly before John B. Zoe and I were discussing place-names, when he said that he thought the place-names beginning with *ndè*,[4] usually attached to the names of a series of islands, may be where Beaver followed Yamǫǫ̀zaa and where Yamǫǫ̀zaa was supposed to have laid logs. I later asked the elders about this connection but never got a definitive answer. Rather, they told the story of the old man who walked and named many of the locales so that people could find their way to resources. He walked and named the places as he came to them. This, they said, happened during the time when all was harmonious—after Yamǫǫ̀zaa gave all beings their own place and explained their social relations and responsibilities within the dè.

In May 2002, Georgina Chocolate and I were staying with Phillip Nitsiza in Whatì when Jimmy Martin stopped in to visit. I told Jimmy and Georgina about an experience I had had with a raven while in the bush. After carefully listening to me, Jimmy told the six Raven stories that he had heard from his grandfather. The one that stays with me, however, is the story I first heard from Joe Mantla on 5 August 1994, when he came to visit me at my cabin. Joe had been the community k'àowo for Gamètì when I arrived in 1993. For the position of k'àowo, Chief Henry Gon replaced Joe in the spring of 1994 with a man who, although known as a very caring and helpful person, liked to travel to Yellowknife and so was not considered to have the character and temperament to be community k'àowo. Most people prefer a community k'àowo who "stays around," taking only short trips to the bush, so that he is in the community when people need him. Furthermore, the community k'àowo organizes hand games and drum dances and tells community members what is going on. My cabin was next to Joe Mantla's. He and Sally Anne Zoe visited specifically so that Joe could tell the story of Wolf and Raven.

At one time, Raven could eat anything. He could hunt animals for food. Then Raven became very greedy. Raven could fly and could see everything and so was very knowledgeable. Others depended on Raven for knowledge of where animals such as the caribou were traveling. Raven was responsible for the survival of others who were restricted to the ground. Raven and Wolf were brothers-in-law because Wolf's sister was married to Raven, and Raven's sister was married to Wolf. Both Raven and Wolf were k'àowo for their camps. Wolf was a good hunter, so he had many people following him. Even though he killed a lot of caribou, the meat was gone in no time because so many people followed Wolf. Raven was more powerful than Wolf because Raven was *k'àowodeè* (who knew everything because Raven could see everything from the air). He flew and could see everything. He had the ability to provide people with information because he knew everything.

There was no food, and everyone was starving.

It is said that Wolf and Raven would meet and tell stories; everyone listened. One time they met at Wolf's house. They took turns telling stories. Wolf noticed that Raven was happy. He said, "Raven, my brother-in-law, you are happy, yet we are starving. We will starve to death unless we find food. You, who are flying around, do you know where all the caribou are? You are happy about something. What is it? I can hardly make it around I am so hungry for food."

Raven denied that he knew anything. "My brother-in-law, there is nothing around. We both are in the same predicament; there are no caribou around."

Wolf could not understand why Raven was so happy, so when Raven was telling a story, Wolf went out and told the kids, "Find Raven's pack-sack, look in it, and see if there is anything there. He may be carrying caribou meat with him. So look." The kids looked, and they found dried meat.

After a while, Raven said, "My brother-in-law, it is getting dark, I'm going home. My home is very far."

Wolf said, "Yes, it is time. It is late."

Raven left.

Wolf told two men with ʔįk'ǫ̀ to work together. Each had the ability to see a long way, so they watched where Raven went. The men watched Raven travel toward the sunrise. Finally, after one put charcoal on his eyes and the other wiped it off, the one with charcoal could see farther. He saw where Raven was hiding all the caribou, and he saw that they were contained behind a snow fence.

Wolf sent for Fox and told Fox, "Go and find the fire. Put your tail in the fire, and free the caribou." Fox traveled to the caribou. When he arrived, he lit his tail on fire and walked among the caribou. The smoke bothered them, and they ran away from the smoke even though the snow bank was high, and they do not like the snow touching their bellies. That is the reason Fox now has a black tip on his tail.

Raven was upset when the caribou ran free. He felt like they were his; he had become greedy.

Wolf spoke strongly to Raven, "We are living here together. We are here to help each other, and because you are greedy, you are not help- ing others. I am your brother-in-law. Do you want your sister to starve? Do you want my sister, your wife, to starve?"

Wolf and the other people put Raven in a circle and talked to him. They talked and talked to him. They knew they would have to be harsh because the people had almost starved. People who deliberately hide or steal food from others should be excluded from the group. Finally, after listening to everyone, Wolf decided Raven could eat only decomposing food after that because he had caused so much distress by hoarding fresh meat.

Wolf said, "When the animals die, you will eat them. People will live around you, and you will eat their garbage. You can no longer kill for food."

That is how Raven lives now. When water is poured outside, Raven drinks the dirty water. When garbage is put out, he will eat it, and that is how he survives. What a thing to happen! It is pitiful for a hunter to lose his right to hunt! That is what happened to Raven. It was very "pitiful" and is very degrading for a great hunter, who had also been an important k'àowodeè.

That is how powerful k'àowo were in the old days. They are the ones who are supposed to take care of the people, but even k'àowo can be- come confused and greedy. When this happens, the people can no lon- ger depend on them. People who do not think about others should not be followed.

I have heard from several elders and hunters that caribou did not always migrate to the Tłı̨chǫ region and that then the people depended on fish and rabbit. Then a hunter had a dream, and he walked to the caribou and invited them to come.

It is said that during the temporal eras known as whaèhdǫǫ̀, "a long time ago," and gotso, "time of our ancestors," the k'àowo and yahbahti were very powerful. They could find animals through their dreams and their visions. Sometimes the k'àowo just got up and moved to where the caribou were. He would not say anything, he would just move, and the people could follow if they wished. It is said, only by being intelligent did a k'àowo have the confidence to move to where food would be found.

It is said, during the whaèhdǫ̀ period human beings were led by great yahbahti with very powerful ʔįk'ǫ̀. Yahbahti had the intelligence to know and to care for the people in a way that affected the whole dè. Not all local bands had a yahbahti because only a few people are capable of such great intelligence while also being strong physically and mentally. They could be warriors and could use their strength to help or destroy others. Each of the regions had at least one yahbahti, and all bands had k'àowo for the tasks that needed doing. Yahbahti had a camp k'àowo, who would tell the people in the camp what needed to be done. The time was good for all beings; they lived well at this time.

It was at this time that an old man walked through the dè and named all the locations so people could find their way. He walked and named the places as he came to them. Life was good; there were plants to eat and to use for medicine. All beings knew their relationships with others. Tłįchǫ either walked or used birch bark canoes to travel to the caribou. In the spring, they would camp at favorite fishing spots that also had many birch trees. They would build caribou fences on the ice, fish, and make birch bark canoes while waiting for the ice to melt. If the caribou walked toward them, they would kill many. In the fall, they would gather and fish for the winter.

During this time, there were plenty of fish, birds, bark for canoes and dishes, and there was moss. Our elders had place-names and an abundance of stories to explain how to use all that lived within the dè. Our grandparents' stories told us how to survive. It is said, life was peaceful, and although they were afraid of the Inuit because they did not know them, sometimes they met with families of Inuit in the fall at a place they both used, called "Kǫ̀k'èetì." The Kitikmeot Inuit used this place in the summer, and the Tłįchǫ traveled there in the fall to hunt caribou. Sometimes the Inuit and Tłįchǫ families camped near each other, visiting and getting to know one another.

In February 2000, the Kitikmeot elders came to an initial Bathurst caribou herd–co-management meeting with their leaders. The meeting was sponsored by the government but held in Behchokǫ̀. At the end of the first day, a meal was provided for these guests under the direction of the Tłįchǫ elders. The two groups visited—telling stories—until three in the morning. The Tłįchǫ and Inuinnaqtun translators were exhausted. They had to translate from their own languages into English and back to their own languages. Although most of the elders could understand both Tłįchǫ and Inuinnaqtun, those who were of middle age and younger could not. But those of us sitting, listening, and eating, we were able to think about how the Inuit and Dene have developed close friendships yet continued to be wary of one another.[5]

We learned about people and places that both groups knew from dwelling on the tundra. Many of these stories were reminiscent of Margaret Lafferty's story of how some Tłįchǫ had visited with the Kitikmeot Inuit. Although Margaret first told this story on 27 October 1995 to Sally Anne while documenting the Wekweètì elders' thoughts on BHP's proposed diamond mine for the Environmental Assessment Review Panel (Dene Cultural Institute 1996), I also remember her telling the story in 1999 at the fall camp at Deèzàatì. She told the story immediately after Elizabeth Chocolate from Behchokǫ̀ mimicked Inuit drumming while singing a song she had learned while camping with Inuit at Deèzàatì as a young woman. Margaret said, "We roamed on the tundra. Traveling close to the Inuit around Kǫk'èetì. The Inuit came back with our elders. Just straight across from here—on the other side of Deèzàatì. That's where the Inuit lived with our elders. The Inuit came back with them by wooden sleigh. The Inuit followed them and lived with them, and then they were heading to Behchokǫ̀; therefore, our ancestors lent them dogs, a sleigh, and a dog harness, and they took a trip to Behchokǫ̀ with our elders. After they went to Behchokǫ̀ and came back here, they lived with us for a while, and then one day we went our separate ways. They went toward Kǫk'èetì, and we went to the trees; that's how it was."

While visiting with the Inuit after the meeting in February 2000—the Yellowknives and the Chipewyan Dene had also been invited to eat with the elders, but they returned immediately to Yellowknife—the Tłįchǫ elders told stories to the Inuit elders about how Edzo and Akaitcho had made peace.

For a long time, life was hard but peaceful, until Akaitcho and his band, who were Yellowknives Dene, started raiding Tłįchǫ camps for furs and food, when life became very difficult. Sometimes Akaitcho's followers would take the women too. Tłįchǫ had more powerful ʔįk'ǫǫ̀, which allowed them constantly to think about where Akaitcho's band would be.

It is said, Tłįchǫ people respect those who use their minds. For this reason, they always tried to follow the most intelligent k'àowo and yahbahti who are capable of protecting them, the old folks, and the

Figure 2.4. From left: Margaret Lafferty, Elizabeth Chocolate (from Behchokǫ̀), Bella Zoe, Elise Simpson, and Rosalie Martin at fall hunting camp at Deèzàatì, 1999. They stopped telling stories to watch the hunters coming up from the boats. (Photograph by the author)

children. ʔɪk'ǫ̀ provided the Tł̨chǫ with the means to stay out of the way of violence because certain people could see where the Akaitcho band was traveling. Some of the great yahbahti such as Sahtso could use their power on Akaitcho's band, and it is said that Akaitcho's band feared Sahtso and knew how his camp looked, and they would say, "Sahtso lives here so let's run away."

During that time, a Tł̨chǫ camp was attacked, and they killed everyone except a Tł̨chǫ woman known as "Whanɪkw'o," the woman who found "whites."

This story made an impression on me the first time I heard it because it is similar to the Stolen Woman stories published elsewhere (see, for example, Cruikshank 1983). Amen Tailbone told the story on 30 March 1993 in conjunction with both the Muskrat story and the one of how Yamǫ̀ǫzaa created social order. He led into the events involving the woman by saying, "After all that [referring to what happened to Muskrat and Yamǫ̀ǫzaa], how can some humans continue to disobey the laws given to us by Yamǫ̀ǫzaa, and how can they forget to respect the place of others?"

A few days later, on 2 April 1993, Alphonse Quitte used the story of the Tłįchǫ woman Whanıkw'o to emphasize the importance of understanding change due to the demands of new technology. I had been using my hand-held electronic organizer in the office where we were discussing language when Alphonse and Marie Quitte, considered senior elders, came to visit. They teased me, calling my electronic planner "Allice's *élan*." An élan is a small skidoo that trappers use for easy travel on small trails in the bush. Alphonse, who is known to have a good memory for stories and songs, then told the story of Whanıkw'o.

Long before Akaitcho's bands raided Tłįchǫ camps, some Cree raided and killed all but one Tłįchǫ woman. Those men decided to save her so she could mend their moccasins. She saw that they had the scalps of her family. She had depended on her older brother, and when she saw his streak of white hair, she did not feel like living. She cried and cried when she saw her brother's hair and her father's hair. They took her; and before she knew it, she was a long way from home. One day they told her to stay at camp and that they would come back for her when they were finished trading. She followed them because she noticed that they were taking the scalps of her family. She had heard them joking that they were going to tell the white traders that her family's scalps were the furs of an animal that lived under the water. She cried and cried.

Whanıkw'o was very capable of living off the land, which she had learned from being isolated and taking care of herself during menarche. It is said that it is very important that women stay by themselves during their menarche so that they can learn to take care of themselves if they are ever alone without their families. They learn to put up their own tents, find food, and sew. At this time, the women are not always alone because their grandmothers come to them and tell them stories. Whanıkw'o had lived on the land, learned well, and listened, so even though she was sad and felt hopeless, she knew what to do.

When Akaitcho's men left the next morning, she followed them. She saw them walk into a large rock. She was surprised and initially did not know what to do. She noticed that a very pale woman kept coming and going from the rock, and so she called her a "Kweèt'ıı." It seemed that these very pale people lived in the large stones. She decided to go to the house and talk to the woman. The woman did not speak Tłįchǫ, but because the Tłįchǫ are good communicators and know how to use words, Whanıkw'o communicated to this woman. She explained, "The furs are the scalps of my relatives; they are not the furs of animals that live under the water."

The woman went and got her husband and introduced Whanıkw'o. After hearing her story, he went back to Akaitcho's men and told them, "We will wait until tomorrow morning to complete the trade. Stay in the house tonight." But the house caught fire, killing those who had kidnapped her.

Whanıkw'o remained with the trader and his wife for two years. She learned their technology and learned about trading. As was consistent with the way she was brought up, she learned and thought about everything she was experiencing with her head and her heart, so she could carry the knowledge always. She had knowledge about how Kweèt'ìı behaved and about their technology.

After two years, she took matches, traps, and guns and left to find her relatives. As she prepared to leave, the trader and his wife were worried about her. She explained she would know her place when she started to walk in the area where the trees were small. They told her that whomever she met first would be the first k'aàwı, or "trading boss."

The first people she ran across were Chipewyan, who held their bows on her. They were afraid because she had a gun. She told them her story, and they became the first k'aàwı. She continued traveling toward her own place. She found her people near a good place for fishing. When she walked toward them, she shot a couple of times in the air with the rifle. They said, "Who threw the fish eggs into the fire? Who's making all the crackles?" When they saw her, her people were afraid. They thought she had died.

Whenever I have heard this story, tellers stress that Whanıkw'o brought to the people knowledge of a new technology and the skill to use it. According to most of the elders, the story of Whanıkw'o is especially important because she helped the people through difficult times by bringing them Kweèt'ìı knowledge and technology. After she brought this knowledge to her people, regional bands started traveling annually and setting up camp together near the trading post. Her husband became the first k'aàwıdeè, a trader who understood and had access to ʔık'ǫ̀ǫ that was particularly powerful over the factors at the trading posts and therefore who traded the furs of those who followed him. The followers usually stayed behind in the camp because they trusted the k'aàwı and k'aàwıdeè, who understood Kweèt'ìı and would negotiate good trades for them. The people always chose to follow k'aàwı and k'aàwıdeè who had the character to be stubborn and would not give in.

After the land claim agreement-in-principle was initialed in Gamètì in 1999, an office was set up in Yellowknife for the Tłįchǫ negotiating team as well as for the four chiefs and their band councillors and staff to have their own place to meet while attending various committee meetings. This office quickly became a gathering place for people from the Tłįchǫ communities, students attending school in Yellowknife, and adults in various wage-earning positions in Yellowknife.

In January 2002, I heard the story of Whanıkw'o from Louis Whane, a senior elder from Wekweètì. He walked into the Tłįchǫ office in Yellowknife and came to where I was sitting and then asked Georgina Franki to translate. He expressed his concern that young people were forgetting the importance of Whanıkw'o and how she had brought Kweèt'įı̀ knowledge to the Tłįchǫ people. He emphasized that to survive, all people should be open to learning and that women's knowledge is important as well. He had expressed this same concern to other elders in Whatì in 2000. In Whatì, he used the story to emphasize that young people were not respecting women and their knowledge. In 2002, however, he pointed to a public-relations poster associated with the land claim. He was very concerned about how Tłįchǫ history was being portrayed and how it was used to tell the stories. Louis felt that the picture showed that only men were important. He pointed out that all people have knowledge — including women — and that Whanıkw'o had done "something big for the people."

After the agreement-in-principle was initialed, the elders became concerned that several places were not protected: Mǫwhìtłį,[6] ʔezǫdzìtì, and ʔedèezhìì. As of 2006, ʔezǫdzìtì officially became "Edzǫdzìtì" as a protected area through the Tłįchǫ Agreement. The Tłįchǫ and Dehcho Dene leadership worked together to protect ʔedèezhìì because the plateau is used by trappers from both Dehcho and Tłįchǫ nèèk'e. In the early 2000s, it was given interim protection under the NWT Protected Areas Strategy (2006). In official protected-area documents, ʔedèezhìì is known as "Edéhzhíe," its Slavey name among the Dehcho Dene.

Andrew Gon told Sally Anne Zoe, Madelaine Chocolate, and me the story of ʔezǫdzìtì.

It is said, during those chaotic times when Akaitcho's band had been killing so many people, the Tłįchǫ could avoid them because they knew the trails and places so well. Sometimes they were surprised, or there were too many young and old people to hide, so the Tłįchǫ decided to retreat to ʔezǫdzìtì, where the fish and small game are plentiful. Only the hunters traveled away from that place so they could get caribou.

The people were so afraid for their children. While at ʔezǫdzìtì, Edzo's father, a yahbahti who had thirty-two sons, decided to teach his sons to use their ʔı̨k'ǫ̀ so they could put a stop to the killing. Only one of his sons was unable to learn and eventually died.

Edzo's father was pleased he had other sons who could learn, and he thought, "If I work with them, they will learn the knowledge that comes from the time of Yamǫ̀ǫzaa, and we will be able to take care of Akaitcho and his followers, and the Sahtu Dene—Bear Lake Slavey—and we ourselves can live in peace."

He said to his boys, "Our enemy, Akaitcho and his followers, are pitiful people; do not bother them. If they are insolent toward you, just snarl at them."

Alphonse Quitte, who was renowned among the other elders for having a good memory for detailed storytelling and singing the very old songs, told the story of Edzo on several occasions. The most memorable version was his telling while at the summer camp at K'ı̨ahkw'àı̨kaà in 1994. It was there that the elders asked him to tell the story as well as to sing the old songs so that young people visiting the camp could learn them.

It is said, when the sons grew up, Akaitcho's followers became afraid of this family. Edzo's father was especially proud of his eldest son, Edzo. If Edzo lived in a camp, Akaitcho's band wouldn't raid it. It is said that they were so afraid of Edzo that if they visited an empty campsite and realized that Edzo had been there, then they would leave and go home. Edzo never thought about killing in retaliation. Edzo always thought about peace. He used the Yamǫ̀ǫzaa stories that had taught them to respect others and to know their place, to think with. Edzo, who was the last great yahbahti, knew that Akaitcho's band had forgotten their place within the dè. They had been greedy for furs. He also knew Akaitcho was a powerful yahbahti and knew that Akaitcho said he wanted to kill Edzo and eat his flesh. He knew people feared Akaitcho. Akaitcho could be kind. He had saved Sir John Franklin from starving, and Edzo's own sister lived in Akaitcho's camp. Even though as a yahbahti Edzo was a great warrior, he avoided his enemy until one day when Edzo and his followers were around Gots'ǫkàtì.

Edzo belonged to the Gots'ǫkàtìgot'ı̨ı̨ regional band. Even so, they usually stayed far to the west, with only hunters traveling toward Kǫ̀k'èetì and Deèzàatì to fish and hunt caribou and musk ox if there were no caribou and only if a yahbahti traveled with them. On this occasion,

Edzo was traveling with his family as well as several hunters. Edzo traveled toward Łìhtì, which he considered his home. And he traveled toward Kǫk'èetì and Deèzàatì. Edzo was tired of fighting, and he knew that if it continued, no one would survive. They had passed Akaitcho around Gots'ǫkàtì in the night, and Edzo, who knew the area so well, had passed Akaitcho without being heard. He and his band were resting on the island known as "Wek'ehàɨlųdìi," but that night when he was getting ready to move, he thought, "We can't live like this forever. It can't be like this all the time."

He said to the people in his band, "I am tired of living like this. I feel like Akaitcho has a knife at my neck all the time. I am going back to see him. Tell me what you think and whether you will come with me."

All the members of Edzo's band knew where Akaitcho was camped. They had traveled around his camp to avoid him. The people following Edzo talked for a long time. Edzo listened and again explained what he thought. His two brothers decided to follow him because their Ɂɨk'ǫǫ̀ complemented his. The others chose to leave him and to continue traveling west.

Edzo said, "OK, go on, but remember to travel only at night and do not have a fire."

They left. Edzo hid his wife and little son on an island and told her to wait for four days.

It is said that he told his wife, "If I do not return within four days, travel at night with our small son and join the others." He took his older son as a witness.

Edzo's sister was married to a Sahtu Dene named K'atehwhì. They lived in Akaitcho's camp because K'atehwhì was Akaitcho's k'àowo. That night Edzo crept into the camp and crawled under the flaps of his sister's tepee. They talked.

Finally, K'atehwhì returned, and Edzo said, "I am tired of the killing and fighting. I want to put an end to it, and I need your help."

They devised a plan, and because K'atehwhì was camp k'àowo and everyone in Akaitcho's camp listened to him, he was able to tell all the people to go near the shore just before Edzo arrived. They were away from where Edzo planned to meet Akaitcho. One of Edzo's brothers was to control their minds while his other brother controlled any metal weapons.

The next day Edzo and his brothers entered Akaitcho's camp. As planned, one brother controlled the minds of Akaitcho's followers, all of whom were at the shore, and the other paid attention to all the metal weapons in the camp. Edzo concentrated on Akaitcho's mind. He sat down facing Akaitcho, saying nothing, and even though Akaitcho threw a knife at Edzo, it only landed between his legs because Edzo's brother controlled the metal.

Then Edzo turned his back to Akaitcho, who had started talking of killing him as well as all the Tłı̨chǫ people. Edzo kept his back to him. Akaitcho continued yelling about killing and eating the flesh of Tłı̨chǫ, especially Edzo. But Edzo said nothing. Edzo knew that if he kept quiet and used his mind to control Akaitcho, Akaitcho would slowly think of peace. Akaitcho repeated himself several times, yelling. Akaitcho's words slowly softened, and he started to talk of peace. Edzo turned around and faced him.

It is said that when Edzo spoke, he said, "What? You no longer want to eat my flesh?" Then he talked of peace; his words were so strong that the trees started to shake, and they cracked. Those trees are still standing at Gots'ǫkàtì. You can see the power of Edzo.

After Edzo and Akaitcho met, it was decided that there would be no more fighting. There would be peace so that all the children and grandchildren would have a good life. They said that if anyone from either side raided, hurt, or killed people from either nation, they could go and kill all the persons who did that. The Tłı̨chǫ people could do that to Akaitcho's band, and Akaitcho's followers could do that to the Tłı̨chǫ. Once peace was made, Edzo went back and collected his wife and child. Everyone danced for several days and nights.

During the last week of August and the first week of September 1988, I was fortunate to be among those who traveled with the Tłı̨chǫ back to Gots'ǫkàtì. We danced all night under the light of the full moon—dancing around the circle, continuing to deepen the track started when Edzo and Akaitcho made peace. We walked to the rock where Edzo had left his son to witness the events. The hunters killed many caribou. Much of the caribou meat was dried, but most was sent back to the community freezers for winter. While at the camp, every adult there stressed the importance of the Edzo peace agreement. They would say, "It is also said, to this day Tłı̨chǫ people live under the Edzo peace agreement, which is a big law because Edzo was a great yahbahti. He was a great man because he made life easier for the Tłı̨chǫ. Today Tłı̨chǫ are expected to live under Edzo's law."

Tłı̨chǫ are similarly expected to live according to the agreement with the Canadian government made by Mǫwhì in the early 1920s. It is difficult to establish the context in which I first heard Mǫwhì's story. I heard parts of it as it was wrapped up with stories of trading. When Alphonse Quitte told us of the meeting between Mǫwhì and the treaty commissioner, I had previously heard it, but never as he told it.

Since the time of Whanıkw'o, the people have followed a k'aàwı. According to most of the elders, there were two k'aàwı from each region. They would meet annually, several miles from the trading post, and would talk about who would be best among them to negotiate the trading deal. Only a few people went to the post.

If the man ʔek'aàwıdeè was among them, the people always wanted him to trade with the factor at the post. The Tłıchǫ were able to do this because of the knowledge brought back by Whanıkw'o. He, like other k'aàwıdeè—"big trading bosses"—had ʔık'ǫǫ̀ for Kweèt'ıı̀ and therefore understood and knew factors better than anyone. It is said, if he touched anything that came from Kweèt'ıı̀, his medicine would kill him. Many people followed him when he was traveling to Behchokǫ̀ to trade. Because ʔek'aàwıdeè knew the Kweèt'ıı̀ so well, he was instrumental in helping to select who among them would talk to the treaty commissioner.

Word came that the treaty commissioner would be traveling to Behchokǫ̀ and asking the Tłıchǫ to sign a friendship treaty. The Tłıchǫ people gathered and discussed this matter and discussed who would talk to the commissioner for them. It is said, at trading posts they had heard stories about how the treaty commissioner would make promises, write them down, but never keep them. It is said, if they lose the paper or if they do not read it all the time, Kweèt'ıı̀ forget. The Tłıchǫ discussed this matter and talked about selecting a person with a strong character to speak for them. Rather than following a k'aàwı or k'àowo or yahbahti, they selected a person to talk for all of them.

It is said, Mǫwhì was suggested by his uncle.[7] For more than six days, the Tłıchǫ people gathered and talked together so they could draw on everyone's knowledge. They developed a strategy and discussed who would be the best person to talk for them. They discussed Mǫwhì's character; they discussed all his strong points as well as his weaknesses. Everyone agreed he would be good because he was stubborn and would not give. They thought he would protect them against the Kweèt'ıı̀'s taking their place, as set down by Yamǫǫ̀zaa. They thought he could protect them against the Kweèt'ıı̀'s taking Tłıchǫ nèèk'e for their own use, as they had done south of Tıdeè. ʔek'aàwıdeè knew Kweèt'ı̨ minds, and he thought that Mǫwhì could stand up to them. The people selected Mǫwhì, and they knew ʔek'aàwıdeè would advise him.

When asked to speak for them, Mǫwhì did not answer immediately. Rather, he listened to the people as they discussed his character, both his strengths and his weaknesses. He then said yes and sat with his uncle, who had taught Mǫwhì as they traveled together.

His uncle said, "Be careful, do not say yes until it is your way. Kweèt'ı̨ do not listen very well, so they can twist your words. Do not agree until you are sure that they have heard you."

Mǫwhì trusted his uncle, who had knowledge of Kweèt'ı̨. His uncle warned him, saying, "Someday Kweèt'ı̨ will take over our place within the dè, just as they have done in other places, and so you must make sure not to agree to anything unless the treaty commissioner has really listened to you. Only then agree. Make sure it is your way or not at all."

Mǫwhì spoke for the people. Mǫwhì was stubborn, and after several days of talking he walked away from the treaty commissioner. It is said, Mǫwhì followed ʔek'aàwıdeè's words. During the treaty talks, the Yellowknives traveled to Behchokǫ̀, with the k'àowo Sangris, who supported the words Mǫwhì spoke and recognized Mǫwhì as k'àowodeè. Sangris worked cooperatively with the other k'àowo and k'aàwı under Edzo's law. They supported Mǫwhì, who did not take the treaty money until his words were understood.

It is said Bishop Breynat cared for the people. He traveled north with the treaty commissioner to ensure the people were heard. It was the bishop who talked to Mǫwhì after he walked away. The bishop explained that it was all right to sign the treaty, that it would be better for the people if Mǫwhì signed the treaty, and that the people would have "the land" as outlined by Mǫwhì, and that all would be the same as long as the river flows and the sun shines. On the fourth day, Mǫwhì signed the treaty. It is said that there is now a "Big Agreement" with the treaty commissioner and the queen. And as Mǫwhì's uncle had warned, there would be a river of Kweèt'ı̨ that does not turn back, and as Romie Wetrade said, "They are like a river flowing forever onto our place."

Tłı̨chǫ have always followed those who are intelligent and encourage people to work cooperatively. Since the coming of the traders, they chose k'aàwı whose task was to take their furs and trade with them because the k'aàwı were the ones who understood the factors. They spoke for those whose furs they had.

Mǫwhì was the first k'àowodeè to speak for all Tłįchǫ people — the first time the Tłįchǫ chose one person to talk for them. They did this because they knew that they had a huge task ahead of them. And just as they listened to the k'àowo they chose to follow, they all listened to and supported Mǫwhì to protect Tłįchǫ nèèk'e from the increasing flow of Kweèt'ı̨.

Before the treaty, most people would stay at the village on ʔįhdaak'ètì, and only the k'aàwı and k'aàwıdeè would go to the trading post. When they heard the treaty commissioner was coming, most people went to Behchokǫ̀ to talk about what they would do. It is also said that several of the elders who now live in Gamètì were at the treaty signing — they were children then. After the "papers" were signed, the treaty commissioner chose Mǫwhì as the grand chief, and the people chose the two k'aàwı from each region as their chiefs. Initially, the grand chief selected his successor. Mǫwhì was the first grand chief until his death in 1936, and he selected Jimmy Bruneau as the second. Bruneau was grand chief until 1969.

It is said, neither the queen nor the federal government lived up to the agreements in the treaty. Even though Mǫwhì talked about everything, he did not realize just how strong was the government's ability to twist words. He did not realize that Kweèt'ı̨ would try to change their agreement or that, for them, "land" did not mean everything. For the Tłįchǫ, all agreements should be honored, which is why it is important to remember the past and the stories that tell of the past.

Mǫwhì had used the stories to think with; he had listened to the people. He had made a huge agreement under both Yamǫ̀ǫzaa's social rules and Edzo's peace agreement. Both provided rules on how to live peacefully with other beings, including other humans. He talked to the treaty commissioner in a way that would allow the Tłįchǫ to continue living where their ancestors had "walked," while sharing their knowledge with a new group of people and while learning the knowledge and skill of the Kweèt'ı̨. He wanted his people to continue surviving within the dè.

Many elders tell of how the government made and changed laws without telling the Tłįchǫ. David Chocolate tells of a time in the 1930s when he was trapping and he found some meat on the trail. He thought the caribou meat had fallen from someone's sled. It never crossed his mind that it would be poisonous, so he fed it to his dogs. They all died. He feels fortunate that he did not eat the meat, but losing his dogs could have caused him to freeze or starve to death. Life was becoming chaotic once again.

It is said that when Mǫwhì died, he left a message that Jimmy Bruneau would be the next grand chief. It was Grand Chief Jimmy Bruneau who said, "If we are to remain a strong people, we must educate our children and grandchildren in both our ways and those of the Kweèt'ı̨̀, so they can say, 'We are strong like two people'."

Romie Wetrade is a quiet man whose words I usually remember because they are said with a great deal of thought. I especially think of his words when I think of the stories I have heard and the importance of leaving stories to the youth. Although many academics have written down and many Dene have spoken the words Romie spoke publicly in September 1994, his words had the most power for me. I remember him saying: "Mǫwhì drew the map with his mind—as long as the sun rises, as long as the river flows, as long as this land shall last, and nothing will change for the people, that is what he [Mǫwhì] said. That is an important agreement that he made for us, and we can't let it go. He did big things for us, and we came all this way, and we raised our children, and we have been raised on this dè. To this day, we still raise our children on it."

I also think about Romie's comment to Madelaine Chocolate and me in November 2003: "Here we sit with gray hair, and we speak because we have obeyed our parents. The ones who have not obeyed their parents have been left behind. When our people talk, they are truthful."

Contextualizing and Temporality

Concerning my question "What does it mean to be knowledgeable if you say you are from the land?" four anthropological issues arise from the narratives told in this chapter. The first issue is time, the second tension, the third personhood, and the fourth context. Together, these narratives depict particular aspects of the Tłı̨chǫ sense of time, contextualizing periods of tension and methods of achieving harmony. The occurrence with Yamǫ̀ǫzaa and his brother, Yamǫ̀ǫgaà, provided all beings with a place and the rules associated with their relationship with other beings—creating differences between all beings. The stories, then, are more than a rationalization of the present (Rosaldo 1980, 91); they present a perspective.

The Place of Temporality

Anthropologists generally accept that northern Dene narratives contain knowledge of considerable time depth, which archaeologists have been able to draw on to their advantage (Nicholas and Andrews 1997). Christopher Hanks (1996, 1997) and June Helm (1981a, 296) match the written records of explorers and historians to occurrences remembered in oral narratives; and Julie Cruikshank (1998, 1–24; 2001) considers divergent perspectives when comparing the oral narratives of Yukon First Nations peoples with scientific and historic written records. Helm argues that although Tłįchǫ recognize events that occurred long before the coming of Kweèt'ìį, they did not conceive these events as falling into a temporal sequence until they had incorporated the European system of time into their own system (2000, 221).

Helm (2000) divides Tłįchǫ temporality into two eras, which she refers to as "floating time" and "linear time." A summary of these eras confirms that the Tłįchǫ have a sense of temporal sequencing with considerable time depth and that although each era can be associated with the replacement of tension by harmonious relations, eras are not bounded. Rather, events and occurrences that took place in the past continue to unfold as they surface in the present. Furthermore, Tłįchǫ have incorporated linear time into their framework as a way of understanding and working with Kweèt'ìį. The two temporal systems run parallel.

As stated earlier, each oral narrative originates within one of four eras. All Tłįchǫ adults know when a specific story originated. As described earlier, gowoo was the era when all people and animals were human and when Yamǫǫ̀zaa and his brother were growing up in a tense, chaotic world. At the end of this era, Yamǫǫ̀zaa set down a number of social rules for behavior that provided language and established specific relationships between all beings.

During whaèhdǫǫ̀, which is often referred to in English as "when the world was new" (Blondin 1990) or "the time of Yamǫǫ̀zaa," all beings became distinct, with different strengths based on the place from which they experienced the dè, and in so doing developed close reciprocal relations, including the ability to communicate with one another. It seems that during the time of Yamǫǫ̀zaa beings became cognizant that they were "of the dè" and belonged to places.

After this period came gotso, "the time of our forbears." The elders I worked with heard from their ancestors that during this period tensions between their ancestors and the Yellowknives started about three generations before they were born. In response to this tension, Edzo's father trained his sons to use ʔık'ǫǫ̀[8] to reestablish harmony. Edzo is credited with reestablishing harmony with the Yellowknives. Like other oral narratives, stories of Edzo originate in places. As people travel trails, they tell and retell these stories in places where they are intertwined with all that had occurred before, providing Tłıchǫ not only with the social rules as set by Yamǫ̀ǫzaa, but with the agreement of peace between the Chipewyan and the Tłıchǫ. As shown in chapters 5 and 6, incidents with Kweèt'ıı̨, such as the interactions between Mǫwhì and the treaty commissioner, also influence the flow of these relations.

Tłıchǫ elders themselves have been living within dìı, "the time of one's own memories." Throughout this period, the Tłıchǫ have maintained their relationships within the dè, within Tłıchǫ nèèk'e, and have consistently sought to maintain the right to personal autonomy while working cooperatively with others.

In discussing occurrences from the past, Tłıchǫ will use the specific names of people or groups of people, other-than-human beings, and events as well as the terms for eras and in so doing give a sense of temporal longevity and validity to the happening recounted. Stories originating in the past are remembered through the telling and retelling and are brought to the present when experienced. The process is the same whether the event occurred yesterday, several decades ago, or during the time of Yamǫ̀ǫzaa. This bringing forward of occurrences through experiencing the narratives one has heard is the same regardless of whether the story originated before or after the introduction of Kweèt'ıı̨ lineal time. If the listener only hears the narratives and dismisses the importance of the narratives' growing and changing with those who experience them, then it is possible the listener will have the impression that, for the Tłıchǫ, narratives float through time.

Based on my experience, I think the idea of floating time is misleading. Rather than floating, time and place of origin ground the stories. While firmly grounded, the stories travel with the individuals who tell them, thus allowing the occurrence and information in the narratives to be experienced in the present. The stories, then, are rooted in place and grow with the individuals who carry and tell them.

Just as the Tłıchǫ emphasize the importance of knowing more than one way and of thinking about the ways of other beings, and just as Jimmy Bruneau directed all Tłıchǫ to know the way of the Kweèt'ıı̨ as well as their own way, they have incorporated two systems of considering temporal sequencing. The linear system introduced by Kweèt'ıı̨ is used when required alongside their own system, which enfolds the past and the future into the present—a system that Henry Sharp calls "simultaneous time" (2001, 63).

Linear time is not, strictly speaking, an era, as Helm describes it. Rather, it sits alongside the Tłıchǫ temporal system. The two are parallel yet linked through relations and through the knowledge that all beings, including different human beings, experience different places and therefore have different ways of perceiving the dè. Tłįchǫ continue to enfold past events with present happenings, while also accepting linear time. They have incorporated linear time into a framework that is open to other perspectives. It is not uncommon for societies to have several concurrent temporal systems. Joy Hendry (2000), for example, found that the Japanese are continually incorporating different ideas about time and do not necessarily change or drop old ways in adopting new ones.

Contextualizing the Story

Roy Dilley reminds us that "context is expandable," encompassing connections and disconnections that may be relevant to any given situation (1999, 39). I have often heard the stories related in this chapter in situations in which there does not seem to be any apparent reason for the telling. However, there has always been a setting in which I "heard" the story and remembered it. I have also heard these oral narratives told in response to some stimulus, such as the arrival of caribou, an individual's behavior, a question that has been asked, or a visit to a particular locale. Stories are told after a trip in which a task was accomplished, especially when those who are younger tell of their experience to a group of elders, who then interweave this occurrence with stories originating in the past. Greg Sarris similarly shows how the storyteller encourages "interlocutors to examine presuppositions that shaped and are embedded in their questions" (1993, 19).

It is interesting to note that in the 1950s Helm heard the story of Whanıkw'o—the woman who first found whites and brought their technology and the idea of trading to the Tłįchǫ—more often than any other story. Reflecting on her observation, I realized that she heard this narrative when Chief Bruneau was stressing that every Tłįchǫ person should learn both ways so they could be strong like two people.

In comparison, I heard the Yamǫ̀ǫzaa story, in which he gave all beings their own place from which to establish social relations within the dè, more often than any other stories in the period between 1993 and 1995, when Tłįchǫ chiefs were negotiating self-government together with land claims. It was also in this period that the elder George Blondin wrote *Yamoria the Lawmaker: Stories of the Dene* (1999). It is difficult to ignore the context in which the elders were emphasizing the importance of understanding the basis of Dene laws.

The elders told the story of Edzo—a Tłįchǫ responsible for making peace with Akaitcho, a Yellowknives Dene—more often than other narratives during the late 1990s, when the Yellowknives and Tłįchǫ were discussing overlap issues in preparation for the settlement of their respective land-claim agreements with the federal and territorial governments.

Important narratives are told in the context of large issues such as the earlier examples and are told during specific interactions with other-than-human beings, such as caribou, or with humans, such as when hunters or politicians return from carrying out their activities; and stories are told as individuals sit around fires. Stories, then, are a mode of discourse used to assist oneself and others to consider happenings that occur on a daily basis, and for this reason I think of them as providing a perspective from which to live in the right way or, as the elders say, to "think with." Ingold, in seeking to place human beings in the world where their everyday tasks are part of the landscape, similarly argues that stories are not "metaphorical representations of the world, but a form of poetic involvement" (2000, 57). Storytelling is thus an outcome of being involved in a world that continually opens to both the person who knows and the audience.

Oral narratives provide the basis for the Tłįchǫ perception of the dè. I observed stories being told to children and grandchildren, to other adults and elders, and within the context of political negotiations. These narratives are told to toddlers seemingly to provide a basis for how to perceive and interact with their surroundings as they grow and for how to take action to deal with tasks in everyday life as well as with chaotic and disharmonious relationships in general.

In considering the stories, I see the emergence of four key points. First, the vast majority of narratives I heard tell of occurrences and happenings in which Tłįchǫ considered a predicament or problem and took action to solve it. In taking action, individuals can take part or not—that is a personal decision. However, those who do take part work cooperatively to ensure a successful outcome. Second, these narratives are told on a regular basis to people of all ages, including toddlers. The consistent telling of the stories takes the listener repeatedly though happenings and occurrences in which individuals take action—the repetition of this notion molds the Tłįchǫ character. Oral narratives are not necessarily told in context—they are just told. Third, knowing the temporal aspect of the occurrence is relevant to being knowledgeable and is incorporated into the telling, just as is the locale of the happening. It is also important to stress that Tłįchǫ oral narratives are not bounded. Parts of events are told as complete stories, just as often as two or three occurrences are told as one story. Fourth and finally, just as the story is not bounded, so the temporal eras of the Tłıchǫ past are not bounded.

Nevertheless, as noted, Tłıchǫ recognize at least four distinct eras: "time when all beings were the same," "time when life was harmonious and places acquired their names," "time of our elders," and "time of living memory." Many younger people do not discuss the first period and refer to the later three as "time of Yamǫǫ̀zaa," "time of Mǫwhì," and "present time." As in English, so the terms used in Tłıchǫ also vary from community to community. Most people understand that knowledge, agreements, and events originated or occurred at different times and that part of knowing something is comprehending that knowledge from the past is brought to the present for use in the future.

If one does not know whence an occurrence originated, the significance of the happening can be diminished—it can "withdraw from the mind"—because it will no longer be brought to the present through experience. There can be no present context if the origin of the story is forgotten. Furthermore, if one does not know the origin, one will find it more difficult to understand what one is experiencing. Significance is attached to the era whence the story came as well as to the locale in which it is experienced. This significance can increase as the event is hooked through each of the eras to the present. One cannot understand Tłıchǫ epistemology without understanding their perception of time and temporality, just as truth is not brought forward without experiencing places.

CHAPTER THREE

Dwelling within Dè and Tłįchǫ nèèk'e

We are of the land.
— GABRIELLE MACKENZIE-SCOTT, DECEMBER 2003

In July 2002, several Tłįchǫ from Gamètì and I stopped for lunch during a day's outing to Semǫ̀tì, a lake south of Gamètì. We ate fish and duck while elders narrated occurrences and happenings within Tłįchǫ nèèk'e. Phillip Zoe shared his experience of seeing northern lights go into the water and cause a whirlpool when he was traveling on Wetł'aezǫtì as a young man and how K'àowo Jimìezhìa told them to go to shore so that the interaction between the spirits of the northern lights and water would be left alone. We were quiet for a moment, contemplating this interaction, and then Laiza Mantla began singing love songs. I asked why she sang to a place rather than to an individual. She replied, "Because the place makes you." And then smiling, she teased, "Go ahead, Charlie, sing to Gamètì — that's where Ilì belongs [and grew from]."

For me, Phillip's story about spirits interacting and Laiza's love song to a place encapsulate much of what it means to dwell and interact within the dè. Dwelling within dè entails a relationship between all beings, a demonstrated respect for entities that dwell in places, as well as a relationship with the place where one belongs. Richard Nelson has noted among the Koyukon the practice of singing tender, loving songs to places (1983, 253), and other Tłįchǫ elders have mentioned it. In 1995, when discussing the probability that BHP would develop a diamond mine near ʔek'atì, Louis Whane narrated how he remembered the diamond rush in 1992 and how prospectors had staked claims all over Tłįchǫ nèèk'e. In telling the importance of traveling trails and occurrences at places, he said, "Whenever we reach Wekweètì [the lake], someone always sings a lullaby." People sing to places because they love them; the place nurtured them as they grew.

Anthropologists discuss the close relationship Dene have with place. Julie Cruikshank shows how Dene in the Yukon think about place when they think about their identity (1998, 17). Thomas Andrews (2004) emphasizes the relationship with place in his description of the land as being like a book, and Keith Basso (1984a, 1996) talks of wisdom sitting in places. Helm considers larger places rather than specific locales in discussing the ties that members of regional bands have to an area in terms of a subsistence base and the kinship ties that extend to others in and outside the regional group (1981a, 295–97; 2000, 10). Relevant to any discussion of Dene places are traveling trails (see Andrews, Zoe, and Herter 1998 on Tłįchǫ) and experiential knowledge (Goulet 1982, 1998; Rushforth 1992; Sharp 2001, 55; D. Smith 1973, 1998).

In this chapter, I build on these anthropological understandings and on Ingold's argument that all hunting-based societies live with the environment by discussing how Tłįchǫ dwell as part of the dè within Tłįchǫ nèèk'e. I emphasize the importance of observing while experiencing and how all beings—not just the Dene—watch and know the character of others with

Figure 3.1. Northern lights on the trail of the ancestors. (Photograph from Tessa Macintosh Photography)

whom they reciprocate and to whom they are meant to show gratitude. The relationships between beings and their place within the dè are basic to understanding Tłıchǫ epistemological and ontological systems.

First, I describe Tłıchǫ nèèk'e and how Tłıchǫ dwell throughout the year. This is basic to understanding Tłıchǫ's role within the dè, which they share with other beings. I then discuss how respectful behavior prepares Tłıchǫ for the unpredictability that can occur with other beings if harmonious relations within the dè are not maintained. I go on to explore the importance of experiencing and observing as mechanisms to knowing— knowing the dè *and* knowing beings with whom one has a relationship as well as their place within the dè. I then discuss in more detail the importance of showing respect to Tłıchǫ ancestors, whose knowledge continues to be passed to the current generation. The last section of this chapter describes how all of these factors play out in the traveling of trails.

Tłıchǫ nèèk'e

When flying over Tłıchǫ nèèk'e, people watch. In the winter, when temperatures can drop to −45°C (−49°F), the pilots fly low so passengers can see the caribou wandering among the open coniferous woodland of the boreal forest or see them traveling in single file across the lakes. We just as often see only their tracks and evidence of where they bedded down on the lakes the night before. Also obvious are skidoo tracks over the frozen lakes and through the tamarack, birch, willow, and black and white spruce. During my first flights, I saw and marveled at the vastness and the amount of ice, wondering, come summer, what I would see.

In the summer, the temperatures may go as high as 35°C (95°F), but average around 16.5°C (61.7°F). The landscape looks like forested islands surrounded by continual lakes connected by rivers and streams. In flight, I could see some but not all of the portages bypassing rough river water or connecting the many lakes that people use to travel through Tłıchǫ nèèk'e. I could also see the bedrock and tundra of the taiga shield as well as the muskeg and plateaus of the taiga plains—all of which makes up the Tłıchǫ nèèk'e.

During my flights to the tundra, I was always fascinated at how the tree coverage becomes increasingly sparse. I could clearly see the long eskers left by the retreating glaciers eight to ten thousand years ago as they wind through the hummocky muskeg surrounding the large lakes. In the tundra, Tłıchǫ camps are often located on whagweè—a flat area consisting of

Figure 3.2. Esker associated with ʔewaànıt'ııtı̀ on the tundra showing its length as it winds through the extensive northern water bodies, 2001. (Photograph by the author)

sandy soil and sparse vegetation—adjacent to eskers. People walk the dry eskers to kw'ia (a small stand of black spruce trees) to find firewood or to look for caribou and watch for grizzlies or simply to marvel at the beauty, as Tłıchǫ so often do.

Like humans, caribou prefer walking on the eskers in the summer, where they can avoid the numerous, bothersome mosquitoes and black flies in the ts'oo (muskeg). Caribou also like to forage in the ts'oo, so hunters follow the caribou trails that are deeply entrenched there. While the hunters are walking, the hunting k'àowo quietly points out what he observes—as much to himself as to those around him: the names of grasses and sedges eaten by caribou in the summer and fall; where caribou have rolled in the mud to coat themselves, making it more difficult for the bugs to reach them; the age of different animals' stools; good fishing spots; and the location of wolf and fox dens in the eskers. Upon returning to the camp, individuals sit near the fire, relaxing while eating a meal and sharing their observations. The oldest elders listen intently, connecting the daily happenings to occurrences in the past through oral narratives. Regna Darnell has also noted this process among the Cree (1974, 336).

As I listened again and again to the people's oral narratives, my mind slowly stopped seeing a static landscape and started seeing people traveling trails throughout Tłįchǫ nèèk'e. As shown on map 1, trails extend east past Kǫk'èetì, Ts'eèhgootì, and ʔedaàtsotì in the tundra; north around the southern and eastern shores of Sahtì; and west reaching into the lowlands toward Dehcho and up along ʔedèezhìì.[1] These trails and shared oral narratives describe the extent of where Tłįchǫ travel and continue to hunt, fish, trap, and gather, both in the boreal forest and on the tundra.

Ebb and Flow of Seasonality

The ebb and flow of seasonality are important as throughout the year and in various locales Tłįchǫ interact with other-than-human beings. And successful interactions with unpredictable entities are contingent on respectful behavior among all beings.

Tłįchǫ have five seasons: the time when the wind gets cold, the time of thin ice, the time when the days are short, the time when the land starts to thaw, and the time when the water and sun are warm. They also refer to two biannual periods: the time when the days are long and the time when the nights are long.

The time when it gets darker—more or less August and September—is the time[2] of large gatherings and community hunts, where relationships are reestablished. Stories are exchanged, keeping everyone abreast of past occurrences and current changes. Discourse centers on where communal caribou hunts will be located on the tundra. Communities take turns hosting the week-long annual gathering that includes the political assembly. People travel by canoe or plane or vehicle if the gathering is in Behchokǫ̀ and they are coming from Yellowknife. Many stay on in the host community for an additional week or so after the gathering to visit with family and friends, slowly moving home before traveling to the tundra for the community caribou hunts.

Before a group leaves for the tundra, it selects a camp k'àowo. But once settled at the camp, hunters break into small hunting parties following their favored hunting k'àowo, who is usually a father, uncle, brother, or brother-in-law. As caribou meat is brought to camp, both women and single men cut meat in thin strips to dry. The women dry fish and caribou meat full-time, using the smoke from smoldering willow branches to keep the flies away and to decrease the drying time. They hang the fish and meat from poles brought from the Tłįchǫ communities. After hunting all day, single men dry meat for their own use. They usually hang it on ropes attached to the single men's tent. Dried and fresh meat for the community freezer is wrapped in caribou hides and sent back on floatplanes that are continually arriving with men and women. Although most delicacies, such as marrow and tongues, are eaten in camp, some are included in bundles sent back for family members who are unable to travel—in particular the senior elders. Dried fish is also sent to the community.

Community hunts coincide with the young people's return to school. Attempts to tie the school year to the round of hunting and gathering activities rather than to the farming seasons of southern Canada have never been successful. The Tłįchǫ Community Services Agency encourages teachers and students from Chief Jimmy Bruneau High School to join those canoeing to the tundra as part of their curriculum. Elders lead the way, telling stories while camped at teaching places. The school trip is designed to keep the trails alive in the minds of all Tłįchǫ by feeding young people stories while they travel trails. It is also meant to expose non-Tłįchǫ who work for the Tłįchǫ to the relationship between their stories, places, and ancestral trails.

Figure 3.3. Madelaine Chocolate preparing to leave fall camp at Deèzàatì by floatplane, 1999. (Photograph by the author)

Sometime after the middle of September, community freezers are full. Chiefs and community k'àowo feel assured that the community will have enough meat—for any family in need and for any community feasts— until the time when the days are short and the caribou arrive in the boreal forest. Most family freezers are full of caribou, but they also hold fish and waterfowl that are harvested as they migrate south for winter. Freezers also contain caribou hides that have been prepared for tanning. Women continue to make dried meat and dried fish and to pick berries.[3] In all four communities, men are busy stockpiling firewood. Behchokǫ̀ residents often sell cords of wood to Yellowknife residents.

With this preparation, all is ready for "freeze-up" or "the time of thin ice," the length of which varies from year to year. As lakes and rivers begin to freeze in November and December, residents of fly-in bush communities are restricted to walking near the community or to traveling by air. Only a few community members travel out and then usually to go to meetings in Yellowknife, Edmonton, Calgary, Vancouver, or Ottawa. At this time of year, the band chief and councillors are more likely to accept invitations to international indigenous meetings and conferences or to mine sites in Australia or the United States that have been operating over an extended period. Most international travel seems to correlate with the difficulty of getting to "the bush." Most people stay in their home community, though, preparing skidoos, toboggans, snowshoes, and clothing and footwear for winter.

During the time of thin ice, the residents of Behchokǫ̀ continue to travel into Yellowknife and more frequently to Hay River, Fort Smith, Grande Prairie, and Edmonton to purchase items, but most often to visit family members who attend technical college or university. During the late 1990s and early 2000s, several men from Behchokǫ̀ took seasonal employment, clearing and burning sections of the bush to straighten and pave the highway between Behchokǫ̀ and Yellowknife. The taking of temporary employment is most pronounced during this time of year because trappers and hunters are waiting for the lakes and rivers to freeze sufficiently so that they can move to their trapping camps and for caribou to move to the boreal forest. This is the darkest season as days become shorter, and with limited snow and ice there is little for the moon and northern lights to reflect from to make travel easier.

The time of short days usually means that lakes and rivers are now frozen, which makes travel by skidoos and dog teams safe unless successive heavy snowfalls have insulated the ice against freezing properly. As the lakes freeze, men move out to their trapping areas, fishing nets go back in the water under the ice, and barren-ground caribou begin to arrive in the boreal forest. If lakes and rivers do not freeze properly, individuals return from the bush telling stories of stuck skidoos, wet footwear, and dangerous spots. The locations of where these events occurred are shared because they are relevant for others' safe travel across lakes and along rivers. Some trappers return to their communities every couple of weeks; others stay at their camps until Christmas. Weasel, mink, fox, wolf, lynx, wolverine, beaver, marten, and otter are trapped, with most trappers focusing on what brings the highest price. Drying racks—in homes and smokehouses—begin to fill as caribou meat and some fish are once again dried, and frames with stretched furs begin to appear in porches and sheds. Successful hunters' freezers are kept full, and food is shared with those less fortunate. A large pot of boiled caribou meat continually sits on the stove in these homes. Caribou or fish is eaten when a task is finished or when visitors appear. Ptarmigan are hunted, and hares snared, especially by the young and the elderly.

Few meetings are organized in the communities during December, and many temporary positions end as everyone begins thinking of Christmas, New Year's, and the return of the trappers. Women sew intensely for Christmas—making beautiful beaded jackets, footwear, gloves, and mittens for family members. Those living in the fly-in communities make at least one trip to Yellowknife to purchase items for Christmas. Some people do not return to their home communities for Christmas, but like the Scots, who probably first introduced these holidays, most return for the New Year's feast and dance because they have a family focus.

After the New Year celebrations, men return to their traplines, young people return to school, and others find temporary work. Several men are hired to help build the ice roads connecting Gamètì, Wekweètì, Whatì, Behchokǫ̀, and the Mackenzie Highway. Hares are snared and ptarmigan hunted, fishnets checked and firewood gathered. Caribou are hunted throughout this period, with associated talk and tension over their whereabouts. In 1998, several Tłı̨chǫ hunters traveled to the Chipewyan community of Łutselk'e to hunt because the majority of caribou had migrated south and east of Tıdeè rather than west–southwest to the Tłı̨chǫ communities.

While the ice roads are still open, families drive between the four communities, visiting friends and family, especially those who live in a community where a large number of caribou are wintering nearby. Most trucks are loaded with a skidoo and sledge in case of a vehicle mishap or if fresh caribou tracks are spotted and there is an opportunity to hunt. People make weekly trips to Behchokǫ̀, where teenagers attending high school stay with relatives or at the residence attached to the Chief Jimmy Bruneau School in Edzo and where many elders are housed in the seniors home, usually referred to as the "Old Folks." Travel from Behchokǫ̀ to Fort Smith, Grande Prairie, Edmonton, and Yellowknife is common because in these larger centers people can purchase supplies for summer projects and transport items such as new appliances, furniture, vehicles, skidoos, and whatever else is needed back to the fly-in communities without paying high costs for air freight. Trips south include visits to friends and relatives in technical colleges and universities, at times to Cree medicine people, whose knowledge of root medicine is extensive according to the elders, and to other friends met at residential school or at the Lac St. Anne annual spiritual gathering.

Several hunting camps are set up along the northern roads, in particular the ice roads, and many travelers stop to visit, drink tea, and eat as they drive between communities. These camps are particularly happy affairs because there is always a supply of fresh caribou meat and at least one elder whose oratorical abilities are highly esteemed. And the local chief—sometimes the grand chief—is often visiting and informing people of political events. Semi–trailer trucks ("semis") also travel the ice roads hauling in fuel, dried goods for local stores to sell over the next year, and material for new houses and oil and gas installations.

Tłı̨chǫ who live away from Tłı̨chǫ nèèk'e are also drawn home while the caribou are in the boreal forest. When Ted Blondin and Violet Camsell-Blondin were at the University of Lethbridge in southern Alberta, Canada, they drove to Behchokǫ̀ and back—a fifty-hour drive—after they were told caribou were in the area. They brought back fresh caribou meat for themselves and their children.

During the time when the land starts to thaw, there are more daylight hours. Given their love of travel (cf. Andrews, Zoe, and Herter 1998; Gillespie 1970, 67), Tłı̨chǫ take advantage of the ease of travel while the earth is frozen, the sun is warming, and their children are out of school during spring break. This usually occurs in March but can be in April. When these three factors come together, several families travel by skidoo and dog team to the Sahtu community of Délı̨ne, where a large annual spiritual gathering led by Charlie Neyelle is held. Some families travel by vehicle over the Mackenzie Highway and ice roads to Délı̨ne while visiting Slavey friends in both the Dehcho and Sahtu regions along the way. People return from this spiritual gathering rejuvenated and full of hope for the future.

Although one might say life begins when the dè is thawing—with snow melting first on the bedrock and other exposed shorelines from a warmth that brings smiles, stories, and laughter—Tłįchǫ elders say that this season is a time when many people become sick and old people die.[4] The oldest elders say these things happen because people are melting just like the ground and the air. During this time, the caribou begin migrating back to their calving grounds. They move slowly as they grow tired from walking in the slushy, heavy snow, are thinner from their winter diet of lichen, and are blind from the glare of the sun on the snow. The ice roads are closed, but many younger men continue to travel between communities in their trucks or by skidoo—in some years even until late May.

Near the end of April and into May, spring camps are set up in snow-free areas. People continue to hunt caribou and keep their fish nets in strategic locations. Around Gamètì, spring camps are set up on exposed bedrock in favorite family locations that can be reached because the lake ice is still thick enough to travel by skidoo or by foot. Throughout the boreal forest, camps are also set up on whagweè (sandy, flat areas with sparse vegetation) accessible by boat. Whagweè around Behchokǫ̀ are accessible by side roads off the main access road between the Mackenzie Highway and Behchokǫ̀ or off the Mackenzie Highway itself. Most are not noticeable from the roads. Women dry meat and work on caribou and moose hides. People tell stories and eat half-dried caribou meat roasted over open fires. This is the time when the air is warm, when there are no mosquitoes, and when travel is easy because of the long hours of sunlight, and the sun is warm as it beats down and reflects off the solid ice.

This is also the time of year when many men take canoes in their toboggans behind skidoos to areas where they "go for beaver and muskrat." Skidoos are eventually covered with tarpaulins and left where they can be retrieved once the land is frozen again. Just before the ice begins to break up, fishing nets are brought in and mended for summer use, skidoos are stored properly, and boats—both metal motorboats and canvas freighter canoes—are examined and mended if necessary.

Once the rivers and lakes are ice free, usually around the end of May or the beginning of June, people are again able to travel by boat. In some years, the ice stays late. Stories are told about the importance of camping near large fisheries and where migratory birds are likely to land; these places provide food even if the ice remains unsafe into June. Tepees are put up, and the black spruce boughs are used as floor covering. The boughs are constantly refreshed to keep everything clean. Meat, fish, and skins are smoked in these teepees while visitors are offered food cooked over the smoking fire. Visitors and hosts share stories. Some build smokehouses out of the packing materials in which goods were shipped to the community

Figure 3.4. Àąwąą explaining to Elsie Mantla, Sally Anne Zoe, and Phoebe Wetrade the importance of camping where whagweè is prominent. They had just finished walking around Nįdzįįkaà on Semįtì noting such things as wolverine dens, rabbit runs, and plants used for medicine, 1998. (Photograph by the author)

over the winter. Everything is used. In Behchokǫ̀, smokehouses attached to each unit at the Old Folks are full as relatives bring meat, hides, and fish for the elders to prepare for drying, smoking, and sharing with visitors.

During the time when the water and sun are warm, in June and July, there are relatively few meetings outside the communities because almost everyone is enjoying the bush, including those who have nine-to-five work in the band office, nursing station, local stores, cafes, and Old Folks in Behchokǫ̀. The Forestry Division of the GNWT hires several of the hunters and trappers to watch for fire from their communities. Companies working on the Mackenzie Highway hire people—usually from Behchokǫ̀ and the Yellowknife area—as flag persons and truck drivers. In some years, individuals stay in such jobs all summer; in other years, there is a frequent turnover in personnel—all depending on "the boss." Fish nets are put back in favored locations in the lakes. Women gather most of the plants, roots, spruce gum, and tamarack bark. Men collect most of the rat root from private locations in lakes. Many people move to their bush cabins or favored locations or set up summer camps in places where they have not been for several years.

At the end of July, many Tłįchǫ travel to Lac St. Anne, a Catholic spiritual gathering place just west of Edmonton, Alberta. First Nations members, who are mainly from western Canada and the northwestern United States, gather there to share food, music, dancing, and stories. At times, Dene from farther afield attend, as they did during the 2001 Lac St. Anne gathering. Diné (Navajo) arrived wanting to meet and share stories with Dene from northern Canada. Stories and food were shared. Interest in sharing oral narratives was so high that few Diné or Tłįchǫ left the festivities to attend the evening prayer being said in one of the many aboriginal languages—Cree, Chipewyan, Slavey, Tłįchǫ, Blackfoot, to name a few. From Lac St. Anne, families travel to Edmonton for favorite activities such as shopping, gambling, and visiting.

On returning home from Lac St. Anne, community members prepare to travel to the annual gathering during the first weeks of August. The first Tłįchǫ Annual Assembly was held in 1992 in Behchokǫ̀, then in Wekweètì, Gamètì, and Whatì in the following years and returning to Behchokǫ̀ in 1996 and again in 2000. As agreed among the political parties and stated in federal legislation, the Tłįchǫ Agreement became legally effective on 5 August 2005, at which time the annual gathering and associated assembly were held in Behchokǫ̀. There was some fear that annual gatherings would end with the finalizing of the Tłįchǫ Agreement, but they have continued.[5]

Several people from each community canoe to the annual gathering. Canoeists meet in a designated location that is close to the community where the gathering is held and arrive together on a particular day. Those already in the community form a long line to welcome the paddlers by shaking hands with each person—young, old, Tłįchǫ, non-Tłįchǫ. Then people visit throughout the community, sharing food while telling stories of their trip. A drum dance, hand games, and other events begin the first night and continue each evening after meetings are held. Sometimes a "rock and roll" dance, with music from local musicians, is held before the drum dance.

Throughout the year, most men rise earlier than others, put on coffee and tea, stoke fires, and go about their tasks. People are constantly busy making items such as drums, ice scoops, mittens, gloves, jackets, and rope to sell or to use. Except during freeze-up and break-up, fish nets are checked; except when the water and sun are warm, snow is collected from special places for tea water. People spend a portion of every day visiting. They make trips to the community offices and individuals' homes in the three smaller Tłįchǫ communities and to the Old Folks and coffee shops in Behchokǫ̀. Groups, especially the elders, often play or watch checkers; gambling at night is a notable pastime.

Tłįchǫ daily tasks and relations within Tłįchǫ nèèk'e change with patterns of dwelling through each season. No matter how people choose to make a living or where they go to university and school or the number of meetings they attend, they are influenced by the seasonality associated with Tłįchǫ nèèk'e. They are also influenced by the unpredictability associated with other-than-human beings that come and go with each season and by the entities that inhabit places along trails.

As my view of Tłįchǫ nèèk'e changed, I could see people doing tasks that maintained relations with other entities as well as between themselves and in this way creating a pattern of dwelling activities or "taskscapes," as Tim Ingold has conceptualized them (2000, 154). "Taskscape" is the closest English concept I have encountered to describe what Tłįchǫ mean when telling of their interactions and relations with other beings who dwell within dè, as set down by Yamǫ̀ǫzaa. The term *taskscape* gives the sense that dè is not so much in a constant flux as in a constant exchange—each of its inhabitants, human and other-than-human beings, giving and taking through established relations that involve the tasks and skills of living. Dè includes everything because all entities are in the state of existing and have spirit.

Preparing for the Unpredictable

Seasons bring a general predictability to the ebb and flow of beings whose places are conjoined with Tłįchǫ nèèk'e, but relations are never taken for granted. Caribou move into the boreal forest in the winter, returning to their calving grounds on the tundra each spring. Migration between tundra and boreal forest is predictable, but their migration route and resulting distribution pattern during the winter are unpredictable due to various factors. Temperatures, ice formation, snow consistency and depth, and wind velocity are unpredictable, requiring that travelers be prepared for a number of scenarios whenever leaving their own community. Preparation means considering many important things, such as appropriate clothing and equipment, traveling with a knowledgeable k'àowo, and being prepared to constantly observe one's surroundings.

Equally relevant is an understanding that a great deal of power can be drawn from the dè and that any number of entities, who have copious amounts of ʔįk'ǫǫ̀, are willing to assist humans who show gratitude and appropriately use what the dè has to offer. When first traveling on the land, I was told to "pay the land" out of respect and in gratitude for my good fortune and in recognition of the numerous and varied entities that may assist us as we travel to our destination. People usually leave on site something they value and use, such as coinage, spruce boughs, or rosaries. A student once gave a pencil because it was important to her success in school. If human beings ignore rules and do not show respect, they will probably have a difficult time because these entities may withdraw their assistance. In my experience, the demonstration of respect and gratitude is never overstated or overtly obvious; it is just done.

The understated quality of appreciation was exemplified one time at K'įahkw'àįkaà, a summer camp, when there was need for birch bark. The location offers a gentle sloping bedrock shore that allows people to dock boats and fetch water easily, a refreshing breeze off the lake that keeps mosquitoes and black flies to a minimum, and a clean, pest-free space for cutting and gutting fish and waterfowl. K'įahkw'àįkaà is relatively close to Gamètì, so those with nine-to-five employment can visit in the evenings and on weekends or stay and commute to their jobs. The site has numerous birch trees, good fishing, and easy access to places frequented by moose and waterfowl. During our time at K'įahkw'àįkaà, birch bark was used extensively to make containers of all sizes because bowls and cups were needed with the coming and going of people from the community. Larger birch bark containers were used to hold bannock, water, cooked and dried fish, and dried caribou meat.

On the last day of our stay on this particular occasion, I noticed an awl in the joint of one of the birch trees. Being new to Tłįchǫ ways, I thought it had been forgotten by Phillip or Bella Zoe, who had used the awl to make holes in the birch bark that had been warmed over the fire and shaped into the form of whatever container was required. Phillip told me to leave it, though, that they left the awl out of respect. He quietly showed appreciation for the bark the tree had provided. The awl is an important tool to a man like Phillip, who makes drums, snowshoes, and other items that his family or others require.

Most adults in the camp had the know-how to make birch bark items, to take migratory birds and fish, and to use spruce boughs for the tents' flooring. They shared their knowledge with those of us who did not have the skill. As we sat around the fire, we heard stories of people traveling in birch bark canoes, the locations of good birch stands, and places where caribou like to travel if they are in the area—stories of making canoes while fishing, of waiting for the caribou and migratory birds to arrive, and of what happens if one

Figure 3.5. Bella Zoe and Laiza Mantla making birch bark containers and dishes for visitors from the community of Gamètì. Summer camp at K'įąhkw'ąįkaà on the lake Gamètì, 1996. (Photograph by the author)

of the beings do not come. After Phillip told me to leave the awl, he added that I should not pick up anything else left in the camp. Although I did not see anything else, I knew the land and all the entities that assisted us over the weeks we stayed at K'įąhkw'ąįkaà were shown gratitude.

Tłįchǫ narratives usually tell of other people's successes due to their ability to hunt, fish, and trap and to their respect for the reciprocal relationship between beings. Embedded in these narratives is information about how most beings are unpredictable and may not appear for any number of reasons, including limited food sources and inability to smell food, which often affects caribou after forest fires or around mining sites, where the smell of fuel is strong.

Humans are the least prepared of all beings to survive. They learn how to live as beings that depend on other-than-human beings and spirits that dwell in places. Successful humans remain flexible and prepared. They do not brag because others can observe what they accomplish. These successful people are seen as knowing something, which in itself is considered respectful. Braggers are considered ignorant because they do not understand that they are significantly less intelligent than the beings they depend on for food, clothing, and shelter. Nor do they understand that their bragging will "go back on them," creating a life of hardship.

Part of respecting is to know the place of the beings with whom you have a relation. The interplay and tension between the predictable and unpredictable is ever present, with a flow of occurrences and stories encapsulating both. The wind is said to dwell in a hole in the tundra, and when it comes out, especially in the winter, it travels every which way, creating a relationship between the ground and the fluxes of the atmosphere. Joe Suzi Mackenzie was quite matter-of-fact about the predictability of the wind in the tundra when he explained it to us:

> Since the beginning, there have always been four winds in the world. Everyone knows this. Towards the south side, when there's wind from the south, it's called Sazhı̨nı̨hts'ìì. When the wind blows to the south from the north, it's called Chı̨k'ènı̨hts'ìì (from one side to the other). When the wind is blowing from the tundra toward the tree line, it is called K'àbatsǫ̀ǫ̀nı̨hts'ìì. When the wind blows from the tree line toward the tundra lakes, it is called Nàą̀nı̨hts'ìì. There are four winds. It's been like that since the beginning. When we walk in the tundra, you are not without wind. There's always wind, wind, wind since there's no trees to prevent the wind from blowing and blowing. In the tundra, there is no break from the wind. It's like that in the tundra, in the summer and winter alike, it's the same seasonally (it comes from all directions). As we sit here, I am talking about the wind, what it is like. (Chocolate et al. 2000, 8–9)

Yet as predictable as the four winds are, travelers acknowledge that when and where the wind picks up are fairly unpredictable. When it does pick up, travel can come to a halt, with fall hunters unable to leave the main camp on the tundra. If the wind is strong enough, it is impossible for floatplanes to arrive or leave. A teacher who on one occasion canoed with the elders and teenagers to the annual gathering in Wekweètì told me of her experience shortly after she arrived: "We were camped at one of the teaching places when a wind blew up, so we couldn't leave. We were grounded, so the elders talked about the place and told us stories about wind throughout the boreal forest and the tundra and on the large lakes. After two days, the elder Nick Black built a raft, placing burning spruce boughs on it, preparing to pay the entities responsible for the wind. As he pushed the raft into the lake, he asked for calm winds and a safe journey.

It only took two hours for the wind to die down. We continued" (personal communication, August 1994).

Spirits can reside in water, wind, rocks, places, or just about anywhere and are shown respect when people "pay the land." Harmonious relations are maintained as contingency to appease these entities, whose power can disrupt travel or any number of human activities if ignored.

People must honor the caribou when the caribou offer themselves. Disrespect in use is immoral. People must place caribou bones, hair, and guts in appropriated locales, such as crevasses. Caribou want to assist Tłıchǫ. As elders say, caribou travel away from the tundra and to the boreal forest to give of themselves, returning to the tundra to give birth so that their young will know their own place. They travel outward along trails, helping human beings, allowing their bodies to be used, and if humans respect them, they return. If not respected, they will travel elsewhere.

On one occasion when Tłıchǫ were starving and there were no caribou in Tłıchǫ nèèk'e, a man had a dream. In the dream, he saw caribou. The Tłıchǫ were starving, so he walked toward the caribou and invited them to travel to Tłıchǫ nèèk'e. It is accepted that caribou do not have to come, nor will they if not treated with respect.

The concept of giving when need is expressed or observed is ever present among Tłıchǫ. In September 2001 during a trip to ?ewaànıt'ııtì, the

Figure 3.6. Fall hunting camp, Gots'ǫkàtì, 1988. (Photograph by the author)

caribou did not come close enough for hunting to be viable. Hunters sat around the fire and the cooking stove, where the women made bannock and fried fish and pork chops. Everyone sat together discussing the problem and what might be causing the caribou to veer away. After several hours of storytelling that focused on reasons why caribou had not come to them in the past, the group agreed that probably the caribou did not think they were needed by the people in the camp. K'àowo Jimmy Martin directed everyone to consume all the pork in the camp and to send my cow leather pack back home on the next floatplane bringing hunters in. The pack and the pork chops demonstrated to the caribou that they were not needed by the people in the camp.

Within hours of ridding the camp of these items, the caribou arrived, traveling close to the camp, giving themselves to the hunters. As caribou were harvested, caribou rugs and dry meat were made, hides were scraped of hair, and everyone happily consumed great quantities of fresh meat. Fresh and dried meats were sent back on any floatplanes arriving with new hunters; planes were full both when they arrived and when they departed. It is said by the most senior elders that if caribou are not needed and used appropriately, their spirit will die.

Figure 3.7. Phillip Zoe making a caribou rug at Deèzàatì fall camp, 1999. Using everything to ensure the spirit of the caribou stays strong and returns. (Photograph by the author)

Senior elders emphasize that one should never bother any other-than-human being unless it is needed and never take more than is needed. In 1988, when I first participated in a fall hunt with the Tłįchǫ on the tundra at Gots'ǫkàtì, a couple of young men shot more caribou than they could carry back to camp. They returned, bragging about the number they had shot. After several adult men went to get the meat and carried it back to camp, the hunt was stopped while caribou stories were told, all of which emphasized the relationship between poor behavior and the disappearance of caribou from the area. Joan Ryan states that in discussions of traditional justice and specifically rules associated with game, elders emphasized the basic rule of killing and taking only what is needed (1995, 27).

All beings have relationships that contribute to the well-being and harmony of others, as set down by Yamǫǫzaa. If one does not pay attention, loss will occur. For the caribou, it means paying attention to their surroundings, including how they are treated by humans. If the caribou spirits are treated well, they will continue to return, providing human beings with meat and hides. If respected and used properly, the caribou spirits will thrive. From the Tłįchǫ perspective, the caribou travel toward them willingly as long as people use and treat them in an appropriate manner, which includes becoming increasingly knowledgeable of them.

Tłįchǫ with whom I worked made a point to listen, understand, and know what happened in the past. They also know there are unpredictable occurrences that require knowledge and stories to think with that will assist them to find solutions. When people travel or use resources, they show respect and gratitude; when entities require appeasing, oral narratives are drawn on to find the most appropriate responsive action. It is commonly held that it is arrogant to think one can know the future. Most prepare by learning the stories, observing their surroundings, "paying the land," and treating other-than-human beings in a manner that strengthens relations rather than diminishes them. Preparing for the future differs from predicting the future, an activity that is considered arrogant unless coming from a prophet who has true dreams and visions. Prophets use their dreams and visions to assist others in need.

Experiencing and Observing

From an early age, Tłįchǫ are taught that other-than-human and human beings acquire knowledge from the places they inhabit. They see, feel, smell, and establish relations from their own place. Beings have their own knowledge and resulting perspective that differs from that of all other beings. Most Tłı̨chǫ depend on knowing other beings by observing them. As Gabrielle Mackenzie-Scott explained, "When we were at ʔǫhtsı̨k'e, my father [Joe Suzi Mackenzie] pointed to a ground squirrel. He said this is the animal who knows everything about what is going on under the ground, just as Raven can see what is going on above ground. He told us we must pay attention and learn from both as they have different knowledge; they are from different places" (personal communication, 27 November 2003).

The Tłı̨chǫ are keen observers and have sophisticated, objective understandings of the dè and of methods for using and sharing its resources. They observe occurrences and happenings from their own place, which provides them with a perception of the environment that goes well beyond what most Western scholars define as empirical. For the Tłı̨chǫ, those experiences include dreaming and visions. This ideology is fundamental to their subsistence base and their knowledge system; it is as tangible as the practice of setting a trap or holding an election.

Each entity sees the dè from a different place, creating a conglomerate of knowledge the Tłı̨chǫ can learn by observing other-than-human beings while doing their own tasks. The interconnections create the continually changing taskscapes of the dè. Life in Tłı̨chǫ nèèk'e is an interplay between encountering the unpredictable and unknown and maintaining harmony by showing gratitude toward other entities and using those entities when there is a need. To demonstrate respect for what has been given, humans benefit from using all that is given: food, clothing, shelter, and other items for oneself and to share with those who have less. To use without waste, one must be aware of precisely what is needed and how it will be used. One must watch, listen, and think with stories while experiencing life because there are twists and turns within the unpredictable dè. One must have sufficient knowledge to know when another's skills and know-how are more appropriate to the task than one's own. And one must acknowledge that other-than-human beings, whose paths Tłı̨chǫ cross, are more intelligent than humans because they have more access to ʔı̨k'ǫǫ̀ than humans. To know what one needs, how to acquire it, and how to use it, one must be extremely observant.

Tłı̨chǫ are intensely observant of all that is around them. They observe caribou while thinking about what "caribou beings" are currently doing in comparison to what they observed on earlier trips or to what they heard from their elders. Tłı̨chǫ harvesters observe what caribou beings are eating by inspecting the mouth of any caribou they shoot, looking for the remains of food, and then they think about what they see. They observe and think about how and where caribou travel on their trails, how the caribou k'àowo, a middle-aged female cow caribou, leads the younger caribou to food, how they return to the calving grounds, and how they know where the water crossings are located.

Tłįchǫ watch how caribou interact with their young, how and when they move into the boreal forest, how and why they move to the tree line, only to move back to the tundra before migrating south to the forest. Tłįchǫ hunters observe, think about, and discuss with elders where caribou cross large lakes and wide rivers. They observe and think about which caribou the others follow and why, what they had been eating when they were killed, and exactly what the caribou eat on the tundra and in the boreal forest. Tłįchǫ observe that the caribou know how to live on the tundra and in the boreal forest, and as Johnny Eyakfwo said, "It's like the ʔekwǫ̀ [caribou that migrate between the tundra and boreal forest] has two separate ways of being knowledgeable" (personal communication, 17 April 1997). Most Tłįchǫ adults make similar comments. For them, caribou know the plant communities and water systems of the tundra, where they forage mainly on grasses, sedges, and bushes. These caribou also know their winter habitats and associated plants, in particular the much-needed lichen that lies under the snow in the boreal forest.

Key to becoming knowledgeable is the ability to find one's own personal truth while maintaining personal autonomy and having the ability to work cooperatively with others. Important aspects of being a responsible individual within a tightly knit group are learning both to observe while having one's own experience and sharing these occurrences while following those who are an authority in any given situation. The Tłįchǫ encourage younger people and the inexperienced to "watch" and "share what they experienced."

People rarely interrupt this behavior; they guide the learning of others through sharing their observations and experiences. During the winter of 2002, I stood watching caribou with Therese and Louis Zoe. Louis is a full-time hunter and trapper. In pointing out several middle-aged female cows, all leading small bands of five or six younger caribou, he was helping me to understand caribou behavior and showing me that caribou teach their young just as people do. Quietly mentioning what he saw to Therese and me was Louis's responsibility, given that he was the most knowledgeable of our group.

It is by experiencing and discussing that experience that younger people are taught to observe all that surrounds them, including locales, trails, water, wind, and people in various situations. All people, whether hunters or not, gather in particular homes—usually, but not always, those of older men who are respected as hunters and k'àowo and who were or continue to be active in the political arena of the dominant society. These homes usually have coffee and tea available and family members, including grandchildren, who are willing to serve visitors.[6]

People also gather to share stories at Old Folks, at favorite community gambling houses, and at the community government office. Individuals hear and share information on many different subjects in these places, such as local, regional, and national politics or something they saw on TV about the treatment of wildlife. People listen, visit, and share their experience and observations, providing others with verification that all is as it should be or with observations of what has changed but should be the same (such as damaged burial sites).

These narrations are regularly repeated, and individuals are expected to listen (not get bored), to remember the details, and to consider the narrative in relation to their own experiences. When people go out, they are expected to observe and verify for themselves what they heard, gaining their own personal knowledge by using the stories to think about what they are observing. The way of learning about caribou is consistent with ways of learning about other beings, other events, and other places.

The act of becoming knowledgeable is valued over a stagnant mind that thinks it knows. Most Tłįchǫ have been taught of the unpredictable entities that dwell within the dè. Tłįchǫ carry with them oral narratives that contain information of what has been observed before and information on being prepared—both for what is expected and for unpredictability. One never knows what has happened until one considers the occurrence from a position in the future.

Within the context of experience and storytelling, there are personal knowledge and group knowledge. After traveling "out" from the community in the bush, on the tundra, to meetings, or on visits in another location, people are expected to share their story when they return for the benefit of all. People share what they have observed. They tell about things such as the state of berries while picking, the condition of fur-bearing animals and trapping expeditions, caribou fitness and the state of caribou habitat, the health of fish found in fishing nets, and meetings with government or trips to Australia or Arizona to visit mines. People listen to the stories and remember. These discourses intertwine past and present to form a conglomerate of observations made during occurrences and happenings that can be used for future decisions and actions.

Each being occupies a different place in the dè and therefore contributes to the whole. Each being experiences the dè in a different way and contributes by sharing that knowledge with other beings. Tłįchǫ experience and observe others from Tłįchǫ nèèk'e. Beings intertwine, intimately and gratefully using each other, but they also stay separate from each other to ensure that they and their places are respected, that each remains who it is and within its own place as defined by Yamǫ̀ǫ̀zaa.

One way to acquire the knowledge of other beings is to observe and listen to what they have to tell. Another way is to become them, taking on their physical forms and experiencing the world as they do. Individuals with specific access to ʔįk'ǫ̀ǫ̀ can take on the physical manifestation of an other-than-human being. During that time, they experience that being's place in the dè, observing from the place of the being whom they have become. In so doing, they learn what that being knows. While in this state, their spirit remains their own, but they observe through the eyes of the other-than-human being. They experience relations, trails, and locales through the other being's physical senses. They are of that being's place. Knowledge acquired in this fashion is much more immediate, direct, and complete than that acquired by observing another being through one's own human eyes.

But dangers come with changing one's physical appearance. The most obvious is being shot by a hunter who mistakes the physical manifestation for the real entity, not a human person who has shape-shifted. Moreover, if the human takes on too much knowledge, he or she can "become the other," including in spirit. George Blondin (1996) tells of a Slavey man who remains a caribou; Cruikshank tells of a man who learned too much about being a caribou and risked staying with them, but his family kept him from returning to caribou (1998, 54–56). The version I heard tells of a man who could become a caribou and manifested himself as a caribou for longer and longer periods as he tried to learn everything the caribou knows. His spirit eventually changed, and he could not return to his human form; his spirit had changed, and he became a caribou. His spirit changed because he had too much caribou knowledge; he had more caribou knowledge than Tłįchǫ knowledge.

Tłįchǫ elders with whom I worked are concerned that their descendants will learn too much Kweèt'ıì knowledge, thus losing their Tłįchǫ spirit as they forget their ancestors' knowledge and ways of observing and experiencing. Tłįchǫ elders consider Kweèt'ıì as part of the dè, and they know that Kweèt'ıì perceive the world differently. Tłįchǫ do not see life as a dichotomy, but as all being essential parts of the interactive web of life.

All beings have spirit and knowledge, but this does not mean that they all are the same.

Persons—Beings—Entities

As Tłįchǫ narratives tell, it has been since the time of Yamǫǫ̀zaa that all beings acquired their own identity and place, gaining the capability to live in harmony and to acquire their own knowledge. Although all entities are perceived as having agency, I have never heard or observed anything that would suggest that beings other than humans are persons. Elders talk about the dè as being "like their parents" because the dè provides everything. And, as Rosalie Drybones explained, "Caribou are not people. They are not human, but like prophets. They can foresee everything that's in our part of the dè. . . . People don't do things without the caribou being aware of it" (personal communication, 5 February 1998).

These analogies may suggest that Tłįchǫ personify other beings, but this is probably not the case. Rather, they are raising the status of some humans to that of the other-than-human beings. Tłįchǫ elders are emphasizing that other-than-human beings are more than human beings—more than persons. Few humans can emulate entities such as Muskrat, who found the ground and brought the earth to the surface of the water. Oral narratives tell of only a few humans who are capable of contributing to the well-being of others on such a scale, and these humans have very close relations with other-than-human beings and have access to ʔįk'ǫ̀. Yamǫǫ̀zaa and his brother, Yamǫǫ̀gaà, who are remembered for using their intelligence to create social relations within the dè, originated—in the stories I heard—from between the cleft hoof of the caribou. And caribou have the ability "to know what is ahead of them" and to help humans so long as they are treated with respect. Caribou know what has occurred where they are about to travel, whereas humans, except prophets, can never know what will happen in the future. Yahbahti Edzo, who made peace with the Yellowknives' Yahbahti Akaitcho, was from a family with considerable intelligence. Edzo had access to ʔįk'ǫ̀ that could control minds, which he did while waiting for Akaitcho to stop threatening and to want peaceful and harmonious relations.

The narrative of Yamǫǫ̀zaa teaches that at one time all beings were the same as human persons, and chaos occurred because no one understood their place or their relationship to the others. Rather than respecting each other, they killed and devoured each other without thought of mutual need, use, or respect. Yamǫ̀ǫ̀zaa set "laws" governing the relationships between all beings and provided social and spatial parameters that gave beings the know-how to live as a continuum within the dè.

Each being is who it is, with its own way of perceiving its surroundings, its own knowledge, and its own intellect. I have never heard other-than-human beings referred to as *dǫ* or "person."[7] Like Roger McDonnell, who worked among the Kaska Dene in the Yukon (1984, 42), I found the idea of "*dǫ*" or "Dǫne" to be very slippery. I found it can denote different classes of humans and at times to separate humans from other-than-human beings. I did not ever hear the term used to include all moving things, no matter what discussion or situation. "Dǫne" is often used to separate Kweèt'ı̨ from "First Nations," and Tłįchǫ from other First Nations. I more often understood the elders to use the term *dǫ* when describing a person who knows the stories and can use them to think with—a fully functioning human being.

Elders do, however, say "like a prophet" or "like the creator" as they describe otherness. I found that Tłįchǫ emphasize the relations that all beings have with others, including human beings, and that humans require the help of other entities to survive. Although human beings are part of the dè and have relations with other-than-human beings, they are different because they are less capable, less able to survive without help. Other-than-human beings have access to more ʔį̀k'ǫ̀ǫ̀ than human beings, except prophets, who can dream for others and are therefore more intelligent than most people.

Feeding the Fire; Respecting Prophets and Ancestors

Michael Asch writes that the idea that only some individuals can "dream true" is long standing among the Dene (1988, 31). Pat Moore and Angela Wheelock (1990a) have discussed how among the Dene in northern Alberta dreaming can increase a person's ability to be successful. I heard several Tłįchǫ elders I worked with tell narratives of gotso, "the time of predecessors that one's elders knew," when there were k'àowo who would dream where the caribou were traveling and would get up and go, leaving the others to follow. Prophets are dreamers who are able to see what ordinary people cannot, and their abilities increase as they become mature adults.

During the summer of 1994, the elders took some Tłįchǫ friends and me to visit the grave of a prophet near our camp at K'ı̨ahkw'àį̨kaà. The prophet is the sister of Romie Wetrade, Jean Wetrade, and Madelaine Drybone. Her grave is on a high bluff near the lake. The younger men cleared the bush so that travelers passing in their boats or on dog sleds or skidoos could see it. They removed weeds and other growth from around her grave and fixed the fence.

We then sat facing her grave and the direction of the rising sun—the direction Yamǫǫ̀zaa walked when traveling the world to tell beings who they were, where their places were located, and how they should relate to one another based on their characteristics and place within the dè. The rosary was said and a prayer given for the prophet. Several individuals privately visited her grave and "talked with her," asking for assistance and leaving money, rosaries, or special stones "to pay her." The rest of us feasted on caribou, bannock, fish, and oranges and listened to Madelaine tell her sister's story. "Our father had found my sister a good husband, but although she explained to him that she had had a dream that if she married, she would be dead before spring of the following year, our father insisted he was a good man. My sister was a prophet and knew she would die, but she was married. She died that winter" (personal communication, July 1994).

As Madelaine told the story, she referred to her sister as a prophet—a person who had visions and could tell the future. When Madelaine finished her story, we fed the fire for her sister. People acknowledged the relationship with her and showed respect, allowing them to continue using her ability as a prophet.

The spirits of predecessors continue to dwell in places within Tłįchǫ nèèk'e and, if shown respect, are willing to assist people. Tłįchǫ clean graves and regularly tend graveyards, whether in the community, in the bush, or on the tundra. They feed the fire to show gratitude for the ancestors' assistance and as a reminder that it was these ancestors who gave them the stories they currently use to think with—the stories that give the basis for living well and thinking about new situations.

Each time I observed the feeding of the fire, it varied. There was always extensive discussion to ensure the process was right for the time and place. The first feeding of the fire I observed was 31 October 1993. The community k'àowo in Gamètì, Joe Mantla, visited several homes announcing that there would be a feeding of the fire and a drum dance at Amen Tailbone's old cabin. Everyone brought food from home. I was simply told to bring some food I really enjoyed.

Before the drum dance, a fire was built in the woodstove. As food was collected in a large metal bowl, Jean Wetrade (church and elders' k'àowo), Joe Mantla (community k'àowo), and Phillip Zoe (eventually church

Figure 3.8. Feeding the fire for the ancestors buried in the graveyard at Nįdzįkaà, Semį̀tì, 1998. (Photograph by the author)

k'àowo) discussed how to proceed and who was to feed the fire. They selected two female and two male elders to put the food into the fire.

They collected food in four roasting pans and added caribou fat. Before each pan of food was put into the fire, a prayer song was drummed, and all four individuals—the person holding the pan going first—circled the small kitchen table placed near the stove, moving from near the fire to their left around the table. A prayer song was also drummed as the food was put into the fire. The k'àowo put additional fat on the fire so it would burn well. The cabin was very full, most community members attending the feeding of the fire.

After the feeding, the drummers warmed their drums, and the dance started. Within the hour, people were dancing in unison. Throughout the night, the harmonious pulsating was felt as most community members moved between circles of lines. As I left the dance, I was told to set my table for the number of people in my family. The following day no one talked about what appeared on his or her own plate, but people talked about what was on other plates. Most people found small particles of dust or fur, interpreted as "good luck" on the land and when trapping.

The feeding of the fire at the prophet's grave in July 1994 was different. First, no one collected the food, nor was anyone selected to put the food on the fire. After cooking fish, caribou, and duck on the fire, we ate while listening to narratives, but all of us left something on our plates. Then Andrew Gon, the oldest male elder, directed us to feed the fire. One at a time, people got up, went to the fire, and let the food on their plate fall gently into the fire while speaking their thanks to the ancestors for their good fortune. They approached the fire from the right, moving toward the east. Phillip Zoe, the church k'àowo from Gamètì, stirred the food in the fire so all of it would burn.

During the 1997 Tłįchǫ annual gathering in Gamètì, the young men who were helping the community k'àowo at the feast collected a bit of food from everyone after being directed to do so. These pieces of food were valued. Between the time of the feast and the drum dance, a fire was built in a large oil drum outside the new recreation building where the feast was held. Eddie Weyallon, community k'àowo from Behchokǫ̀, and Phillip Zoe attended the fire, and a few people stood around it. Eddie and Phillip conversed continually until the fire became steady and strong. A prayer song was sung to the sound of the drum, the rosary was said, and only then did those present slowly slip their food into the fire. A prayer song was drummed while the food burned.

A feast and a feeding of the fire took place on the last night of all of our spring, summer, and fall camps. In 1999 at the fall caribou camp at Deèzàatì, Jimmy Martin, the camp k'àowo, instructed Joseph Whane, the youngest man in camp, to collect all the food in one of the larger pots. Joseph was given constant instruction while collecting the food and while putting it into the woodstove that was used to keep the tent warm. Phillip Zoe, church k'àowo, said a prayer before the food was put into the fire.

The lengthy discussion among community and church k'àowo on how to proceed in each particular situation and the directions they issued to their younger assistants seemed to be intrinsic to the process throughout the feeding. On each occasion, everyone kept a portion of the food on his or her plate—a favored piece. If the fire was passed by or circled, people walked from east to west, and as each one put the food in the fire, he or she spoke a prayer or words to the ancestors. Gratitude was expressed for all that had been shared and for a successful trip or event. Conversation is key to considering the right way to feed the fire: who should do what and how it should be done.

While attending to the ancestors' graves, Tłįchǫ remember the words they heard while walking with their predecessors and the stories they listened to while sitting and sharing food with them by fires. These memories help individuals to know their place—the extent of Tłįchǫ nèèk'e within the dè—and to remember that the extent of their land within the world as

Figure 3.9. Feast on the last night of fall camp at ʔewaànıt'ıtı̀, 2001. The youngest men in the camp are responsible for serving food to others—in this case, Johnny Simpson under the direction of his elder Pierre Beaverho from Whatì. (Photograph by the author)

defined by government and industry is not the limit of their place within the dè. Knowing who is buried where also helps people to remember that their predecessors are willing to assist them if they are respectful.

Feeding the fire shows respect for those who have shared their knowledge through oral narratives and who continue to walk the dè. It is these ancestors whose stories have guided the Tłı̨chǫ to think about how to maintain relations with both other-than-human beings and human beings. Feeding the fire shows respect for all predecessors who passed stories to the current generations, who guided them to places where they were able to experience other beings, and who encouraged them to observe and be aware of their surroundings without pushing their will on others, who taught them to take a story and use it to think with.

Placing Beings within the Dè

The elders with whom I worked often stated that all entities, whether human beings or other-than-human beings, should know their place. The concepts attached to place are old. Within the Tłı̨chǫ cosmos, Yamǫ̀ǫzaa assigned a place to all beings when he gave them their character and explained their relationship to others. As I spent time with Tłıchǫ, it became increasingly apparent that Tłıchǫ nèèk'e is part of the dè and that the dè is part of Tłıchǫ nèèk'e.

During a meeting on the issue of "land as home," Phillip Zoe spoke of dè in the following terms: "There are no empty spaces. All spaces are used by something: fox, fish, trees, humans, wind, northern lights. It might look empty, but all the dè is used" (taped meeting, 15 October 2004). All space is filled with places within which beings inhabit. For the Tłıchǫ, there is no empty space. The dè is an assortment of entities dwelling within their own places and interacting together. Places such as Tłıchǫ nèèk'e and Hozìi?ekwǫ̀ nèèk'e—the place you expect to find barren-ground caribou—are large and overlap in space. Yet they are separate. Trails that belong to beings within the dè connect and crisscross but remain distinct. Locales—whether geographic locations or places within the mind—are situated along the trails where beings carry out tasks, including the task of resting before taking on other activities.

The place one belongs to and grows from determines the way one lives, the relations one has, and the knowledge one acquires. Human and other-than-human beings—Tłıchǫ and Kweèt'ıı̀, woodland and barren-ground caribou, raven and ground squirrel, tundra and mountain grizzly—have different perspectives depending on their place within the dè.

Separation and connectivity are defined through relationship as set down by Yamǫ̀ǫzaa. Both the Kitikmeot Inuit and Tłıchǫ have used the area called "Kǫ̀k'èetì"—Inuit in the winter and Tłıchǫ in the fall. And both have stories based on their own experience in this area and told from their own perspective. They use the same space but inhabit different places because the knowledge one needs in the winter or spring differs from the knowledge required in the summer or fall. One might say that their respective places merge, but because they require different knowledge to occupy the same space, they in fact perceive and inhabit different places.

Trails can take the Tłıchǫ to places where you would expect to find other-than-human beings such as wolf, fox, caribou, squirrel, and beaver as well as other human beings such as the Inuit, Slavey, Chipewyan, and Yellowknives. Trails come together in particular places, but each being sees its surroundings from its own perspective—from its own trail, from the place where it belongs. According to the Tłıchǫ elders, all beings have deep trails and memory of the places they have traveled. Caribou beings, like human beings, show their young the trails and places they need to survive.

Trails allow the continual movement of beings. Beings can and do interact at intersections, but locales do not become congested. It is as if beings have parallel lives that periodically intersect. Each being has its own perspective based on its own trails and its own experiences, so that intimacy is provided even while beings remain separate. There is movement, both outward divergence and inward convergence.

From the Tłįchǫ elders' perspective, spirits exist with or without a physical manifestation. But to survive, all entities require a place to which they belong. A discussion between the elders Romie Wetrade and Amen Tailbone about whether rock spirits die exemplifies this idea. They narrated their own experience, their own observations.

Romie Wetrade stoked the fire in the woodstove, and he related the oral narrative of the continuing death and decay around Rayrock Mine. He reminded us that Rayrock used to be another place known as "Kwetįį?àa." It was once filled with happy spirits, where hunters who traveled and hunted would feel like singing. But, he explained, the happy spirits disappeared when mining of uranium began in the 1950s, and even though the mine is now closed, the happiness causing one to want to sing has not returned. From these elders' perspective, rock and stones have spirits, but to maintain their spirit they require place. Their narrative suggests that a spirit—whether a rock spirit, a human spirit, or a caribou spirit—will become homeless and slowly lose its character rather than die when its place is destroyed. Similarly, water and wind beings have spirit and their own place within the dè and should be shown respect if life is to remain balanced and in harmony.

Tłįchǫ begin life listening to stories, usually told by their grandparents. Stories help them to perceive and interpret their surroundings. An individual's personal trail begins at home and expands as she or he carries out tasks within Tłįchǫ nèèk'e and while interacting with other beings within the dè. Individuals leave their mark as they use and live at places and on the trails that connect places. Beings are continually moving out from their place, traveling and performing and completing tasks along trails. Trails are considered in their totality, not separate from the locations and homes along them. To emphasize this point, Margaret Lafferty said, "As long as we shall last and as long as our descendants shall last and as long as our children shall last, we want them to use this land as their father and mother, this is what we think about this land. . . . We love this land. It's like a mother to us and a father to us" (as quoted in Legat et al. 1995, 9).

For the Tłįchǫ, "to use and share" is morally correct; "to abuse" is wrong. Using another being—a human person or an other-than-human being—in a way that is reciprocal and appropriate indicates respect toward those who have more ability than oneself. To have knowledge of other beings allows humans to use them in respectful ways. Using another human person also demonstrates respect of that person's capabilities. Individuals who are successful and give of themselves—hunters, fishers, seamstresses, wage earners—are respected for being knowledgeable and for maintaining relations with those who are less successful.

As human beings dwell and experience their place, they tell of that place and the trails that connect it to the places of other beings. Not only are all these places connected by the trails you can see, embedded within the earth from years of travel, but the stories and songs are also trails connecting human beings and places in their minds, including those places associated with ʔįk'ǫǫ̀.

The elders say that all beings should know their place and that all should respect the place of others. If there is no knowledge or respect, reestablishing harmony is required. It is often said that Kweèt'įį have forgotten their place, which is the reason why they feel a need to take and control the places of other beings. Sir John Franklin's behavior at the Tłįchǫ fishery adjacent to Délįne, described in his 1828 journal, exemplifies this abusive behavior.

Tłįchǫ fishers had told Franklin's men about their fishery; as was appropriate, they had shared their knowledge with those new to the area. According to Franklin's records, his crew fished at the Tłįchǫ fishery much of the summer and into the late autumn and so had a fair cache. Therefore, when Tłįchǫ started to arrive at their fishery, most fish were gone, and so they asked Franklin and his men for fish. Franklin says that Tłįchǫ "begged" when they were unable to get sufficient fish in the fall (1828, 62–63). Given the Tłįchǫ perspective on sharing and on how the successful should share with the less fortunate, it is more than probable that the Tłįchǫ were not begging but demonstrating need to Franklin for the fish his men had taken. Due to Franklin's unwillingness to share the fish taken from the Tłįchǫ fishery, he is remembered as abusing that place by taking more than he needed and as being greedy and ignorant when not sharing with those who needed the fish to survive.

Dwelling within the dè and Tłįchǫ nèèk'e is a social environment full of entities that are aware, have feelings, and provide assistance or withdraw, depending on humans' behavior. As beings travel, they mingle with other beings, creating and re-creating taskscapes within the dè. They carry out activities and use and show respect to those who can offer assistance and who are more intelligent and skillful. The Tłįchǫ perceive themselves and others as being of the dè and growing from places. It is the working, traveling, resting, thinking with stories, and philosophizing that provide the nourishment necessary for people to become responsible adults by the time they are in their midforties.

CHAPTER FOUR

Experiencing Kweèt'ı̨ı̨

Traders, Miners, and Bureaucrats

*We did not conceive that they did not see the world as we do. The Dene
had no experience of a people who would try to control us, or who would
say that somehow they owned the land that we always lived on.*
　　　　　　　　　　　　—STEPHEN KAKFWI, IN DENE NATION,
　　　　　　　　　　　　　　　Denendeh: A Dene Celebration

On 23 July 2002, Madelaine Drybone died at the age of ninety-seven. Madelaine was one of four elders who initiated the traditional-governance research
in 1993 in the conviction that continually listening to and sharing stories
are vital to the survival of her descendants as well as of the entire Tłı̨chǫ
people. Madelaine was the last of the four to die. Upon her death, Georgina
Chocolate, whose son is married to Madelaine's daughter's daughter, said
to me, "She is pulling everything in." Georgina's statement reinforced how
philosophical and strategic the Tłı̨chǫ are about epistemological matters.
The Land Claim Agreement-in-Principle had been initialed with the federal and territorial governments concerning the Tłı̨chǫ's land claims and
self-government. For Madelaine, her descendants would be living under a
new agreement. She and the other elders had left their stories, and now it
was up to their descendants to use those stories and the elders' experience to
think about how to live life under the Tłı̨chǫ Agreement.

In this chapter, I move back through time to consider the relationships
between Tłı̨chǫ and Kweèt'ı̨ı̨, with a focus on exploration and government.
This relationship is an important part of the context within which the oldest elders initiated the first traditional-governance project and how they
directed the Tłı̨chǫ Knowledge Program. It is also key to understanding
why the elders and leaders decided on negotiating a regional land claim.
In the consideration of events from the past, the importance of remembering what has occurred becomes clear. I draw mainly on written sources
wherein Tłı̨chǫ elders remember and share many occurrences through

stories about their own and their predecessors' experiences with Kweèt'ii. For the Tłıchǫ with whom I worked, remembering the past and using the stories to think with are basic to finding solutions to problems and ensuring that harmony is maintained in the present.

Julie Cruikshank emphasizes how in the telling of events through oral narratives or in written texts, some aspects are suppressed, whereas others are highlighted (1998, 1–24). I have selected events that demonstrate how Kweèt'ii increasingly took control of the land for resource development, while Tłıchǫ individuals and their chiefs—along with other Dene and Métis leaders—attempted to reestablish and maintain personal autonomy, group sociability, and self-determination.

Kweèt'ii involved with exploration and government have historically considered northern Canada as a frontier of wild empty spaces containing resources for the taking and as a land to be feared until managed and controlled. Henry Sharp describes the fear and loathing the white population have of the land of the Chipewyan. Referring to Margaret Atwood's (1995) study of the image of the North in Canadian literature, Sharp shows how the dominant population's attitudes are shaped by the idea of a nature that is to be feared (2001, 42–43). The ideas of emptiness and of the need to control nature while building a safe cultural landscape are widespread in Canada, as revealed in a poem published in *The Beaver: A Journal of Progress*:

EMPIRE BUILDERS

Earth's empty spaces call them where
    the mind is free to roam,
And build its phantom cities near the
    grey wolf's distant home.
They see the prairie waving with the yet
    unplanted grain,
And hear the silence echoing the harvest
    Song's refrain.
For them rocky wastes pour forth rich
    treasures still unmined,
They bind the mighty rivers to the service
    of mankind.
Their railways feed the valleys, cross the
    mountains, span the streams—
Till the wilderness is conquered through
    these empire-builders' dreams. ("Empire Builders" 1920, 20)

The Tłıchǫ view is very different. They consider the dè to be fully inhabited. The dè is not to be managed, controlled, or changed but to be lived in and respected so that harmonious relations can be established and maintained.

Many others have written about various aspects of the relationship between Kweèt'ıı̀ and the Dene. Kerry Abel (1993) provides an in-depth history of northern Dene east of the Mackenzie Mountains. René Fumoleau (2004) has written the most complete and informative work on events associated with Treaty 8 of 1899 and Treaty 11 of 1921. Mark Dickerson (1992) considers the political events associated with the process of devolution from Ottawa, and Glen Coulthard (2003) discusses the importance of the relationship between self-determination and cultural identity, demonstrating how devolution and the desire to bring democracy to northern Canada not only supported but also advanced the colonization process. John Sandlos (2003) provides a succinct historical overview of environmental legislation designed to protect the last wilderness from "wanton" indigenous hunters. Michael Asch (1984, 1997) draws on his own experience with the Dene to discuss the legal, historical, economic, and political aspects of self-determination as well as the enactment of aboriginal rights within the context of the 1982 Canada Act. He explains the definitions of self-determination and inherent rights put forward by aboriginal organizations and expresses his concern that without an adequate understanding by governments, aboriginal rights will be only symbolic. He recognizes and explains policy changes since 1969 and demonstrates the need for a better understanding of existing aboriginal and treaty rights.

When one considers journal records of explorers and traders and oral narratives of the Tłıchǫ elders, it should not be surprising that the interpretations of the events are based on cultural perspectives that more often than not diverge rather than converge.

The Arrival of Kweèt'ıı̀

The Tłıchǫ had relatively late contact with Kweèt'ıı̀, although stories and goods preceded explorers and traders. June Helm refers to this period as the incipient-early stage, defined by the introduction of European knowledge and goods, but without face-to-face contact (2000, 106–8). Tłıchǫ oral narratives tell of their becoming aware of the European presence through Whanıkw'o, the Tłı̨chǫ woman who spent two years learning about trading after escaping from the Yellowknives, who had kidnapped her after killing her relatives.

In the late eighteenth century, Samuel Hearne wrote of a Tłı̨chǫ woman who, until she was taken by the Cree, had never met Kweèt'ı̀ and had only heard of Kweèt'ı̀ goods and technology (1795, 262–67). When one of Hearne's companions found her in January 1792 and brought her to his camp, she had been on her own for at least seven months after escaping from her captors. She eventually lived with a Chipewyan man.

Father Émile Petitot, an Oblate priest and ethnographer, recorded subarctic Dene oral narratives while making numerous journeys to the Mackenzie Mountains, the Coppermine River,[1] the Arctic Ocean, and Great Slave Lake (Tıdeè) between 1874 and 1878 (1976, 14; see also Savoie 2001). Petitot recorded a Chipewyan version of the story of a woman, Jumping Marten, who lived with Hudson's Bay Company traders. He was told how the Cree took her as a slave in the early 1700s. According to this story, she was the first to describe the traders, who lived in a stone house at York Factory (also see Abel 1993, 49–53). Abel points out that by the mid-1700s a number of French–Cree Métis men had made their way north and married Tłı̨chǫ women (1993, 76). These men probably shared their stories on trapping, trading, religion, and Kweèt'ı̀ in general. The stories of Kweèt'ı̀, their technology, and their practices of trading—wherever these narratives originated—followed the trails throughout Denendeh.

The Hudson's Bay Company built Fort York and later, in 1717, Prince of Wales Fort near Churchill, Manitoba. The company wanted to attract Chipewyan Dene, who used the northern Hudson Bay drainage system over which the company had a legal monopoly. They also wanted to attract Yellowknives, who had access to a source of copper at the mouth of the Coppermine River (Abel 1993, 65–87). Peter Pond, a Canadian free trader, pushed past the limits of the area legally owned by the Hudson's Bay Company while he was wintering on the Athabasca River in 1778–79 (Helm 2000, 127). During this trip, he traveled as far as Great Slave Lake. Based on information from Peter Pond, Alexander Mackenzie ventured down the waterway that came to be called the Mackenzie River in July 1789, encountering about thirty Slavey and Tłı̨chǫ Dene just south of the mouth of the Great Bear River (Mackenzie 1970, 183). In that same year, Peter Pond and other free traders formed the North West Company, opening posts from Great Slave Lake to the lower Mackenzie River.

Exploration and Fur Trade

Trading posts came and went, usually in the same vicinity and often with more than one company operating at a time (Usher 1971). Between the free traders' establishment of Fort Resolution in 1786 and the establishment of (Old) Fort Rae in 1852,[2] the Tłı̨chǫ traded at Whatì as early as 1789 (Krech 1984, 105; Russell 1898, 69–70) and at Fort Resolution sometime after 1823 (Helm 2000, 113). David Smith found that from 1823, when the old North West Company outpost of Fort Providence was abandoned, until 1852, when the Hudson's Bay Company opened (Old) Fort Rae, all native people living in the vicinity of Great Slave Lake came to Fort Resolution to trade (1982, 56). After (Old) Fort Rae was established, it was used almost exclusively by Tłı̨chǫ. They did trade elsewhere, however. Bands residing closer to Great Bear Lake traveled north to Délı̨ne (Fort Franklin) when it was established after 1808 and to Tuht'a (Fort Norman) from 1810 (Helm 2000, 27). Tłı̨chǫ who belonged to the Tsǫ̀tigot'ı̨ı̨ and Tahgagot'ı̨ı̨ regional bands (see map 3) traveled to Fort Simpson after it was established around 1803 (Krech 1984).

Soon after the Yellowknives became middlemen, they started raiding Tłı̨chǫ camps. The elders told me that Tłı̨chǫ never really had trouble with the Chipewyan, who lived around Fort Resolution. Their real adversaries were Akaitcho and his band of Yellowknives from the east and north of Great Slave Lake, whom the Tłı̨chǫ call "T'etsǫt'ıne,"[3] a name also used for the Yellowknives in some of the early literature (Mason 1946, 12; Richardson 1851, 245). Akaitcho's band continually raided Tłı̨chǫ camps, killing everyone except a few women, whom they took along with the furs. Although trade occurred around the Whatì area into the early 1790s (Krech 1984, 106), it would have been minimal due to the threat of attacks. To avoid the raids and loss of life, Tłı̨chǫ from the Whatì region moved closer to Fort Simpson. They eventually tired of being bullied, however, and retaliated by killing several Yellowknives in 1823 (Gillespie 1981, 287; Krech 1984, 131). Tłı̨chǫ elders tell of several other retaliations, such as the one at Ɂı̨ts'èetì, just east of Ɂezǫdzìtì, the area to which several bands—including that of Edzo's father—had retreated. The area is south of the western half of Great Bear Lake. By traveling west and north, the Tłı̨chǫ were better able to avoid Akaitcho and his followers, but not always—Akaitcho also raided the Slavey living around Great Bear Lake (Gillespie 1981, 286–87; Hanks 1996, 704; Helm and Gillespie 1981).

Franklin credited the Hudson's Bay Company with brokering peace between Tłı̨chǫ and the Yellowknives (1828, 9); however, all Tłı̨chǫ credit

Edzo with creating peace with Akaitcho. Helm narrows this occurrence to 1829 (1981a, 296), but tension and fear continued to exist between these groups until the mid- to late 1830s (Gillespie 1981, 288) and surfaced again during the winter of 2001–2002 when overlap and boundary issues were being negotiated for the land claim.

Throughout the early to mid-1800s, the North West Company and the Hudson's Bay Company were vying for furs from Dene throughout Denendeh. The two companies merged in 1821. They built their forts on well-traveled water routes, and it was not until 1852 that a post was built at (Old) Fort Rae on an island in the North Arm of Great Slave Lake. The Oblate missionaries arrived the same year, and despite their unsuccessful attempts to abolish "medicine power" (Mason 1946, 40), the Tłı̨chǫ embraced these missionaries due to the apparent similarities of their beliefs (Ryan 1995, 3). Helm (2000, 9) and Ryan (1995, 3) agree that contact was slow and not traumatic even with the arrival of both missionaries and traders. However, socioterritorial relations shifted as Tłı̨chǫ placed increasing value on items obtainable at the trading post (Helm and Damas 1963). Although there were few problems at first, the problems that did exist were exacerbated with the establishment of Catholic institutions, particularly when children were moved to Catholic residential schools, where they could no longer be educated through oral narratives (Ryan 1995, 3).

Shepard Krech argues that if dependency is measured only by economic indices, then disruption would appear to have been slow and nontraumatic, but, he argues, trade did indeed interfere and disrupt the lives of many Dene. According to Krech, the need to acquire goods both supplanted and added to traditional items. He also considers the need to visit the post to exchange goods as behavior that progressively undermined the indigenous foraging economy (1984, 138–42). Diseases to which the Dene were susceptible were brought to them from outside the region. Hostilities between Tłı̨chǫ and Yellowknives, sparked by the fur trade, and the Dene's enthusiasm for trading and trade goods led to fairly lengthy and ever more frequent visits to the trading post. If hunters became ill, they could not hunt, causing serious problems in the camp. Krech emphasizes that with the advent of fur trading, the desire for goods and thus the contact with disease varied from one individual to the next and from one band to another, as did the effects of trade.

From a review of the literature, one gets the impression that trapping and trading have an historical beginning and end and that the tie to trading posts increasingly separated the Tłı̨chǫ as well as other Dene from their hunting and fishing activities. Oral narratives tell that Tłı̨chǫ continued their foraging activities, even though they also chose to take part in the wage economy. Slobodin shows that the Gwich'in made choices about taking on wage positions and that hunting currently takes up at least half of their time even when they are trapping (1962, 22–23). Debbie DeLancey (1985) makes the same argument for the Slavey Dene.

The Tłı̨chǫ themselves consider the task of trapping as an extension of the kinds of tasks they have always done; they think of themselves as hunters, trappers, and fishers. And they think carefully about entering into mining and other activities related to industrial development. During a conversation I heard in 2003, several young men talked about returning to trapping as a viable endeavor that is "better" for them than the mines. Trapping continues to be viewed as an important land-based activity, even though it is not as economically viable as it once was.

Just as the fur trade has to be understood within its historical context, so must our understanding of why traders and explorers made and continue to make both positive and negative impressions on Tłı̨chǫ people. Samuel Hearne and John Rae are remembered as individuals well able to look after themselves as well as to contribute to the camps they stayed in. Sir John Franklin and company are remembered as having been disrespectful and greedy. Franklin camped in at least two locales where Tłı̨chǫ encountered him: Fort Enterprise and Fort Franklin.[4]

Sir John Franklin noted that Tłı̨chǫ who lived in the area around Fort Enterprise had named most of the lakes, rivers, and "remarkable hills." He remembered them as treating women with respect and liking to dance, sing, and joke (1823, 291). On their return to Fort Enterprise, Franklin and his men were starving, so members of Akaitcho's band brought them provisions, and, according to the oral accounts, Franklin and his men were literally carried out and asked not to return. Franklin reports in his journal that "the Indians treated us with the utmost tenderness, gave us their snow-shoes, and walked without themselves, keeping by our sides, that they might lift us when we fell" (1823, 470).[5]

Some Tłı̨chǫ remember the stories of Franklin. In 1987–88, several elders from Whatì told Randy Freeman, the territorial toponymist, why starvation hit Franklin's expedition. When Franklin and his men returned to Beʔaıtì from their journey to the coast, they found that bears had broken into their cache and eaten all the caribou. The bears were taking revenge on Franklin and his men because they had killed some bears earlier and had been disrespectful by hanging the bears' heads in trees and putting silly grins on the bears' faces. One of the Whatì elders went on to tell Freeman that his ancestor had been part of the group that had come to

Franklin's rescue. Because they did not trust him to leave their land as he had promised, they bound his feet and hands and carried him to old Fort Providence.

During Franklin's second trip in the mid-1820s, his winter base camp was adjacent to a Tłįchǫ fishery on Great Bear Lake (Hanks 1996). His journal entries (1828, 51–63) explain the location as an old North West Company site known to have a fishery able to secure food for up to fifty people. Because he had in excess of thirty men, he kept five to twenty nets in the water until December 1, when most were removed due to a lower daily catch. Until the nets were removed, however, they were yielding between three hundred and eight hundred fish per day. He notes in his journal that around this time Tłįchǫ returned from hunting to spear fish at the head of Bear Lake River but were unable to catch many. Franklin states that the Tłįchǫ were not diligent in their fishing, preferring rather to beg. He goes on to say that he provided them with nets to encourage them to greater exertion, but instead they proceeded to empty his nets. Franklin was indignant, feeling that he had been robbed and deprived of his expedition's catch. He felt compelled to withhold all supplies to ensure that his own men would not starve, an act that eventually caused Tłįchǫ families to leave.

Charlie Neyelle, a Sahtu Dene from Délįne to whom the Tłįchǫ—in particular those from Gamètì—are close, told archaeologist Chris Hanks that Tłįchǫ depended on this fishery to secure sufficient food to last the winter because the water here does not freeze. In sharing the fishery with the Franklin expedition, they thought that Franklin should reciprocate because his nets were taking most of the catch. Neyelle also explained that Franklin's men were too free with the Tłįchǫ women. Once the Tłįchǫ adults realized that Franklin would not reciprocate, they moved to another locale so that they would have sufficient fish to feed their families and would be able to protect their women from Franklin's men. Charlie Neyelle went on to tell Hanks that when Franklin found there was another location that would yield fish, he immediately sent men with nets and lines. Franklin and his men felt that Tłįchǫ should share their favored fishing spots but were irked when they themselves were expected to reciprocate (Hanks 1996, 21). George Blondin, a Sahtu Dene elder who married a Tłįchǫ woman and settled in Behchokǫ̀, said to Chris Hanks in 1995 that he "wished his ancestors had better understood the British concept of property before they freely helped explorers like Franklin." For Blondin, the tangled threads of Dene involvement in the "discovery" of northern

Canada are still being sorted out today in land claims and self-government settlements (Hanks 1996, 13).

Helm refers to this period as the "contact traditional stage," when interactions with Kweèt'ı̨ı̨ took place predominantly through the fur trade, the church, and explorers (2000, 106–8). During this period, Helm suggests, Dene gatherings at the various posts created a venue for intermarriage and linguistic exchange, precipitating intergroup amalgamations. According to Helm, the Sahtu Dene grew out of intermarriage between the Tłı̨chǫ and Hare[6] with an infusion of Mountain Dene, who traded into Tulita and Délı̨ne during the mid-1800s. Had these forts never existed at either end of Great Bear River, Helm speculates, the genealogical mix of descendants of Hare and Tłı̨chǫ Dene would never have emerged as the Sahtu Dene with a unique Slavey language dialect (2000, 16).

Exploration and Government

Traders did not try to control or protect the Dene, nor was it Hudson's Bay Company policy to do so. Trading companies wanted the furs that could be procured more easily if the people were living in the bush. Canadian government policy, however, reflects the need to control and extract resources from First Nations' traditional territories and was designed to restrict their movement. The Tłı̨chǫ have never moved onto reserves, but their rights over Tłı̨chǫ nèèk'e, their place within the dè as defined by Yamǫ̀ǫzaa, were progressively curtailed. Legislation such as the Royal Proclamation of 1763 and the Indian Act of 1874 was justified as necessary to protect and restrain Canada's First Nations: to protect them from settlers and developers and ironically to restrain them from destroying the last frontier. The Royal Proclamation forbade settlement on Indian lands without those lands being obtained by purchase or without aboriginal populations' giving up their rights to their territory. The Indian Act was created to protect First Nations people and Indian lands by enabling the federal government to administer the affairs of First Nations through landholding and land transfer. But, in fact, there was little protection.

The British and Canadian governments made decisions affecting all First Nations, including the Dene. Exploration, coupled with policy and legislation to protect the last frontier from the ways of indigenous people, who in actuality depended on it for their survival, placed considerable constraints on the Dene (Sandlos 2003). The naturalists who pressured the government to protect northern wilderness also wanted the north to be economically viable and productive (Sandlos 2003, 405–7). In 1763, when the Royal Proclamation was passed, few explorers had traveled as far as Denendeh. But the British and Canadian governments encouraged exploration that would inevitably lead to resource development and settlement. Fortunately for the Dene, fur was the only resource deemed worth pursuing between the eighteenth and early twentieth centuries in Denendeh. This land of muskeg, bedrock, and numerous rivers and lakes was useless for farming, and not until the late 1930s did minerals begin producing more revenue than the fur trade. In 1921, when Treaty 11 was signed following the official discovery of oil, the NWT commissioner enacted the "Entry Ordinance," named four councillors, and held the first session of the Northwest Territories Council on 28 April 1921 (Fumoleau 2004, 198–99).

After World War II, the Canadian government felt the need to give the North a bureaucratic presence and to pursue the minerals there—in particular uranium—that it deemed important for national safety and sovereignty. By the late 1950s, the government was planning to devolve governing responsibilities for northern affairs to the North. Most related government initiatives came in the 1960s, with the formation of a territorial government, day schools in many Dene communities, and more reliable medical services.

Treaty 11 was not signed until 1921, yet legislation and policy began to affect Dene lives earlier. In 1917, the Northwest Game Act stipulated a closed season on caribou between October and November and from the beginning of April to the end of July. The policy stipulated that Dene hunters could take caribou during closed seasons only to prevent starvation. And the Migratory Birds Convention Act of 1917 effectively denied native northerners legal access to many species of the game birds they depended on during the spring and fall. In response to these legislated controls, on 18 July 1920 Chipewyan, Slavey, and Tłįchǫ refused treaty payments associated with Treaty 8 in protest against the decisions being made by remote policymakers in Ottawa that were causing them to starve (Sandlos 2003, 405–7). Just as in the case of the encounters with Franklin remembered through oral narratives, people remember interactions with government: bureaucrats speaking for the federal government who were sent to establish control yet lacked the authority to think outside policy guidelines or to finalize agreements. All this is remembered. Madelaine Drybone turned to those of us attending the first land-claim negotiating session in 1993 and said, "Their bosses should come to our communities, so we can talk to them. Nothing will be solved. They will talk, go away, and when they return, their words will be different." Oral narratives coupled with experience similarly caused Tłı̨chǫ adults to be cautious when dealing with the treaty commissioner. As told in the oral narratives and as documented by Fumoleau (2004, 233), the Tłı̨chǫ carefully and anxiously considered the outcome of Treaty 8 in preparation for clear communication with the treaty commissioner in 1921.

Treaty 11

The Royal Proclamation of 1763 and the Indian Act of 1874 were created under the guise of protecting the indigenous people and their lands by enabling the federal government to administer the affairs of First Nations through land holding and land transfer. The establishment of oil claims in 1914 near Norman Wells, just west of Great Bear Lake (Sahtì), gave the federal government the impetus to establish treaty relations with Dene living north of Great Slave Lake. Chief Mǫwhì signed Treaty 11 on 22 August 1921 for the Tłı̨chǫ at Behchokǫ̀. Those present understood the treaty to be a mutual understanding of peaceful relations. None of the Tłı̨chǫ understood that in actuality they had surrendered the land to the government (Fumoleau 2004, 273). The Tłı̨chǫ, along

Figure 4.1. Mǫwhì in Behchokǫ̀, 1935. (Courtesy of Glenbow Museum Archives. Photograph no. pd-338-31 from the G. R. Reid Collection)

with other Dene and Bishop Gabriel Breynat, understood that the government would reciprocate with goods and medicine while its representatives lived within Tłįchǫ nèèk'e (Breynat 2004). When oil and gas were
subsequently found in Alberta, where transportation costs were cheaper,
the development of oil reserves in Denendeh was put on hold, as were the
Canadian government's promises.

The Catholic Church set up health services to deal with measles and
tuberculosis epidemics and built a mission hospital in Behchokǫ̀ in 1940.[7]
Children attended the residential schools in Fort Smith, Fort Resolution,
Fort Providence, and Inuvik until the 1960s, when community schooling
was initiated. Bishop Breynat lobbied the government and made several
trips to Ottawa in the hope that the federal government would live up to
its treaty commitments to educate, house, and provide medical care to the
Dene. Before his death, he wrote an article entitled "Canada's Blackest
Blot," which appeared in the *Toronto Star Weekly* on 28 May 1938 and
the Quebec City newspaper *le Soleil* on 3 July 1938. The article begins:
"The story of the white man's invasion of the Canadian Northwest may
be named by future historians as one of the blackest blots on the pages of
Canadian history. It is an ugly story. A story of greed, of ruthlessness, and
broken promises" (Breynat 2004, 494).

K'àowo, K'aàwı, Chiefs

Once Mǫwhì had signed Treaty 11, the federal government named him
grand chief, and several other "headmen" who were trading at the Hudson's Bay Company became chiefs. The Canadian government imposed
this structure through the provisions of the Indian Act, which assumed
that leadership is based on title or being "in authority." In contrast, the
Tłįchǫ themselves recognized individuals as leaders by virtue of their skill
and knowledge. They are not so much "in authority" as "authorities of" a
task. It was on this basis that the Tłįchǫ selected Mǫwhì to represent and
speak for all of them.

At the time of the treaty, Mǫwhì was a k'àowo or "boss" who had a
following owing to his knowledge of the bush and the trails. He was also
considered a k'aàwı, a "trading boss," who worked and traveled with his
uncle, who was a respected k'aàwıdeè, an important and successful trading
boss known for his understanding of Kweèt'ı̨̀. All Tłįchǫ k'aàwıdeè had a
large following when traveling to the posts because of their knowledge of
trading and of the factors at the post. Tłįchǫ k'aàwıdeè were expected to be

hard bargainers who understood the value of their furs and who sent their assistants—k'aàwı in training—ahead of them with "tally sticks" to provide accurate information of the worth of what they carried. Tłıchǫ k'aàwıdeè learned quickly that they gained more respect from the post factors if they had a large following, so their followers were completely committed to them while at the fort (J. Smith 1976, 76). The same tactic was used when meeting with the commissioner: one speaker with many followers.

Although the federal commission appointed Mǫwhì as grand chief after the signing of Treaty 11, the Tłıchǫ themselves had already selected him to speak for them and followed him because of his knowledge and skill. K'aàwı likewise were named as chiefs of their regions. The position of chief continues to be held by a Tłıchǫ who has knowledge of Kweèt'ıì ways. Nevertheless, the issue of whether a chief should be a person who understands Kweèt'ıì ways or a person who has spent a great deal of time in the bush remains a topic of discussion. For the elders, an ideal chief is a person who knows both.

Mining in Tłıchǫ nèèk'e

In spite of the signing of Treaty 11 and the appointment of chiefs who were to be informed about the coming and going of Kweèt'ıì, the Canadian government did not fulfill its treaty responsibilities or inform the Dene of its intentions with regard to development. Until recently, most government personnel perceived their federal title and bureaucratic position as giving them an authority superior to that of the Dene. The history of development is riddled with a lack of realistic consultation and information exchange.

From the research done by Gabrielle Mackenzie-Scott (2001), we know that after silver and pitchblende were discovered in 1930 on the east shore of Great Bear Lake (Sahtì), approximately three hundred prospectors entered the area. By 1939, more than four hundred prospectors had claimed some five thousand properties between K'àatì and Tıdeè. Uranium and gold extraction began in Tłıchǫ nèèk'e in the early 1930s. In 1921, the Aurous Gold Mining Company started the first mine on the East Arm of Great Slave Lake. Between 1931 and 1947, another twenty mines within Tłıchǫ nèèk'e were producing gold, silver, uranium, copper, tungsten, and tantalum. Another seven were in operation between 1950 and 1982. During the 1990s, one more gold mine and two diamond mines opened.

Development, policy, and legislation were going ahead with little consideration to how they would affect the Dene. Kweèt'ıì once again took without reciprocating, failing to explain their actions and to live up to agreements made by the treaty commissioner with the Dene. This behavior was particularly evident during the 1950s in the case of uranium mining. Although the extraction of uranium at the Rayrock Mine was short-lived, it once again demonstrated a lack of respect for the land and the people. During the 1950s, scientists were realizing how handling uranium ore could have serious short- and long-term effects. It was not the mine managers who shared this information with the Tłı̨chǫ who worked at and set up tents and cabins near the mines, but rather other workers who had access to the managers.

On 3 October 1996, Monique Etlonzo from Behchokǫ̀ explained that her husband and other underground workers learned of the potential dangers of uranium mining from a fellow worker, who had left the mine after he heard the managers arguing and expressing fear of the spillage (Legat et al. 1997, 15). The story of Rayrock Mine is told and remembered so the younger Tłı̨chǫ will know it and use it to think with while meeting and negotiating with developers.

Government Policies; Tłı̨chǫ Autonomy

In response to the Second World War and the ensuing Cold War, Canadian politicians felt northern development was critical for national sovereignty and protection. In addition to sovereignty issues, the protective and paternalistic attitudes so prevalent toward First Nations across Canada became much more evident in relations with the Dene, for two reasons. First, Canadian policy governing native people had become apparent to the US military during the war, and the criticism had shamed the Canadian government. Second, Canada was starting to act as an international peacekeeper and power broker for the United Nations and thus could hardly criticize colonial powers in Africa if its own government was just as bad (Dickerson 1992, 61). Government-initiated medical services and social assistance and the idea of day schools in communities were introduced. These initiatives, along with the housing program, were designed to bring people in from the bush. For Tłı̨chǫ Dene, these services were directed at Behchokǫ̀. The number of small businesses servicing the mines increased, government offices proliferated, and government policies protecting wildlife were more systematically applied (Helm 1979, 156).

Along with this increased control, several incidents that occurred in rapid succession between 1962 and 1967 heightened "anti-white" feelings. Nancy Lurie notes that negative feelings were directed not so much to individuals as to the "white institutions" that were trying to control Tłı̨chǫ people (2000, 97–98). These institutions included social services, which many Tłı̨chǫ held responsible for breaking relationships between parents and children, and the wildlife division for conservation policies, which Tłı̨chǫ felt was acting at the expense of those who were trying to secure food for their families.

One incident took place in Behchokǫ̀ on 2 July 1962 when Game Warden Gene Earl announced that because caribou numbers were declining, hunters were not to kill any cows or calves. Helm observed the exchange and described later how both Johnny Simpson, a middle-aged hunter, and Grand Chief Jimmy Bruneau were among those who responded to Earl (2000, 66–67). Johnny Simpson explained that if he saw many caribou, he would not kill cows, but that he, not the game warden, was his own boss. Bruneau explained that he would never agree not to shoot cows and calves and that the Tłı̨chǫ depend on caribou in the winter. As Grand Chief Bruneau stated, "The caribou are ours." "You fellows don't give us anything. . . . We are all living on the caribou. . . . We haven't got any money. We get out in the bush, get a little meat, that's what we eat. You guys all got jobs. You walk in a restaurant and buy food with your money. Out there, the caribou is our money."[8] Helm says that "Chief Bruneau then change[d] the topic, asking a question about the dates for Treaty at other forts" (2000, 67). Although Bruneau did not withdraw physically from the situation, he withdrew from further discussion about caribou by changing the subject.

Donald Gamble (1986) describes a similar incident in the 1960s. As an engineer, he was working on the project to build a new village for Tłı̨chǫ residing at Behchokǫ̀, where several children had died due to poor sanitation and drainage problems. Housing was also sorely needed. Gamble explains that after several meetings between officials in Yellowknife and officials from Ottawa, it was decided that the best solution would be to move the entire community to a location nearer the highway. They then held community meetings, at which Tłı̨chǫ quietly but continually pointed out that they did not need to be near a highway. They needed to stay near their fishing nets on ʔı̨hdaak'ètì. Moreover, they emphasized the cultural and geographic importance of the location of their current place of residence. According to Gamble—and oral narratives—the bureaucrats continually stressed the benefits of moving, pointing out that the community would have safety features such as a park for their children, a cul-de-sac, sufficient elevation for a good drainage system that would alleviate the sanitation problems, and row housing.

Finally, Chief Bruneau told the officials to go ahead and build the new settlement if that is what they really wanted so much, but he warned them that the people would probably stay in Behchokǫ̀. The bureaucrats and consultants took this statement as a local endorsement, and the community of Edzo was built. All government services were located in Edzo, including an elementary school, to which students continue to be bussed (Gamble 1986). Since the 1970s, however, services have gradually been relocated to Behchokǫ̀, where the Tłı̨chǫ remained. Although an elementary school was built in Behchokǫ̀, the school in Edzo remains as a regional high school, with its motto based on Grand Chief Jimmy Bruneau's direction to all Tłı̨chǫ, "Learn both ways so that every individual can be strong like two people."

The building of the new community—Edzo—was testimony to the bureaucrats' and consultants' lack of understanding and their "we know what is best for you" attitude. Bruneau's response conversely demonstrated Tłı̨chǫ respect for personal autonomy and growth. On the one hand, he told the bureaucrats to go ahead and do what they wanted to do. On the other hand, he warned them that "the people" do not "follow" those whom they do not consider knowledgeable. The bureaucratic decision, he explained, was not right for them.

Sewer, water, and sanitation problems were eventually solved in Behchokǫ̀. However, there continues to be a chronic shortage of housing for the population of approximately eighteen hundred. For several decades, the houses and apartments in Edzo were occupied by Kweèt'ıı̨ teachers working at one of the schools. More recently, some Tłı̨chǫ individuals with full-time wage employment have begun to live there. Edzo has become an annex or neighborhood of Behchokǫ̀.

Mǫwhì 's father, Ɂewaı̨hgǫ, was the first to build a cabin at the current site of Behchokǫ̀, and then in 1902 he persuaded the free traders James Hislop and Ed Nagle to set up a trading post there—the Hislop and Nagle Company. Behchokǫ̀ was safer and easier to reach than (Old) Fort Rae, and by 1906 the Catholic mission and the Hudson's Bay Company had moved there as well (Helm 2000, 27). The Tłı̨chǫ never favored the location of (Old) Fort Rae. In 1913, John Mason noticed that Tłı̨chǫ were fearful of crossing the Tıdeè (Great Slave Lake) in their canoes (1946, 13). With the exception of a few families, such as the Blackducks and Rabescas, who have always used the north shore of Tıdeè, most Tłı̨chǫ still do not like traveling on Tıdeè or Sahtì, nor did they feel comfortable in the York boat (Helm 2000, 150).

In 1961, the Mackenzie Highway reached the gold-mining community of Yellowknife, making travel between Yellowknife and Behchokǫ̀ easier, particularly after the seven-mile spur between Behchokǫ̀ and the Mackenzie Highway was built in 1967. The highway also connected the

Tłı̨chǫ with southern Canada, so, being people who love to travel, they took advantage of it to learn more about "the South." By the late 1960s, people were traveling south, establishing contact with other aboriginal people such as the Navajo in Arizona and the Dene Tha Slavey in northern Alberta, where they attended prophet gatherings (Helm 1994). They also attended Catholic spiritual gatherings at Lac St. Anne. In these and other situations, they met people involved in the "Indian," which it was referred to at the time, movement in southern Canada and the United States. They were no longer alone in their frustrations and concerns. Young people were meeting and strategizing with former residential schoolmates and members of First Nations who were also vying for self-government.

David Smith (1992) describes how young people in one Dene community successfully took control of the local government in 1971. By 1975, several Dene ran successfully in the territorial elections. However, early in the session of the new Legislative Assembly, George Barnaby from Fort Good Hope and James Wah-Shee from Behchokǫ̀ noted that many of their people thought the territorial government was not working for native people's concerns and interests. Others felt that if aboriginal people could gain a majority, this problem could be corrected. In 1979, Wah-Shee was elected to the territorial Legislative Assembly, along with four other Dene representatives. Richard Nerysoo and James Wah-Shee were appointed members of the Executive Council, with Wah-Shee becoming the first minister of the Local Government Department (Dickerson 1992, 102).

The Mackenzie Highway brought more than knowledge: alcohol also made its way to Behchokǫ̀. In 1971, Tłı̨chǫ voted to have "dry communities." Theirs was the first region in the NWT to ban alcohol. Before and after the ban, when alcohol was brought to the communities, the community k'àowo would take it and pour it on the ground. The amount of alcohol any one person can have is restricted in Behchokǫ̀[9] and completely banned in the smaller Tłı̨chǫ fly-in communities.

Fly-in Communities: Whatì, Wekweètì, and Gamètì

In the 1960s, several Tłı̨chǫ hauled building material in their freighter canoes across lakes, rivers, and numerous portages in order to build communities away from Behchokǫ̀. They sought places where Kweèt'ı̨ı influence was minimal, where they could be free from the alcohol and the ever-increasing rules, regulations, and controls being administered from Yellowknife. They wanted to protect their families and to live in a way that was right. Families who currently live in Behchokǫ̀ continue to send their children and other family members to these smaller fly-in communities to live with relatives.

Alexie Arrowmaker led the Tłı̨chǫ Dechı̨laagot'ı̨ı̨, "Edge of the Woods People," to settle in Wekweètì, which has always been an important place to them (Helm 1981a, 292, and 2000, 189). In 1969, he was the first chief to be elected rather than selected by consensus. He continued within the political arena as one of the advisers to the team negotiating land claims and self-government until his death in fall 2005. Wekweètì is the smallest of the three fly-in communities, with a population that rarely exceeds 150. Since the 1970s, the community has had a school and band office; it had only one phone number until the mid-1990s, when students and the band office moved rapidly to the Internet. Tłı̨chǫ people from other communities say that the people in Wekweètì speak "real" Tłı̨chǫ because they have no non-Tłı̨chǫ neighbors.

Also in the 1960s, the Apple, Tailbone, Zoe, Wetrade, Gon, Arrowmaker, Mantla, and Chocolate families began settling Gamètì. They

Figure 4.2. Amen Tailbone and Rosalie Tailbone were among those who in the 1960s decided to assist with creating a community at Gamètì so their children would live in harmony and would live life as taught in the oral narratives. Here they are working together, sharing their knowledge as Amen makes a drum frame and Rosalie prepares to go in the tepee, where she will work on a caribou hide that is right for the drum, 1994. (Photograph by the author)

followed Andrew Gon, who became chief, and Jean Wetrade, who became community k'àowo. They built their cabins in a favored spring fishing locale, where they had always gathered to wait for the caribou and where there were birch trees from which birch bark canoes could be built as they waited for the ice to melt. They could fish and hunt as well as prepare for summer travel. Most people living in Gamètì are descendants of the ?et'aagot'ı̨ı̨, "Next to the Other People"; the Sahtìgot'ı̨ı̨, "Bear Lake People"; and the Gots'ǫkàtìgot'ı̨ı̨, "Cloudberry Lake People," who continue to have relations with the Sahtu Dene living in Délı̨ne. The women in Gamètì are known for their skill in preparing hides. The community's population is about 350.

Families also returned to Whatì with the intention of raising their children in a safer environment. Whatì had been community-like since the 1950s, when both Joan Ryan and June Helm taught children to read and write, which allowed them to stay with their families rather than having to go to residential schools. With its population of approximately five hundred, Whatì is known by other Tłı̨chǫ as having the best fish, fresh and dried. Community members continue to have favorite fishing places where they stay on a regular basis.

Many elders express their frustration at the inability of Kweèt'ı̨ı̨ to understand how people can reside in places without digging up the ground and building buildings. To these elders, it seems that in the Kweèt'ı̨ı̨ view the environment is something that humans are destined to build and construct on, filling up spaces rather than dwelling in and using places. This frustration with the Kweèt'ı̨ı̨ perspective lay behind a comment that Margaret Lafferty made on 10 October 1995 concerning Wekweètì: "Whoever those people are that are saying that [we only recently moved here] can't tell me I'm lying because whatever I know, I learned from my elders. . . . The elders used to travel on these trails. . . . To this day, Wekweètì was never without the People, not at all" (Dene Cultural Institute 1996, 10). I have heard similar comments from elders currently residing in Behchokǫ̀, Whatì, and Gamètì.

Education

Tłı̨chǫ are particularly interested in how and what their descendants learn and have a strong commitment to protecting the dè, the places that teach, and their right to govern themselves. They were and continue to be committed to learning the ways of both Kweèt'ı̨ı̨ and Tłı̨chǫ. Like the federal government, they wanted community schools, but for a different reason. The government wanted the Dene out of the bush so that "wilderness" could be both protected and put to use in the interests of economic prosperity and national security. Tłıchǫ wanted their children with them in the community so they could guide their learning.

Education has been on the Dene Nation's agenda since the nation was established under the banner of the Indian Brotherhood of the Northwest Territories in 1968. Dene requested that the school year be scheduled to fit with the annual round of hunting and trapping rather than farming and that regions should have authority over the curriculum. Local school societies were established throughout Denendeh, and the Tłıchǫ Rae-Edzo School Society was the first to open its own school. Chief Jimmy Bruneau Elementary School opened its doors in Behchokǫ̀ with fifteen classrooms and a hundred-bed residence to house young people whose parents were not settled in the community.

The Rae-Edzo School Society immediately began cooperating with the Yellowknife School Society to prepare a series of storybooks for the school that would focus on Tłıchǫ heritage (Abel 1993, 250). Not until 1989, however, was the Tłıchǫ leadership able to approve the establishment of a regional board. In 1973, when the territorial government initiated a teacher-certification program to be taught in Fort Smith, every teacher was required to speak and write one Dene language in addition to English (Abel 1993). Although Behchokǫ̀ elementary school has a Tłıchǫ principal, most teachers in the fly-in communities continue to be non-Tłıchǫ directly out of university. These teachers do not speak the local language or understand Tłıchǫ ways; they also lack teaching experience of any kind. The Tłıchǫ leadership is committed to educating these teachers by offering them opportunities to canoe to the tundra for the fall caribou hunt. Furthermore, communities have Tłıchǫ individuals as teaching assistants who help the students with reading and writing in their own language.

All Tłıchǫ individuals are encouraged to remember occurrences and happenings from the past, including what Kweèt'ıı say and how they behave. Tłıchǫ discuss the importance of equipping their youth to live in an ever-changing world while maintaining strength in their own culture (Barnaby 2004, 529). These open attitudes, however, are not consistent with the Western approach to learning and bring some frustrations. Elders discuss their concerns about growing disharmony among the people, in particular the youth. They fear that young people will have no way forward. Margaret Lafferty, an elder from Wekweètì, expressed this concern succinctly:

Kweèt'įį keep stating that the children should be taught . . . yet our children still do not have jobs, and if they forget about the caribou they will be pitiful. They teach the children how to speak English . . . and teach them only about Kweèt'įį knowledge. They say our children will be poor unless they speak English. They say our children will not have a job [wage-earning employment] unless they speak English. Nowadays, they say it's like that. We don't know how to speak English but we worked the same as our elders did in the past, and we weren't that pitiful. We survived through hardships. We know our people's knowledge. However, even though the children speak English, they do not have a job. What are they being taught? It is as if they are not taught anything. (Dene Cultural Institute 1996, 12)

Defending Land Rights

At the time that education was at the top of the Indian Brotherhood agenda, the Canadian government was keen on building a pipeline to bring the oil and natural gas found in 1967 at Prudeau Bay, Alaska, down the Mackenzie Valley to Alberta as well as south to the United States. In this economic venture, little thought was given to the Dene, nor was the matter discussed with them. It was only through June Helm's attendance at the 1968 Behchokǫ̀ Treaty Days that the venture was drawn to their attention. While handing out treaty payments, the government agent raised the possibility of setting up reserves under the provision of Treaty 11 signed in 1921. Helm wondered why, after forty-seven years, reserves were being suggested. A few months later she understood. The federal government, to implement its proposed pipeline project, needed to complete the process of extinguishing aboriginal title to eliminate native land claims as a factor in negotiations over the pipeline's development (Helm 1979, 156).

The Canadian government was convinced that the pipeline would be built. The Dene, Inuvialuit, and Métis requested an explanation, pointing out that they had had no venue to express their concerns, nor did they have any way of knowing what was going on or what decisions had been made. In response, the Department of Indian Affairs and Northern Development sponsored a meeting for the sixteen Dene chiefs at Fort Smith, NWT. The chiefs decided to organize themselves, with James Wah-Shee, a Tłįchǫ from Behchokǫ̀, being elected as the first president of the Indian Brotherhood of the Northwest Territories (Dene Nation 1984, 35), which later grew into the Dene Nation.

Dene Nation leaders at this time included Georges Erasmus, a Tłı̨chǫ born in Behchokǫ̀ and raised in Yellowknife, who became president in 1974. In 1983, he was elected vice-chief for the northern region of the Assembly of First Nations, the Canada-wide organization representing First Nations. In 1985, he was elected Grand Chief of the Assembly of First Nations.

For Dene, the need to organize to deal with the threat of the pipeline was intimately tied to the 1969 "Statement of the Government of Canada on Indian Policy." Known as the "White Paper," this document stated that Indian claims based on aboriginal rights were no longer significant, but that any breaches of treaty rights would be resolved. The policy called for the termination of the special rights and status of aboriginal peoples. First Nations people across Canada—including the Dene—responded with the "Red Paper," in which they firmly rejected the federal government's proposal. In response, the government appointed a claims commissioner.

By 1970, the federal government was providing funding to the Indian Brotherhood to develop positions and databases to enable the Dene to negotiate both comprehensive and specific claims. In 1972, the government once again offered the Dene reserves and financial compensation "to discharge the Crown's responsibilities as outlined in the treaties" (Abel 1993, 251). The Indian Brotherhood declined the offer, stating that the Dene's oral narratives clearly interpreted Treaty 8 and Treaty 11 as agreements of friendship rather than land surrender. It claimed that the undertakings that had been made to the Dene and under which they had agreed to sign Treaties 8 and 11 were fraudulent and that they had never extinguished their aboriginal rights or title to the land.

The Dene chiefs decided to go to court to stop all developments. In 1973, the Indian Brotherhood decided that Chief François Paulette—a Chipewyan from Fort Smith—would file a "caveat" with the Registrar of Land Titles claiming a Dene interest in more than one million square kilometers (Abel 1993, 251). Judge William George Morrow, who considered the case when the government challenged the Dene's caveat, decided that the Dene had a right to be heard. Although the federal government has never agreed that the treaties were friendship agreements, in 1973 it did agree to negotiate aboriginal rights on the grounds that Dene had never received the full benefits set out in the treaties (Abel 1993, 251; Barnaby 2004, 524).

By the early 1970s, approximately half of the 25,000 to 30,000 people in the (then) NWT were Kweèt'ı̨ı̨, living in the four largest communities of Yellowknife, Fort Smith, Inuvik, and Hay River. About 80 percent of the Kweèt'ı̨ı̨ population was transient. The pipeline's impact would have been principally on the Inuit, Métis, and Dene living along the Mackenzie Valley corridor. The Dene were the largest group, with a population of 6,700 in 1971 (Helm 1981b, 216). In 1975, the federal government responded to Dene, Inuit, and Métis concerns by expanding the guidelines for the environmental review of the pipeline to include social concerns. They appointed Justice Thomas Berger to hold an inquiry into the proposed pipeline. He was known as an outspoken advocate of native rights. During 1975 and 1976, Justice Berger traveled to all communities that would be impacted by the pipeline. He held formal hearings of sworn testimony and took submissions from the applicant pipeline companies, environmental organizations, business and other special-interest groups, and several NWT native organizations.

Berger also held informal hearings in all communities. Tłı̨chǫ statements ranged from asserting their relations within the dè to expressing anxiety, based on evidence from past development, about the damage that might be caused by the pipeline. Two such statements came from residents of Gamètì. The words of Bruno Apple were translated as follows:

> He says, life has not been very easy in the past and it's unlikely it will be any easier in the future. He says, he'd like to say a few words on the pipeline. He says, this land here provides all the meat and fish and everything that they need to live on and he says that we hate to see all these things go when the pipeline gets through and he also said that our real parents have long deceased and this land is like our own father and mother. They provide all the meat and fish, and everything that they need. . . . This pipeline that they are talking about building, they shouldn't build it too close to where the animals live. We, who live this way of life, like living this way, he says. We do not want to see this pipeline built. . . . This land here provides all fur bearing animals and whenever they go trapping, they get their money off the fur. He says, though the money won't last very long, he says we're still against this pipeline. He says, this land here has been very good to us. The little kids here who are now out with their mothers, like the little babies and little boys who are out playing, then in the future they're going to need this land to live on. He says, we love our kids and if this pipeline should be built, the pipeline is going to sweep the animals away from this land. He says, I have said what was on my mind. (from transcriptions in Scott 2007, 63–64)

Paul Drybone added through his translator,

We may talk about the land a lot but it's because we love this land and we don't want to see anything happen to it. He says, sometimes during the cold weather, even though it's really cold, they still have to go out and see their net as they have to eat. It's a very hard form of living but we still love the way we live. That's another reason why we don't want to see this pipeline go through. Many people will benefit from this pipeline but this winter when the trucks go on the winter road, they also have to cross the lake and when they do go across the lake, sometimes they discharge gas and throw away gas on the lake and this kills the fish. We are serious when we say that we don't want this pipeline to go through. He says we have always wondered when the government people would come and listen to them and listen to them and talk to them and talk with them, but now that you're here, they'd like to take advantage of this opportunity to say what they have to say to you. That's about all I have to say. Thank you. (from transcriptions in Scott 2007, 64)

In April 1977, Justice Berger recommended that there be no pipeline for at least ten years to allow for "native claims to be settled, and for new programs and new institutions to be established" (Berger 1977, xxvi–xxvii). Through Berger and Paulette's Caveat case, the Dene were able to put aboriginal rights on the table.

The Declaration of Dene Nationhood was passed at the second joint General Assembly of the Indian Brotherhood of the Northwest Territories at Fort Simpson, 19 July 1975.

Statement of Rights. We the Dene of the Northwest Territories insist on the right to be regarded by ourselves and the world as a nation. Our struggle is for the recognition of the Dene Nation by the Government and peoples of Canada and the peoples and governments of the world.

As once Europe was the exclusive homeland of the European peoples, Africa the exclusive homeland of the African peoples, the New World, North and South America, was the exclusive homeland of Aboriginal peoples of the New World, the Amerindian and the Inuit.

The New World like other parts of the world has suffered the experience of colonialism and imperialism. Other peoples have occupied the land—often with force—and foreign governments have imposed themselves on our people. Ancient civilizations and ways of life have been destroyed.

Colonialism and imperialism are now dead or dying. Recent years have witnessed the birth of new nations or rebirth of old nations out of the ashes of colonialism.

As Europe is the place where you will find European countries with European governments for European peoples, now also you will find in Africa and Asia the existence of African and Asian countries with African and Asian governments for the African and Asian peoples.

The African and Asian peoples—the peoples of the Third World— have fought for and won the right to self-determination, the right to recognition as distinct peoples and the recognition of themselves as nations.

But in the New World the Native peoples have not fared so well. Even in countries in South America where the Native peoples are the vast majority of the population there in not one country which has an Amerindian government for the Amerindian peoples.

Nowhere in the New World have the Native peoples won the right to self-determination and the right to recognition by the world as a distinct people and as Nations.

While the Native people of Canada are a minority in their home-land, the Native people of the Northwest Territories, the Dene and the Inuit, are a majority of the population of the Northwest Territories.

The Dene find themselves as part of a country. That country is Canada. But the Government of Canada is not the Government of the Dene. The Government of the Northwest Territories is not the Govern-ment of the Dene. These governments were not the choice of the Dene, they were imposed upon the Dene.

What we the Dene are struggling for is the recognition of the Dene Nation by the governments and peoples of the world.

And while there are realities we are forced to submit to, such as the existence of a country called Canada, we insist on the right to self- deter-mination as a distinct people and the recognition of the Dene Nation.

We the Dene are part of the Fourth World. And as the peoples and Nations of the world have come to recognize the existence and rights of those peoples who make up the Third World, the day must come when the nations of the Fourth World will come to be recognized and respected. The challenge to the Dene and the world is to find the way for the recognition of the Dene Nation.

Our plea to the world is to help us in our struggle to find a place in the world community where we can exercise our right to self-determination as a distinct people and as a nation.

What we seek then is independence and self-determination within
the country of Canada. This is what we mean when we call for a just
land settlement for the Dene Nation. (Dene Nation 1977, 2–4)

On 25 October 1976, the Indian Brotherhood submitted a position
paper calling on the Government of Canada to negotiate with the Dene
on the matters that were important to them, as stated in the Dene Declaration (Helm 1981b, 233–34). When the federal government refused,
Tłįchǫ once again took action by refusing "treaty annuity" unless the government recognized that the Tłįchǫ had not ceded and surrendered their
land under Treaty 11. In the following year (1978), the Sahtu Dene joined
the Tłįchǫ, and by 1981 half the Dene were boycotting treaty ceremo-
nies (Barnaby 2004). Although land-claim negotiations began in 1981,
the Dene led a national coalition to pressure the federal government "to
make changes to the comprehensive land claims policy and to drop their
requirement for aboriginal people to extinguish their aboriginal rights in
exchange for land-claims agreements" (Barnaby 2004, 528). In September
1988, the Land Claim Agreement-in-Principle was signed by the Dene-
Métis Secretariat, which since 1979 had been mandated to negotiate a
joint land claim. In April of the following year, approximately 24,500
square miles of land was withdrawn for protection from development,
pending land selection.

In spite of known problems, in April 1990 the Dene-Métis leadership
agreed to take the completed Comprehensive Dene-Métis Land Claims
Agreement to the communities for ratification. On 18 July 1990, the joint
Dene-Métis Assembly passed a resolution calling for renegotiation of por-
tions of the agreement and possible court action to force recognition of
aboriginal and treaty rights. Representatives from the Delta and the Sahtu
opposed the motion. The Gwich'in walked out of the 1990 Dene National
Assembly, and the Sahtu delegates were unable to come to a consensus
and abstained from voting. By September 1990, both had withdrawn from
the process and had requested the right to negotiate regional claims. On
7 November, the federal government informed the Dene-Métis Secretariat that the government would no longer negotiate with it and would cut
funding retrospectively to 1 October of the same year. The land freeze
was lifted. The diamond rush began soon after that: prospectors laid claim
to land with little consideration for the Tłįchǫ people. The federal and
territorial governments continued to issue permits and licenses in geographic regions where the Dene refused to sign a final agreement because
that agreement contained an extinguishment provision (Asch and Zlotkin

1997, 223). The extinguishment provision in the Dene-Métis Agreement provided *only* for the extinguishment of Dene and of Métis *aboriginal title* to the lands and resources in Denendeh. The agreement left other cultural and political rights—undefined—alone, at least in principle. The Dene refused to sign because, for them, the land is tied to who they are as human beings. As we have learned since the Tłįchǫ Agreement has been ratified, extinguishment of aboriginal title to lands has serious implications for the content and scope of Dene self-government rights, such as they are.

Dogrib Treaty 11 Council

After the federal government withdrew funding from the Dene-Métis Secretariat, Tłįchǫ leaders traveled to their communities to discuss what community members would like done. This process lasted two years. In 1992, the Dogrib Treaty 11 Council was formed and became a society under the Northwest Territories Societies Act of 1988, with a mandate to negotiate a land-claim and self-government agreement with the federal government. A regional claim was proposed, including a claim on self-government according to S.35 of the Constitution Act of 1982.

In Yellowknife in March 1994, the new Liberal Indian and Northern Affairs federal minister Ron Irwin made a verbal commitment to the Tłįchǫ leaders and elders that they could negotiate self-government as part of their land-claim agreement. In August 1995, the Canadian government introduced a new policy on self-government called the "Inherent Right to Self-Government," providing Tłįchǫ negotiators with a new mandate. By April 1997, the federal government had agreed to negotiate a joint land-claim and self-government agreement with the Dogrib Treaty 11 Council. This was a welcome change of heart for the Tłįchǫ, who had been the first among the Dene to refuse "treaty annuity" because the government would not recognize that the Dene had not ceded and surrendered their land and the right to govern themselves. The Tłįchǫ Agreement was officially signed in August 2005 at the annual gathering in Behchokǫ̀.

Between 1992 and 2005, Tłįchǫ leaders were involved with much more than negotiating the claim with the federal and territorial governments. There were overlap issues to be settled with Yellowknives from Dettah and N'dilo in Yellowknife Bay and with Slavey living in the Dehcho, whose regional center is located in Fort Simpson. By 2002, Tłįchǫ and Dehcho

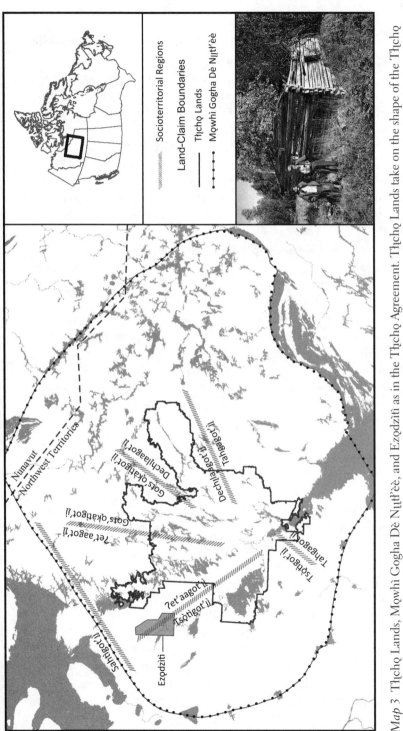

Map 3 Tłı̨chǫ Lands, Mǫwhì Gogha Dè Nı̨ı̨tł'èè, and Ezǫdzìti as in the Tłı̨chǫ Agreement. Tłı̨chǫ Lands take on the shape of the Tłı̨chǫ socioterritorial regions: Sahtı̨got'ı̨ı̨, "Bear Lake People"; ?et'aagot'ı̨ı̨, "Cross the Divide People"; Gots'ǫkàtìgot'ı̨ı̨, "Cloudberry Lake People"; Dechı̨laagot'ı̨ı̨, "Edge of the Woods People"; Tàhgagot'ı̨ı̨, "Follow the Shore People"; and Tsǫtı̨got'ı̨ı̨, "Filth Lake People." Photograph of Adele Wedawin and Pierre Mantla Sr. in 1998 at Nı̨dzı̨ı̨kàà by the author. (Base map courtesy of Mark Fenwick, Land Protection Department, Tłı̨chǫ Government)

Slavey had reached an agreement to work together to protect ?edèezhìì under the NWT Protected Areas Strategy.

Throughout the period during which the land claim was being negotiated, several mining developments were proposed within Mǫwhì Gogha Dè Nı̨ı̨tłèè, the area defined by Mǫwhì in 1921 for traditional use. The caribou calving grounds of the Bathurst area are adjacent to this area. The caribou congregate in early fall along the Deèzàatìdeè (Coppermine River) and in the Deèzàatì (Point Lake) and ?ek'atì (Lac de Gras) areas, where two diamond mines are under operation. While in these areas, the caribou forage on the lush grasses and sedges before migrating to the boreal forest, where they graze mainly on various types of lichen during the winter.

The effects of mining developments on the migrating caribou continue to be a worry for both elders and leaders. In response to the environmental concerns associated with the proposed diamond-mining developments, the West Kitikmeot Slave Study Society was formed in 1996 with representatives from the territorial and federal governments, the Chamber of Mines, and aboriginal parties (Inuit, Tłı̨chǫ, Chipewyan, and Métis). At the same time, the Dogrib Renewable Resources Committee indicated to the Dogrib Treaty 11 Council that their research priorities were caribou, habitat, water, and heritage as well as research leading to a monitoring program based on their knowledge. The committee included harvesters and elders from each of the four Tłı̨chǫ communities.

Taking Action

Since the arrival of government and industry, the Tłı̨chǫ—along with other Dene—continually asserted the importance of self-determination in relation to treaties, legislation, and industrial development. Such assertions were increased in the 1970s with statements regarding devolving federal responsibility to the territorial council; getting ready for land-claim negotiations; thinking about education, health, and wildlife; and opposing the Mackenzie Valley Pipeline. Many of these issues continue.

It is not surprising, then, that when the federal government withdrew funding from the Dene-Métis Secretariat and the land freeze was lifted, the Tłı̨chǫ regrouped. On evaluating the situation, the elders took action by requesting that their oral narratives of traditional governance be heard and recorded. They wanted to ensure that their knowledge could be used after the land-claims and self-government agreement was reached with the federal government. I was asked to participate in research on traditional governance and to use the PAR method.

On 3 December 1992, I made my first trip to Gamètì. On that flight, I contemplated how the recent diamond rush was affecting the Tłıchǫ people. During the summer of 1990, when the Dene-Métis land-claim negotiations came to a halt, the Government of Canada terminated the land withdrawals. It refused to issue another Order-in-Council similar to the one finalized in early 1989 as part of the Interim Measures Agreement negotiated with the Dene-Métis.[10] Lifting of the land freeze provided exploration teams with the opportunity to stake their claims to potentially productive sites. Throughout Tłıchǫ nèèk'e, evidence of these mining claims was found, along with some mining stakes— literally—adjacent to Tłıchǫ homes. I wondered how the Tłıchǫ leaders might be feeling, considering that they, along with the other Dene and

Figure 4.3. Claim stake near grave on esker within walking distance of Ts'ıʔehdaà on the lake ʔewaànıt'ıtì. Ts'ıʔehdaà is important to Tłıchǫ of Dechılaagot'ıì and Tahgagot'ıì as a place where elders, women, and children were left when men went trapping on the tundra. (Photograph by the author)

Métis, had put considerable time into trying to secure their land and their right to self-government.

Most members of the dominant society living in Yellowknife were oblivious to the manner in which the staking frenzy was taking place. Their thoughts were on other things. On 18 September 1992, a bomb set in a mine shaft killed nine men who had crossed the picket line during the strike at Giant Mine. Everyone living in Yellowknife was affected; federal and territorial bureaucrats responsible for northern Dene communities were emotionally caught up in what had taken place in their own community[11] rather than in what was occurring within Tłıchǫ nèèk'e.

During that first flight, my thoughts were on mining. I was both saddened and shocked. Miners were dead in Yellowknife, and prospectors seemingly had little regard for the Dene and their land. I wondered about the diamond rush; I wondered whether a new strategy had been agreed for negotiating a regional claim and whether another regional land freeze was possible. I was also thinking about the Gamètì community's request to use PAR as a method to study traditional governance. My mind was swirling, and over the next few years it continued to spin with question after question as our research eventually led to the anthropological question: What does it mean to be knowledgeable if you say you are from the land?

CHAPTER FIVE

Experiencing Kweèt'ıı̨

Collaborating and Taking Action

Before deciding what to do, leaders need to listen to the people.
— Alphonse Quitte, 1993

Everyone should help each other to think about the problems.
— Madelaine Drybone, 1993

In June 2004, Father Jean Pochat and I sat talking. I expressed my respect for the Tłı̨chǫ elders with whom I worked and for their reverence for the spirit in all things. I also expressed how I love the gentle way in which these elders tell stories to guide behavior. He listened to me. He then told me that as a young man he had learned more from the Tłı̨chǫ elders than he had during his years of study and more than he had taught them, about truly loving and the spirit of God. He went on to say how he could literally see how deeply the elders love and respect the dè. As we parted, he again told me how much he loves listening to the elders.

This chapter is an overview of collaborating and taking action. I focus on PAR as collaborative research that in many ways mirrors Tłı̨chǫ ways of considering problems, finding solutions, and taking action. To exemplify the importance Tłı̨chǫ place on people who, like Father Pochat, contribute and listen to the Tłı̨chǫ perspective when collaborating, I portray a few Kweèt'ıı̨ individuals who are remembered for these characteristics. As in the previous chapter, this historical overview focuses on the value of relations in which personal autonomy is supported and group cooperation is secured.

First, I consider participatory and collaborative research that has been undertaken with the Dene in the NWT because it is based on listening and observing. I then describe Kweèt'ıı̨ who have developed relations with

Figure 5.1. Father Jean Pochat and Jimmy Martin at the Heritage Fair, Chief Jimmy Bruneau School, March 2010. (Photograph from Tessa Macintosh Photography)

Tłı̨chǫ that have been cemented by listening and experiencing Tłı̨chǫ nèèk'e as well as by respecting the personal autonomy of others and giving of oneself. Finally, I discuss why the Tłı̨chǫ requested PAR, how it fits with the Tłı̨chǫ knowledge system, and how it is appropriated to fit Tłı̨chǫ needs.

Since the 1970s, elders and leaders have repeatedly stated that they want their knowledge documented by local researchers so that they can be part of the decision-making and management processes affecting themselves and the dè. The same demands, of course, are being made by First Nations across Canada. The questions are: Why did Tłı̨chǫ elders and leaders request PAR? How did this help them to advance their desire for young people now and in the future to be self-determining? Answers to these questions call for reflection on research approaches used over the previous few decades and the importance that the Tłı̨chǫ place on understanding other systems of knowledge.

Participatory and Collaborative Research

The Dene have been instigating participatory and collaborative research over several decades. June Helm and Joan Ryan began their anthropological inquiries with the Tłı̨chǫ in the 1950s. Ryan started as a teacher and later became an anthropologist, using her skills to train community researchers. By the late 1950s, Helm had completed anthropological research with the Slavey Dene residing in Jean Marie River (Helm 1961). In Whatì, Helm was immediately recruited to assist young people with their reading and writing skills so that they could stay home with their families instead of going to a federally approved Catholic residential school. She did this while fulfilling her academic obligation to document the native subsistence economy (Helm and Lurie 1961).

Helm was particularly interested in change and continuity among the Tłı̨chǫ, who had limited contact with the outside world except other Dene until later. She was interested in understanding how a composite hunting band consisting of unrelated families had come to create a community based on parent–child and sibling ties, as she had observed in Jean Marie River (Helm 1979, 148). Julian Steward had thought the composite hunting band to be originally characteristic of Dene social organization (1955, 143–47). Based on research with Dene throughout the 1960s, particularly in Whatì, Helm (1968) concluded that no singular entity could be specified as "the band" in Dene society. Rather, there were three types of groups, which she calls the "local band," the "regional band," and the "task group" (Helm 1965, 1968, 2000).

During Helm's pursuit of evidence of continuity and change, the Tłı̨chǫ turned her toward ethnohistorical research as they told her rich oral narratives regarding many topics, including socioterritorial organization and leadership (1979, 149). Tłı̨chǫ took her back through the stories, helping her to realize that the changes occurring in the 1960s—the new highway, government policies, and so on—were pressing. Helm designed field research to be carried out by local people while she worked with the Indian Brotherhood of the Northwest Territories (now the Dene Nation). The project's aim was to reestablish Dene control over land use and development through negotiation and the judicial process (Helm 1979, 158).

Deborah DeLancey (1984), an anthropologist who lived in the North Slavey community of Fort Good Hope, used a collaborative approach to document knowledge of fish spawning. Word of this research spread throughout the North and was instrumental in stimulating other participatory research. As in most research projects with the Dene, the Slavey wanted their knowledge to be respected by the federal and territorial decision makers. Also instrumental was the Dene Mapping Project initiated in the 1970s and overseen by Michael Asch, who collaborated with the Dene Nation to document past and present land use (Asch, Andrews, and Smith 1986). In the early 1980s, the community of Fort McPherson and the Arctic Institute of North America, University of Calgary, initiated a PAR pilot project with the Dene Nation and the Departments of Education and Culture and Communications, GNWT, on revitalizing Gwich'in language and culture (Ryan and Robinson 1990).

Shortly after the formation of the Dene Cultural Institute, a participatory research project with Fort Good Hope and Colville Lake was piloted to document traditional environmental knowledge. The project aimed to understand similarities and differences between Dene knowledge and scientific knowledge systems and to find ways to integrate the two (Johnson 1992; Johnson and Ruttan 1993). About the same time, archaeologists working with northern Dene—most commonly those working for the GNWT, such as Ellen Bielowski, Thomas Andrews, Christopher Hanks, and Robert Janes—started using collaborative approaches.

Janes (1983, 1991), director of Heritage and Museums, GNWT, and executive director of the Science Institute during the 1970s and 1980s, argues that participatory research, especially in ethnoarchaeology, provides an understanding of sites based on the Dene's continued procurement from the land. Andrews, GNWT territorial archaeologist, works extensively on documenting culturally significant sites based on both the material items and the stories that belong there (Andrews 1990; Andrews and Zoe 1997; Andrews, Zoe, and Herter 1998). Hanks, a heritage consultant who was subarctic archaeologist for the GNWT and who has worked principally with the Sahtu Dene and Kitikmeot Inuit, consistently uses collaborative approaches in his ethnogeographical and ethnoarchaeological research (Hanks and Pokotylo 1989; Hanks and Winters 1983, 1986). So do Ellen Bielowski, a founding board member of the Northern Heritage Society, and Martha Johnson, who organized interdisciplinary projects on Devon Island during the 1980s. In those projects, youth from across the North worked with Inuit elders, geologists, biologists, and archaeologists. The Gwich'in Social and Cultural Institute works collaboratively with archaeologists to document their heritage sites for social, educational, and environmental purposes (Kritsch and Andre 1997).

The collaborative and participatory research carried out by archaeologists in the NWT was initiated by the Dene and is now connected to a larger movement in Canada. Archaeologists have recognized that their discipline has much to offer to processes such as land claims, environmental assessments, public education, and museum studies. Equally important, archaeologists have recognized that research alongside those whose past is being explored is enlightening both to archaeology and to the community who share their oral traditions. The articles collected in the volume *At a Crossroads: Archaeology and First Peoples in Canada* (Nicholas and Andrews 1997) exemplify the extent to which this recognition has become established across Canada.

These initial collaborative research projects have provided a foundation for later participatory approaches—including PAR. In 2005, the community of Délı̨ne completed a joint project with anthropologists, ecologists, risk analysts, and community health scientists to understand the effects, future risks, and methods of containing the uranium from Port Radium on Great Bear Lake (Indian and Northern Affairs Canada 2006).

Dene have been persistent in their desire to inform others and to be informed by and about others. They share their oral narratives with newcomers to their land and listen to these newcomers' stories. They have always paid attention to what has been told to non-Dene, including anthropologists. The elders with whom I worked knew much of what June Helm's key informant, Vital Thomas, told her in Behchokǫ̀ from the 1960s until his death in 1990. The elders also know of several of Helm's publications. As the elder Àąwą̀ said in the course of discussing local and regional bands at the summer camp near Kǫ̀mǫ̀laa in July 1996, "We know what Vital told her [Helm]; we want you to go past that" (personal communication). The Tłı̨chǫ elders are also aware of who told what stories to Tom Andrews; the focus of the stories told to Martha Johnson, who worked on the traditional-medicine project in Whatì (Ryan and Johnson 1994); and what was told to Aggie Brockman, who worked on the traditional-justice project in Whatì (Ryan 1995). Tłı̨chǫ elders also know the information discussed with and stories told to the linguist Leslie Saxon, such as those associated with place-names (Dogrib Treaty 11 Council 2002).

Remembering Experiences; Sharing Stories

The sharing of oral narratives with non-Tłı̨chǫ provides the newcomer with the perspective necessary to live and work with the Tłı̨chǫ in what the Tłı̨chǫ consider to be the right way. These stories are to be contemplated and experienced. Take, for example, the canoes coming into communities after the walking of trails that is part of the ancestors project (Zoe and

Nevitt 1998), in which young people are taken by canoe to the annual gathering and to the tundra for fall caribou hunting. Teachers who work in Tłı̨chǫ schools are encouraged to take part in these trips. In this way, Tłı̨chǫ elders and leaders can share their stories and skills while providing experience to their descendants and to those who teach their descendants. From the Tłı̨chǫ perspective, it is better for everyone if non-Tłı̨chǫ and Tłı̨chǫ can live harmoniously together. They want social relationships within the Tłı̨chǫ nèèk'e, as defined by Yamǫǫ̀zaa, to be harmonious and respectful.

Just as the Tłı̨chǫ Dene want to share their experiences through stories, they also want to hear stories that originated elsewhere. They consider knowledge from each place to be different and value hearing about different ways of thinking about and describing these places. They value traveling, as Beryle Gillespie has noted (1970, 67). The continual renewal of relations through which oral narratives are shared is key to remembering and using oral narratives to think with. It is also key to understanding and learning more about the perspective of others.

Experiencing Petitot

In 1996, the Gamètì elders selected Kǫ̀mǫ̀ladèa—a desired camping spot across from Kǫ̀mǫ̀laa, the place where their predecessors had exchanged oral narratives with the first priest to come to the area, probably Father Émile Petitot—for their July summer camp. I thought they selected the location for its proximity to the community because most elders brought their grandchildren, and other family members traveled back and forth between the camp and the community where they worked for a wage. But the elders had selected the site so that we could take care of a significant location and experience the importance of an ongoing relationship with the Catholic Church.

Louis Zoe, the camp k'àowo, first helped to set up the wall tents and ensured that the elders present had what they needed for drying meat and fish, working hides, and making frames for drums. He then went with a group of men in search of two spruce trees. They proceeded to peel the bark off the trees. The poles were then planed down into two beautiful six-by-eight-inch pieces of lumber of different lengths with which to make a cross that would replace the cross placed at Kǫ̀mǫ̀laa by the first priest in Tłı̨chǫ nèèk'e. Each worked a bit at a time, on occasion resting, doing other activities, conferring with each other, returning to take a turn. As

Figure 5.2. Canoes arriving at Gamètì for the annual gathering after traveling for ten days from Behchokǫ̀, Whatì, and Wekweètì. The travelers met the night before at a designated place and arrived together, 1999. (Photograph by Madelaine Chocolate)

Figure 5.3. As paddlers leave their canoes, they are welcomed by several hundred Tłı̨chǫ who have flown in from their home communities, 1999. Kweèt'ı̨ı̨ who have taken part in this shaking-hands ritual have remarked that this ceremony is "most powerful" and that when it is over, they feel harmony and a sense of unity. (Photograph by Madelaine Chocolate)

they neared the end of their task, Andrew Gon told the story of Kǫmǫlaa and how after listening to Tłıchǫ, the priest had told them stories of Jesus, which is probably one of the reasons why Tłıchǫ say the rosary at significant locales. Many of the Dene stories have been published in the *Book of the Dene* (Petitot 1976). After a few days, we all boated across the lake to Kǫmǫlaa.

Most of us walked up the path to the place where the old cross had been located, as Phillip Zoe, Louis's older brother and church k'àowo, had instructed. The elder David Chocolate, Phillip's sister's husband, had become blind over the winter, and he was "talked up" because he knew the detailed layout of the trail. Once we arrived, the younger men gave the older elders tea. They then joined the rest of us who were surveying the area to see if we could find further evidence of a disintegrating cross or the poles the cross was made of. After much conferring on the exact location, people came to an agreement, and the young men erected the newly made cross under guidance of their elders, in particular Phillip Zoe and Andrew Gon. Several of these young men were the ones building the new Catholic church in Gamèti under the guidance of Brother Prince, a master carpenter.

Everyone then sat around the cross, praying and saying their rosaries. Andrew Gon repeated the narrative. Again, we were told how their ancestors had brought the priest to this place where they exchanged stories. Andrew Gon emphasized that their ancestors told the priest how much they loved the dè because it was like their mother and father and how Yamǫǫzaa had given them laws to live by and that the priest had told them how much he loved Jesus because Jesus was the son of God. Further stories were exchanged about the current priest—Father Pochat, an Oblate—who had lived among and traveled with the Tłıchǫ since the mid-1950s and resided in Behchokǫ̀. (Father Pochat died in November 2010.) They also told the story of Pope John Paul II's visit in 1987 to Fort Simpson, where he spoke to thousands of people about the importance of maintaining aboriginal culture and rights.

The narratives told by Andrew and other elders reminded all people that Fathers Pochat and Petitot had traveled the trails and listened and in return had shared stories of how they envisioned the world. For the Tłıchǫ, the abilities to share stories and to listen are respected characteristics that indicate a person's level of intelligence, their willingness to create relationships, and their respect for the dè. The stories associated with Father Petitot, who is known to have erected many crosses throughout Tłıchǫ nèèk'e (see also Helm 2000, 160), are firmly entrenched and reaffirmed in the places where the original events took place. His behavior is consistent with the idea of traveling to locales and stopping to learn from them. Phillip Zoe and Andrew Gon were treating the meeting between Petitot and their ancestors as an event that is part of the present. That event established relationships that are ongoing and continually reaffirmed, even though the occurrence originated in the past.

Erecting the cross and telling stories of Father Petitot reminded people of their relationship with the Catholic Church. It also put them in mind of the relationships being formed with the Protestant missionaries settling in Behchokò, Gamètì, and Whatì. There is some concern about the missionaries' more fundamentalist approaches to religion. People's overriding worry is that friends and relatives turning to Protestantism will become confused about who they are. Yet Protestant missionaries have settled in the communities, speak Tłįchǫ, send their children to the community school, take part in traditional activities, and assist in translating the Bible and developing Dene fonts compatible with international keyboards. In 1996, there was quite a bit of talk about the Protestant approaches to religion, which probably, along with the building of the Catholic church, contributed to the context of setting up the cross and telling stories in Kòmòlaa in the summer of 1996.

Since their initial concerns in the early to mid-1990s, most Tłįchǫ I know have accepted that those choosing to follow the Protestant faith have not forgotten who they are. Tłįchǫ, whether Catholic or Protestant, actively encourage others to be proud of the knowledge, skill, and "laws" that originated in the past and continue to assist people to live in the way that is right for Tłįchǫ.

Remembering Petitot reminds Tłįchǫ who they are in relation to the Catholic Church, their own perspective, and non-Tłįchǫ ways of perceiving the dè. It reminds them that sharing through stories is the basis for cooperation while maintaining personal autonomy.

Remembering Tara

Tara was a Kweèt'įį who worked in the social services office in Behchokò in the early 1990s and is remembered as a person with a strong character. Tara was assigned the case when a teacher who had worked in many communities throughout the NWT and Nunavut was charged with sexual abuse. Many of the victimized girls were still under age when the teacher was brought to court.

Tara visited Tłıchǫ homes to explain the legal process to the girls and to their parents and grandparents. She prepared them for the trial that was to be held in Iqaluit and where they were to testify. The trial started, but near the time when the girls and Tara were to travel to Iqaluit, Tara was killed in a car accident. I heard talk that the accident was brought about by "that teacher throwing ʔık'ǫ̀" because he was "that powerful." It is well known that those with the ability to use ʔık'ǫ̀ can do so by throwing it from incredible distances. People were fearful, and the girls no longer wished to testify; their feeling and behavior were consistent with June Helm's ob-servations that Dene will often withdraw from anxious situations because they fear ʔık'ǫ̀. The girls wished to withdraw from having to testify at court. Within a few weeks of Tara's death, though, the accused confessed, and the girls did not have to travel to provide evidence at the trial.

Tara, like many others who have died, continues to walk the dè and help those in need; she is credited with the teacher's confession. She is remembered as having a powerful mind, which she used to help the girls. Tara's picture now hangs in many Tłıchǫ homes alongside the pictures of Jesus and Naedzo, the Bear Lake prophet, who told the Tłıchǫ that "the worst thing you can do is to kill somebody, whether it is by ʔık'ǫ̀ or with a club" (Helm 1994, 29).

Tłıchǫ relationships are often marked by a mixture of harmony and disharmony, with a deep fear of those who use ʔık'ǫ̀ in destructive ways. Although Kweèt'ıì rarely know that ʔık'ǫ̀ is being discussed or that it is being used, Tłıchǫ nevertheless believe that many humans—including Kweèt'ıì—have access to ʔık'ǫ̀ and the ability to use it. But according to most elders I worked with, Kweèt'ıì usually misuse their intelligence because "their minds are all over the place." Tara was respectful and thoughtful about how she listened and talked. Although the story is told only occasionally because it is "too sad," Tara is remembered.

The story of Tara is a reminder that collaboration and respect is pos-sible with all humans, including Kweèt'ıì who have chosen to be bureau-crats, and that the way someone uses power of any kind reflects character.

Respecting Anne Gunn

With the advent of diamond mining in the mid-1990s, the Dogrib Treaty 11 Council wanted Tłıchǫ knowledge of the caribou to be taken into ac-count in decision-making and management processes that would result from development in the Lac de Gras area. The West Kitikmeot Slave

Study Society provided a means to accomplish this goal. The society included representatives from industry, from the territorial and federal governments, as well as from the Dene, Kitikmeot Inuit, and Métis (the Yellowknives declined to participate). The society wanted both scientific and traditional-knowledge research to be carried out in order to establish "base line data" against which the cumulative effects of industrial development could be measured. In 1996, the Dogrib Treaty 11 Council initiated two PAR projects to document Tłıchǫ knowledge, one of which was on caribou migration and the state of their habitat. Responsibility for the latter was delegated to the elders in Behchokǫ̀, who shared their knowledge of caribou and took the researchers on hunting trips within the boreal forest as well as into the tundra. GNWT biologist Anne Gunn also received funding from the West Kitikmeot Slave Study Society to radio-collar caribou cows to track their migration patterns. These two caribou projects were intended to complement each other.

During the 1996 annual gathering in Gamètì, Anne requested and was given time to discuss her project, including why she chose to use radio collars to collect migration data. Prior to her presentation, she had made a point of visiting the elders in their homes, during which she explained her project, including her ethical stance on her research. She discussed her opinions and listened to elders' concerns, thoughts, and values. They did not agree with her approach. They did not think it right for the caribou to be collared, and they were extremely concerned about the weight and potential danger of the collars to the caribou. Nevertheless, because she took time to visit and explain her views, the elders expressed respect for Anne. She is known to share. She is also known to walk where she does research, the calving grounds at Bathurst Inlet, and to travel to where caribou are. She is known to drink tea while sitting around fires with hunters, during which time she listens to their observations and shares her own. Although Anne's research does not involve participatory or collaborative methods in the way of PAR, she does take young Tłıchǫ assistants with her during her field seasons so that they can experience and learn scientific methods. Anne is respected because she shares and is honest about her work and her ethical stance.

Most of the Tłıchǫ individuals with whom I have worked have a remarkably deep understanding of Kweèt'ıì behavior and way of thinking. The Tłıchǫ observe and tell stories about Kweèt'ıì's character and have done so since the 1700s. Conversations taking place on the streets in Yellowknife rarely include in-depth storytelling; rather, Tłıchǫ spend time observing their surroundings just as they do in the bush. Upon returning home or to the Tłı̨chǫ Yellowknife office, they, in particular the elders, share oral narratives. This activity often, but not always, includes current and past observations that take the listeners to occurrences in the past and then bring them back slowly and light-heartedly to the present, a process Regna Darnell also noted among the Cree in the early 1970s (1974, 336).

These narratives often, but not always, include the Kweèt'ı̨̀ whom the Tłı̨chǫ have been observing. Stories are shared about people such as Justice Thomas Berger (1977), who listened to them during the Mackenzie Valley Pipeline Inquiry and suggested a moratorium on all development for a period of ten years, and Justice Morrow, whom Tłı̨chǫ remember as a person who listened and, after considering their oral narratives, suggested that the Dene had a right to file a caveat with the Registrar of Land Titles.

Sharing stories of a positive character is a reminder that when personal autonomy is remembered and stories told, collaboration and cooperation are more likely.

Choosing PAR

Given Tłı̨chǫ respect for sharing and working cooperatively, it is understandable that participatory and collaborative approaches are attractive to them. And given their respect for personal autonomy, the appeal of PAR to them is equally understandable. PAR is a cooperative process that emphasizes thinking about and discussing problems as well as thinking about and discussing solutions prior to taking action. The PAR process as developed by the Dene Cultural Institute and the Arctic Institute of North America includes training and acknowledges the importance of "knowing two ways."

Joanne Barnaby and Joan Ryan developed the PAR model used in Tłı̨chǫ communities. Joanne was influenced by Dene Cultural Institute board members and the Denendeh Elders Council, and Joan was influenced by the work of Paulo Freire (1972) and Sol Tax (1988, 8–15). Ryan explains PAR as "a process whereby all members of the team share power, responsibility, and decision-making and cooperate fully to make sure the goals of the project are realized. It is not an easy process and the group's interaction has to be negotiated so that there is a true sharing of power in all matters. PAR works only by consensus" (1995, 7).

Ryan's mentor, Sol Tax, became convinced that anthropologists should not simply study indigenous people and leave it at that; he thought their work should benefit the people they work with. He called this approach "action anthropology." He emphasized that anthropologists should work to preserve aboriginal identity through pan–American Indian institutions. He also emphasized the "action" aspects, including the support of political action in the form of documentaries (1988, 14–15). Ryan, following Freire, emphasizes the education and training aspect of PAR, which is critical to social reform. Robin McTaggart (1997) argues that it is the researcher's responsibility to go beyond methodology by explaining the political and ethical agendas that may influence his or her work.

For the Tłı̨chǫ with whom I worked, Ryan and Barnaby's explanation of PAR translated as sharing experiences and observations, which inevitably includes one's ethical position on social and political issues. The Tłı̨chǫ— like Freire and Tax—are interested in action that leads to a strong aboriginal identity and education that supports their participation in political and social decision making.

In 1988, the GNWT minister of justice, Michael Ballantyne, approached the Dene Cultural Institute to deliver a training program for aboriginal justices of the peace. Joanne Barnaby, then the institute's executive director, consulted with her board of directors and the Denendeh Elders Council, chaired by George Blondin.[1] They declined the offer but suggested that research be done on Dene traditional-justice systems. They proposed that a documented understanding of Dene justice systems could be integrated into any future changes to justice legislation. The minister agreed.

In 1989, the Dene Cultural Institute proposed at the Dene-Métis Assembly in Fort Smith, NWT, that it and the Arctic Institute of North America conduct a Dene justice research project. Joanne described the PAR methodology first used for the Gwich'in Language and Cultural Project in Fort McPherson (Ryan and Robinson 1990). Chief Isadore Zoe of Whatì indicated the band council's interest in having the research take place in his community (Ryan 1995, 4). Then in 1992, immediately following the justice project, the community of Whatì employed the two local researchers trained in the PAR process to carry out research on traditional medicine (Ryan and Johnson 1994).

In 1991, the elders in Gamètì, led by Jean Wetrade and Andrew Gon, asked their chief, Peter Arrowmaker, for a PAR project to document traditional governance. In May 1992, the chief approached Joanne, who discussed the idea with the Denendeh Elders Council and the Dene Cultural Institute board of directors. They liked the idea and decided to approach the Arctic Institute of North America to collaborate with them and the community. Joanne and Joan asked me to oversee the research. I readily agreed. I knew that community research would enhance my understanding of Dene perspectives on land, knowledge, and the importance of story. As with the justice and medicine projects in Whatì, the elders and elected leadership in Gamètì said they wanted a documented understanding of the "right way" for the Tłı̨chǫ.

The preferred way for Tłı̨chǫ to deal with problems is to listen to those who have experienced the problem, discuss solutions, come to an agreement about what needs to be done, and then do the task. This approach is epitomized in the stories of Yamǫ̀ǫzaa, Edzo, and Mǫwhì as well as in oral narratives such as those of Wolf and Raven. And it was exemplified in the two years it took for Tłı̨chǫ leaders to visit all the communities after the Dene-Métis land-claim negotiations came to an end and before the Dogrib Treaty 11 Council was formed and given a mandate. I have witnessed this approach among hunters, sitting with their wives and elders, discussing where the caribou might be and what action is required to ensure successful hunting. I have also witnessed it among hunters who are discussing how to maintain knowledge and care of Tłı̨chǫ nèèk'e. They live life as a story.

Taking Action

Adults, whether leaders, elders, or active harvesters of what the dè offers, think about how to provide opportunities for young people to travel and experience Tłı̨chǫ nèèk'e; adults share their experience with others in the community. The concerns of elders, harvesters, and leaders resulted in solutions and actions. The hunters decided to travel all the trails, teaching their children and grandchildren not only their own knowledge, but that of hunters who had been raised along other trails associated with other social regions within Tłı̨chǫ nèèk'e. Earlier, but in the same vein, the leaders and elders had decided on using PAR to document and use the oral narratives for current issues and to ensure that the young people would hear them. All had defined the problem, discussed a solution, and planned an action. In so doing, they were taking steps to fulfill their responsibilities as human beings of the "land" to restore harmony while reminding others that Tłı̨chǫ nèèk'e is where they belong.

These harvesters' desire to travel outside places they have known since they were children is well within the ideals of "living the right way," an ideal remembered when hearing Mǫwhì's name and the reason why so many Tłı̨chǫ elders want the Mǫwhì Trail protected. Mǫwhì is remembered for traveling Tłı̨chǫ nèèk'e trails—traveling and reaching outward to learn. He is also remembered for sharing his knowledge with others.

With the PAR process, community members define the problem, carry out the research, discuss possible solutions, decide on an action, and put it into effect. This process continually loops back on itself to reevaluate the success of the action and to redefine what research and actions are still required. In essence, this process is what occurred in Whatì on the justice project as the research team evaluated its findings with the elders' advisory committee—appointed by Chief Isadore Zoe—and the technical advisory committee, consisting of academics and bureaucrats, who were to assist in incorporating the Dene way into justice legislation. The technical committee was the bridge between the community and the GNWT Justice Department (Ryan 1995, 13).

When I arrived in Gamètì in 1992, however, the elders told me that they did not want or need a technical advisory committee, as Whatì had. They agreed that it was the role of their elected chief and council, who are supposed to know Kweèt'ı̀ı̀, to establish this bridge. To make this point, they told the stories of Mǫwhì, who was selected to speak to the treaty commissioner, and of the k'aàwı who understood the factors at the trading posts. The elders also agreed they would be their "own boss," not advisers, as the Whatì elders had been. In Gamètì, the elders were following Jean Wetrade, their k'àowo, who oversaw the traditional-governance project, and saw their task as selecting community members who would learn and experience the stories and document the oral narratives. They also defined their role as selecting the places—the locales and trails—to be experienced so that the "truth" of their stories could be realized. They were always ready to guide the research team and watched to ensure that we undertook the tasks they thought we needed to accomplish in a way they considered appropriate.

The Gamètì elders had their own agenda. First and foremost, they wished to use an approach that was right for them to guide younger people to think with stories. They guided what oral narratives the research team heard, what places we walked, and which tasks we did at which locations. They created a process in which Tłı̨chǫ throughout the community were talking about stories associated with leadership and followership.

Through PAR, the elders decided to take action to ensure that their descendants retained relations with all that is part of Tłı̨chǫ nèèk'e—past, present, and future. The elders had a clear idea of the problem and of the tasks that needed to be done. They had already discussed the problem and had a possible solution. They used the PAR process to give some younger people, now and in the future, stories to think with and to guide them to use both ways so that each of them can be strong like two people. The process would also promote the discussion of occurrences and happenings as told in stories among others who were not directly involved.

The elders used PAR as a step toward restoring harmony to what they saw as increasingly chaotic relations with others. In hearing these stories, more younger people would come to know them. The elders could then say to their leaders and other Tłįchǫ who were meeting with government and industry, "Remember Edzo," "Remember Mǫwhì," or "Remember Bruneau," knowing that all Tłįchǫ, including the young, would understand.

This use of names recalls Keith Basso's (1984a, 1988) discussion of the Apache use of place-names to look forward into space while looking backward in time. To use a name is to allow the listener's mind to travel to where the event took place without pushing one's own thought on him or her. It helps that person think about how to deal with his or her current situation. The name brings people, event, and place together, folding the past into the present, where trails to the future exit.

A different scenario occurred in Behchokǫ̀ when the Dogrib Treaty 11 Council decided to participate in the West Kitikmeot Slave Study Society and to contribute to research for future monitoring. After considerable discussion, the Dogrib Renewable Resources Committee, consisting of elders and hunters, advised the council that caribou, habitat, heritage, and water were their research priorities. They recommended that the council use the PAR method so that community members could be trained in such research and that future actions could be taken to monitor and "care for" the environment in the wake of the impacts of diamond mining. The council members' decision to use PAR was based on observations in Whatì and Gamètì and on the acknowledgment that they could maintain control over the research while working cooperatively with Kweèt'ı̨.

It is the PAR approach that provides communities their rightful place to be involved in any research project connected to them and to define what is relevant rather than making them subjects to be studied, as is the case in most academic research and development projects. Elders and leaders acknowledged that PAR is a Kweèt'ı̨ process that allows people to work cooperatively and to reflect on and recognize issues of concern.

A similar process can be found in the stories of Yamǫ̀ǫ̀zaa, Edzo, Mǫwhì, and Bruneau. They all contemplated the social problems of their time, talked to others, reflected on possible solutions, and took action to reestablish harmonious social relationships.

Figure 5.4. Tłįchǫ youth and elders at Ɂǫhtsı̨k'e, 1998, where the water flows out of Ɂek'atì and where you can always go for caribou and fish. Members of the Tłįchǫ Regional Elders Committee wanted young people to know this place because they feared it would be impacted by the mining development in the area. *Back row, left to right:* Jimmy Martin, Georgina Chocolate, Dehga Scott, Sally Anne Zoe, Darla Beaulieu, Peter John Mackenzie, Harry Apple, Kevin Kodzin. *Seated, left to right:* Roger Champlain, Therese Zoe, Elizabeth Michel, Julie Mackenzie, Joe Suzi Mackenzie, Robert Mackenzie. *Front:* Chris Football and Louis Whane. (Photograph by Gabrielle Mackenzie-Scott)

In all cases—the traditional-justice, traditional-governance, Tłįchǫ knowledge of caribou, and place-names projects—the Tłįchǫ requested the PAR process because it allowed them to engage with Kweèt'ıì in a way they thought was right for both the dominant society and themselves. It allowed past and present relationships to be embedded within the research process, leading to solutions and actions, just as in the past. For the elders, PAR was a way of acknowledging the importance of both Tłįchǫ knowledge and the dominant society's knowledge, as is constantly emphasized in the story of Grand Chief Bruneau.

Several aspects of the Tłįchǫ perspective on social organization and relationships easily allow Tłįchǫ communities to accommodate PAR, as does their ideology of autonomy and group cooperation. The most obvious organizational aspect of PAR is the task group. The group forms for a limited time and for a specific purpose; members listen to and follow the k'àowo known to be an authority on the task to be done. The Gamètì case shows this approach: those who know provide others with open-ended stories to think with so that those doing the task—having the experience—can learn their own personal truths.

Elders guide young people's learning by giving them enough—through oral narratives—to think with. The rhetoric of PAR includes self-determination and skills training. In the projects discussed here, the chiefs focused on the ownership of the research process within their communities as a positive way to work more closely with industry and government. The elders saw PAR as the action necessary for them to guide their descendants. Elders and leaders used PAR both to enhance the possibility of continuing harmony within Tłı̨chǫ nèèk'e and to guide the learning of selected younger people to know two ways, as directed by Chief Bruneau.

Tłı̨chǫ take into account the behavior and character of individual Kweèt'ıı̨ when considering how to cope with ever-increasing resource development and government demands that reduce Tłı̨chǫ capacity to govern themselves and use their lands. They have found that some Kweèt'ıı̨ can listen and establish relations, whereas others are tied to policy without considering the possibility of being flexible. Tłı̨chǫ have observed and met social and biological scientists, bureaucrats, missionaries, explorers, and priests who have listened and shared while establishing relations. The elders in particular continually encourage their juniors to learn about Kweèt'ıı̨ and to speak calmly while interacting or meeting with them.

Donald Gamble (1986) notes that throughout the meetings with federal and territorial officials, consultants, and specialists sent to encourage the people of Behchokǫ̀ to move inland to Edzo in the 1960s, Tłı̨chǫ spoke quietly and continually pointed out the need to stay near their fishing nets on the lake. They didn't need to be near a highway. He eventually heard them, he writes, and began to realize the differences in their approach to living life.

One perspective places humans outside the environment and considers the globe with a detachment that allows both land and resources to be taken; the other perspective comes from a position of experiencing the environment from within (Ingold 2000, 209–18). The elders are well aware that participatory and collaborative research calls for calm dialogue and the continual relating of oral traditions to Kweèt'ıı̨. The leaders realize that many funding agencies and some academic institutions accept the PAR approach endorsed by the Dene Cultural Institute. They are well aware that their knowledge of and relationship with human and other-than-human beings is based on stories different from those told by most Kweèt'ıì. It is the narratives that produce different perspectives. In knowing the past from the perspective of their own oral narratives, Tłıchǫ have been able to think about what action is required to move away from the increasingly chaotic events engulfing their lives.

Tłıchǫ adults say that when a person knows the stories, he or she is capable of thinking while remaining flexible—a capability that is admired and extremely important for survival in the northern boreal forest and tundra. They also admire the ability to know the right way for yourself and for those who depend on you. Knowledgeable individuals are capable of working with others and directing their own lives. For Tłıchǫ, these are the characteristics of self-determination. For the elders with whom I worked, documenting stories and experiencing Tłıchǫ nèèk'e using the PAR process were useful in the modern setting. They felt that their children and grandchildren were losing important characteristics, including the ability to think and take appropriate action when need be. They wanted the stories that help people think to be made available in their own language for when their descendants decided they needed them.

This discussion may appear to imply that the PAR process is always successful. That is not my intent. My experience is that when the elders and leaders learned of the elements attached to PAR, they requested it because the discourse is similar to their own system of working through issues. This system is evident in how harvesters who use the land and elders discuss issues, find solutions, and take actions.

It is interesting to note that once the research on traditional governance in Gamètì was under way, I rarely heard PAR being used and then only when discussions turned to accessing funding while maintaining control of the research. When directing our research, the elders encouraged everyone to work together while thinking for oneself. They were interested in both personal autonomy as well as cooperative behaviors. Since 2004, the term *participatory action research* no longer seems to be used; rather, the leaders discuss the importance of cooperating while working toward a positive future. They use the same stories to emphasize thinking about issues and taking action, and most people continue to stress the importance of documenting stories and guiding the learning of young people while visiting locales and traveling trails.

CHAPTER SIX

Following Those Who Know

In 2004, I was talking with an employee of one of the diamond companies about the company's traditional environmental knowledge research with aboriginal communities in northern Canada. During this conversation, he made a passing comment that the Inuit are much easier to work with because "Inuit elders tend to defer to younger people," unlike the Dene, whose elders guide those younger by sharing stories and by advising how they would like to see tasks done. He felt that the ever-present tension between generations created difficulties for industry. Although I, too, have noticed tension between generations, I have also noticed the manner in which agreement is achieved and tension dissolved, which is the focus of this chapter.

Several anthropologists have written on the institutionalized conflict, tension, and anxiety of northern Dene—the associated withdrawal and controlled release of tension in their interpersonal relations. Joan Ryan (1995) suggests that increased tension in the communities is the result of Euro-Canadian influence. Michael Asch (1988) describes a Slavey community where people who would not have resided together in the bush are now living in close proximity.

Asch argues that this contemporary community coincides with the regional bands of the past that gathered together only periodically to feast and celebrate and to meet potential marriage partners (1988, 35). According to Asch, each cluster of households in the Slavey fly-in bush community corresponds with the local band. This arrangement brings marriageable individuals into close proximity, which is ideologically discouraged among Dene because it is not appropriate to marry someone with whom one resides (36). Asch says that Dene have tried to solve the problem by creating kin out of close allies (37). Nevertheless, the situation has created chronic disputes between households, and members of clusters avoid each other during daily activities. The most difficult of these conflicts, Asch explains, are those between people of the same sex and the same age (55). Jean-Guy Goulet describes the tension caused by alcohol in a community of Dene Tha Slavey in northern Alberta (2000, 55–57). He focuses on how drunken behavior allows individuals to infringe on others' autonomy, which would otherwise be socially unacceptable.

This chapter adds to the anthropological literature on institutionalized tension, in particular on how tension arises between generations when considering who is the most knowledgeable. The idea of following the most capable and skilled hunter has been well documented in the subarctic literature, including the work of Georg Henriksen (1973) among the Naskapi of Labrador; June Helm (Helm 2000; Helm and Damas 1963, 17; née MacNeish 1956) among the Dehcho Slavey and Tłı̨chǫ in the NWT; Richard Slobodin (1969) among the Peel River Gwich'in, whose territory encompasses lands in both the NWT and the Yukon Territory; and David Smith among the Chipewyan of Fort Resolution (1982, 36). In Gamètì, people similarly considered whom to follow—the person most capable to accomplish the tasks necessary to maintain personal autonomy and self-determination.

To focus this discussion, I describe a situation that took place in Gamètì during the first several weeks of the traditional-governance project in the early 1990s. Though the tension in Gamètì focused on the project, its roots lay in different ideas about how to achieve and enhance harmony during a time of unrest between the various Dene people as well as between Dene and the federal and territorial governments. At the center of the tension were the elders' k'àowo and the elected chief.

As events were unfolding in the project and individuals were considering whom to follow, avoidance between the leaders—the k'àowo and the elected chief—and their respective followers was apparent. In this account, I consider the relationships between being knowledgeable, tension, and gaining a following.

The Context

In 1991, the elders in Gamètì, led by Jean Wetrade and Andrew Gon, both in their eighties, asked Chief Peter Arrowmaker for a project to document traditional governance. By December 1992, when funding had been secured to start the project, the Dogrib Treaty 11 Council was formed with a mandate to negotiate land claims and self-government. The Tłįchǫ negotiators had completed their community visits to determine how community members wished to proceed with the land-claim process and were currently traveling to the communities to explain their strategy for negotiating with the federal and territorial governments. Community members—including elders and band councillors—repeatedly stated that they wanted their knowledge documented so that they could be part of the decision-making and management process affecting themselves and all that is part of Tłįchǫ nèèk'e.

The oldest elders were also saying that they wanted their oral narratives documented so that their descendants would have the stories to think with. The events and relations the elders wanted remembered reflected the traditional governing system. Elders wanted them to know: how "laws" came about and how they continue to be applicable; how mining uranium at Rayrock caused destruction and disease; how federal legislation affected their lives; how Justice Thomas Berger had the ability to listen, resulting

Figure 6.1. Jean Wetrade, 1994. Jean, along with Andrew Gon, led five families belonging to Ɂet'aagot'ı̨ı̨ and Gots'ǫkàtìgot'ı̨ı̨ away from Behchokǫ̀ and created a community at Gamètì. (Photograph by the author)

in a moratorium on the pipeline development. They wanted the many stories of the dè told and retold. They wanted young people to remember all that had occurred since the arrival of Kweèt'ı̨ and how life's events led to specific laws and agreements. The elders I worked with often said that although young people think they do not need stories from the past, there will come a time when these younger people will need their ancestors' stories to think with. In anticipation of this unforeseeable time, the elders wanted to tell and retell and to record all the oral narratives they knew.

In considering the goal of ensuring youth have the oral narratives for the future, I find that storytellers do not speak just to their current audience, as Dennis Tedlock suggests in a comparison of oral and written narrative (1983, 10). The oral storyteller may have no more specific knowledge of the future audience than does the writer, even if the elders are recording and telling stories for their descendants. The elders do not know what situation will prompt younger generations to want to draw on the oral narratives, but they want to pass on their knowledge because they think the wisdom of the past may be needed in the future.

Documenting oral narratives for the future is not a phenomenon of the 1990s only; in the 1960s, the prophet Naedzo wanted the anthropologist Beryle Gillespie to tape him so that he could get his true stories on tape. He said, "Pretty near everyone is starting to talk about the whiteman's way. I think the Indian way was better. We didn't have much trouble, not like now, because we listened to one another and treated one another just like brothers. I'll be glad if everyone hears my speech" (qtd. in Helm 2000, 166).

Oral narratives from the past, then, are told so they can be heard in the future by an unknown audience that is experiencing tension and will need to listen to stories that will help them to think about the problem and find solutions.

First Meeting

On 6 December 1992, I attended a Dogrib Treaty 11 Council meeting held in Gamètì. James Wah-Shee, who eventually would negotiate the self-government aspects of the 2005 Tłı̨chǫ Agreement, explained to community members that the negotiators planned to continue pressuring the federal government to include self-government as part of the land claim. He listened to others discuss how the traditional-governance project had been conceptualized. After a few hours of discussion, the newly elected Gamètì chief Henry Gon announced that the Gamètì elders would oversee the traditional-governance project; James Wah-Shee emphasized the project's importance. All was set to begin in January.

The Tension

When I returned to the community on 8 January 1993, all discussion of the traditional-governance project had stopped. Chief Henry Gon explained that he and the band council members were too busy to organize a research office or the Gamètì Elders Committee or to hire researchers and that I would have to organize these things myself. I wondered what had happened over Christmas and New Year's. The band council had held meetings, and although the meetings were open to the public, few were attending. I also noticed that few of the band councillors were attending the Friday night hand games or the Sunday night drum dances.

Because the community had specifically requested a PAR approach so that they could oversee and control the project, I proceeded with caution. To me, the community "felt" tense, but the silence as well as the apparent withdrawal could have been due to any number of factors. It could have been that people did not want to chat with a stranger, especially a Kweèt'ìì, or it could have been due to shyness or any other of the many reasons for withdrawal discussed by Jane Christian and Peter Gardner (1977) in their study of thought and communication among the Slavey.

I spent my time visiting and listening to what was being talked about and getting to know people. I was given one of the old government cabins to make my home. After two weeks had passed, I happened to be visiting Jean Wetrade, the elders' k'àowo and a respected elder, with Therese Zoe. During our visit, Jean explained to Therese that the chief and band councillors had changed their minds. Chief Gon now thought the research funding should be used to develop a self-government model for the negotiating team and that the elders should act as advisers. The elders themselves, Jean explained, still wanted the narratives documented on audiotape and for people to experience places so that the stories would be known to be true and remembered and retold in the future. The elders thought that some young people could be guided now, and others could listen to the taped version of the stories in the future. The elders wanted their descendants to have a varied collection of stories to think with when the stories were needed. I continued visiting around the community as well as at a couple of the hunting camps set up along the ice road.

The Elders

In several situations, I heard the elders Jean Wetrade and Andrew Gon state that they, like the chief, wanted a good working relationship with non-Tłįchǫ. They, however, expressed that the most important factors were to ensure self-determination and harmony with all "beings"— including Kweèt'ı̨—and to enable all Tłįchǫ to learn what had occurred in the past, to experience the Tłįchǫ way themselves, and to build on the knowledge they learned through these experiences by also understanding the "Kweèt'ı̨ way." They referred to the importance of knowing two ways and the importance of solving problems while thinking about others.

They told the stories of Yamǫǫ̀zaa, Edzo, and Mǫwhì, all of whom had learned from their elders and whose greatness had to do with their ability to listen to those who followed them and to act on what needed to be accomplished. Yamǫǫ̀zaa and his brother had learned from their grandfather, had listened to the people, and had established social rules. Edzo had similarly learned from his father, had experienced and listened to others discuss the problem, and had then created peace with the Yellowknives by controlling Akaitcho's mind. Mǫwhì had learned from both his father and his uncle, had listened to the people and the bishop, and then had made a peace agreement with the treaty commissioner. The elders gently emphasized how these men were able to think about what needed to be done to achieve harmonious relations because they knew the stories from the past and intimately knew the dè, through which they worked and traveled. They walked places.

While visiting, I heard several elders talk about how chiefs and councillors are constantly traveling to negotiating meetings and mining sites in other parts of the world, such as on Diné (Navajo) land in the United States. Some elders were saying that these leaders only wanted to travel in order to act like Kweèt'ı̨. Those who made such statements were well aware, however, that traveling to these places was the chief's and band councillors' responsibility, just as interacting and dealing with bureaucrats and industrial personnel were the elected leaders' responsibility.[1] The elders themselves encouraged younger people to travel to where Kweèt'ı̨ live and work so that they could learn Kweèt'ı̨ ways. The elders were also aware that all middle-aged men in Gamètì, including the chief, hunted on a regular basis for their families and that the chief as well as others regularly visited hunting camps set up outside the community.

On still other occasions, the elders were telling the story of the woman who first brought Kweèt'ı̨ knowledge to Tłįchǫ people and how women work well for the community because they are more likely to stay in the community and teach their children and grandchildren. Only later did I realize that the elders were setting the stage to hire women for the traditional-governance research project. And only after the project was well under way did I hear them say that if young women in their twenties to forties hear the stories and learn both the Tłįchǫ and the Kweèt'ı̨ way, then the youth of the future will benefit.

Band Councillors

During my visits around the community in the early 1990s, I heard Gamètì band councillors talk about how the elders make good advisers but do not know the modern world, how the "old ways" no longer apply, and how women do not know the way of the bush. The councillors who made these statements knew perfectly well, however, that most elders residing in Gamètì had been involved in political strategies during the 1960s, 1970s, and 1980s. They also knew the narratives that tell of both positive and

Figure 6.2. Rita Blackduck and Sally Anne Zoe *(front)* at Gamètì, 1993. They were the first Tłįchǫ researchers to be asked by the Gamètì Elders Committee to work with them on the traditional-governance project.
(Photograph by the author)

negative interaction with Kweèt'ı̨ since the early 1700s because they had learned these stories from these very same elders.

They knew that most elders were familiar with the similarities and differences between bush life and life under the rules and regulations set by the federal and territorial governments. They were aware that Tłı̨chǫ elders had participated in and observed the Berger inquiry and had been involved in negotiations and discussions with federal bureaucrats regarding education, wildlife, and the right to live in a way Tłı̨chǫ deem appropriate. They were aware the elders had been indirectly involved in the "Paulette Case" overseen by Judge Morrow, resulting in the renegotiation of Treaty 11 as a comprehensive claim, and politically involved with the Dene-Métis claim. They knew that the elders had experienced problems within the dè caused by "Kweèt'ı̨ ways," such as the Rayrock uranium mine (Legat et al. 1997), and had experienced the influx of prospectors on Tłı̨chǫ nèèk'e (Mackenzie-Scott 2001). Despite all this, the councillors were saying that the elders did not understand the Kweèt'ı̨ way.

The councillors told the same oral narratives the elders did—in particular the stories of Mǫwhì—but used them to justify the role of elders as advisers rather than as "bosses" overseeing the traditional-governance research project. They stressed how Mǫwhì had been advised by his uncle, who had "the power to know Kweèt'ı̨." They stressed how Yamǫǫ̀zaa, Edzo, and Mǫwhì had worked for all Tłı̨chǫ people and not just their own band. Because the councillors wanted self-governance for all Tłı̨chǫ, they reasoned the research should focus on that process.

Being Recognized as Knowledgeable

Both factions were telling the same stories to encourage community members to think about the role of the elders, what tasks really needed doing, and who had the knowledge and skill to lead and accomplish the tasks. However, in telling the same stories, each faction would highlight the skill and knowledge of the individual they thought should be followed. They emphasized different aspects of living life in the right way. Through the narratives, the councillors insisted that, following the chief, the correct tasks would be accomplished by the most skilled individuals—namely, those middle-aged men who had more experience with contemporary Kweèt'ı̨ ways and who continued to know, use, and travel in the bush, unlike the elders, who were "retired harvesters; retired hunters and gatherers." They compared the relevant experience of the chief and other middle-aged men with that of past yahbahti—Yamǫǫ̀zaa and Edzo and the first k'àowodeè, Mǫwhì. They emphasized that their approach would retain personal autonomy by reestablishing the right to self-govern through legislation.

It was during a discussion of these issues that a younger man in his forties said, "Women don't know the land, so people like Madelaine Drybone [in her late eighties] can't advise us." Andrew Gon was present and gave this young man a very firm talking to. Andrew said women such as Madelaine know Tłı̨chǫ nèèk'e better than any men under sixty; that these women have lived and worked and traveled trails all their lives, using both men's and women's knowledge to survive; that younger men had to stop thinking of women as not knowing.

The elders used the same narratives to argue that their k'àowo—Jean Wetrade—would be the best person to follow to ensure that the Tłı̨chǫ understand self-government based on traditional governing principles. They stressed that individuals such as Bruneau, Mǫwhì, Edzo, and Whanıkw'o were successful in helping all Tłı̨chǫ because they knew the stories from the past and had worked and traveled within the dè. They emphasized how these great leaders were capable of drawing on the stories and their personal knowledge to think with whenever they were faced with new situations or when new laws were required to enhance harmonious relations.

They spoke eloquently about Jean Wetrade's commitment to the teaching of young people, how he understood what stories need to be told, and how the new school bears his name. They wove the stories and current events together to emphasize the role of elders as "boss" of the project rather than as "adviser." The elders stressed that self-government would be successful only if personal autonomy and the ability to work cooperatively are maintained in the future, which for them would come from knowing Tłı̨chǫ nèèk'e and from knowing the oral narratives passed down from their ancestors.

Focus of the Tension

Interestingly, the tension was focused around, on the one side, Jean Wetrade and Andrew Gon, who were "like brothers," and, on the other, Chief Henry Gon—Andrew Gon's younger brother's son. As I visited various members of the Gamètì community, I learned that most of the elders, most of the women, and several of the active trappers talked and told stories that supported Jean Wetrade. In contrast, many middle-aged men, active hunters but not necessarily active trappers, spoke for the chief. The chief's father, Andrew Gon's brother Pierre, supported his son. Individuals under the age of forty watched and listened but did not seem to voice opinions or tell stories. This watching and listening among the youngest people in a group is consistent with the observations made by Jane Christian and Peter Gardner, who found that among the Slavey, young people often spread news but do not tell stories (1977, 66–88).

Most people in Gamètì agree that individuals under the age of about forty are not considered to have full adult status. They are still actively learning narratives and gaining experiential knowledge. Older people have enough experience and skill to share their life experiences without bragging.

Withdrawal Continued; Dialogue Continued

During the initial stages of the tension in Gamètì, groups of people avoided each other. As individuals thought about and decided which tasks should be done and whom they would follow, they appeared not to be so withdrawn. Nevertheless, the key players on both sides continued to avoid each other. More and more community members consistently spoke about the importance of a strong community k'àowo, about their respect for Joe Mantla, who was community k'àowo at the time, and about their right to think for themselves on a daily basis. Middle-aged men supporting the chief continued to explain the importance of Tłı̨chǫ self-determination to ensure that the Tłı̨chǫ people would always have a say and to assure others that Tłı̨chǫ territory and their way of life would be secure. For the band councillors, negotiating with government and industry would enable the Tłı̨chǫ people to maintain their autonomy as a First Nations people in Canada and to benefit from rather than "suffer" the consequences of development.

Oral narratives and talk on this issue continued for almost two months. It became increasingly apparent that most of the community agreed that the elders should record the stories of traditional governance so that young people would not forget the past and would be able to use the stories to think with in the future. Only much later did I realize that the talk of what should occur extended out to relatives and friends in other communities and that the chiefs in those communities were actively discussing the issue with Chief Gon.

Elders Taking Action

On Sunday, 28 February 1993, Jean Wetrade announced at church that a feast for the elders would be held at his home. As for larger feasts, community members cooked caribou and fish, and Joe Mantla, community k'àowo, and the younger men who assisted him delivered the food. It is usual that the community k'àowo's helpers—young men in training—also serve the food, but in this case Jean Wetrade's sons served the food and refilled our cups with tea.

Jean asked Therese Zoe to come and to bring me with her. Twenty-eight of the thirty elders attended, and other members of the community—children and adults—dropped in and sat and listened for varying lengths of time. Jean Wetrade and Andrew Gon spoke first, explaining the issue that needed discussing. Then each of the elders spoke. Although most of the discussion was not interpreted to me, others did tell me that the chief and the band councillors were traveling outside of the community on important business. Therese interpreted the Yamǫ̀ǫ̀zaa and Edzo stories, emphasizing the greatness of both men, who had brought an end to chaotic times. After a lengthy discussion, Jean Wetrade announced that the four oldest elders in the community—Marie Zoe (eighty-six), Madelaine Drybone (eighty-five), Andrew Gon (eighty-three), and Jean Wetrade (eighty-four)—would direct the traditional-governance project and that they would be inviting the chief to sit with them. They explained that both men's and women's knowledge as well as the knowledge of all the animals were important. They explained that individuals of their choice would be hired for the project because they knew which families needed a wage earner and which individuals were interested in working closely with the elders.

Chief Gon returned a few days later. Jean Wetrade invited him to sit with the elders, and Chief Gon agreed. Later, at a public feast, Chief Gon informed the community that he had been sitting with the other three chiefs and members of the negotiating team and that they had decided to select one elder from each of the communities to advise them on land claims and self-government. He informed the community that Harry Simpson had been selected from Gamètì. Harry is Andrew Gon's son-in-law, one of two elders on the Gamètì Band Council, and a personal adviser to John B. Zoe, who was chief negotiator for the Tłı̨chǫ claim. He also informed the community that Jean Wetrade would be the k'àowo for the traditional-governance project and named the other three elders (Marie Zoe, Madelaine Drybone, Andrew Gon), who together would form the

Figure 6.3. Andrew Gon, Amen Tailbone, and Romie Wetrade sharing stories after visiting the prophet's grave and feeding the fire on the shores of the lake Gamètì, 1994. (Photograph by the author)

Gamètì Elders Committee, overseeing the traditional-governance project, with Jean as the k'àowo. The elders hired Rita Blackduck and Sally Anne Zoe as local researchers shortly after.

Over the course of several months, Chief Gon sat with the elders on many occasions. He then asked Àąwąą, the other elder on the band council, to sit with the elders; within the year, Àąwąą was replaced on the Gamètì Elders Committee by Harry Simpson. Harry was younger than the other elders, and, being respectful, he listened, taking the stories in and sharing them with the lawyers and the negotiating team. Through Harry Simpson, the elders acted indirectly as advisers to the task group working on a self-government model while still "being their own boss," accomplishing the task they thought was more relevant to maintaining personal autonomy for their descendants and for maintaining harmony within the dè.

Thus, in the end, to summarize, two task groups were formed. One group consisting of elders, with Jean Wetrade as k'àowo, would oversee the documentation of stories for the future and the visits to the bush to experience the stories and walk the locales where they originated. The second group, consisting of one elder from each community and John B. Zoe as chief negotiator, would work to ensure a land-claim and self-government agreement that was right for the people. It was John B. who explained to me that providing the elders with opportunities to tell stories would help to maintain the "Tłıchǫ character" during the negotiating process.

He believed that if the young were curious about the project, they would visit the elders and listen to the stories; they would also become curious about and listen to the events associated with the land-claim and self-government negotiations. He thought the stories would lead people of all ages to think about the negotiations, creating a context within which a better claim could be negotiated. He also thought that through the completion of both tasks—defining a self-government model and documenting and learning the stories from the past—more people would remember and experience the truth in the present. Hearing stories would stimulate more narration and more discussion and heighten awareness as people throughout Tłıchǫ nèèk'e visit and talk among themselves. The formation of two task groups gave everyone autonomy. Most individuals in Gamètì were at least peripherally involved in doing or supporting the task they thought appropriate for the future.

Dog Incident

Shortly after the acknowledgment that both tasks needed doing, an incident occurred in Gamètì that further confirmed both that the stories were needed to think with in the future in order to enhance individual autonomy on a daily basis and that the Tłıchǫ nation needed a workable self-government agreement. It started with a loose dog.

It is rare to see loose dogs—except very small puppies—wandering in Tłıchǫ communities. But in an extremely rare incident a dog got loose and attacked a four-year-old boy. The boy was medivacked to Yellowknife. Immediately after the attack, Francis Quitte went after the dog on his skidoo. He was the only single adult male without children in the community and therefore the only person who could kill the dog. Everyone watched as the chase crisscrossed the lake ice in front of the community. Francis was trying to get close enough to shoot the dog but not close enough to be attacked in case it was rabid. Everyone in the community was concerned that the dog might have been infected by a rabid fox.

Francis chased the dog across the frozen lake in temperatures of –40°C (–40°F), finally shooting it. The nurse had talked to NWT health services and told Francis to put the dog's body in the community freezer. Francis explained that it was not the Tłı̨chǫ way to mix caribou and dog. But the bureaucrat told the nurse that they should wrap the dog in plastic and then it would not be mixed with caribou. They followed these instructions. Once again there was tension in the community—this time because Tłı̨chǫ rules were being broken in favor of government policy and direction.

The following day all the adults talked about the incident as an example of increased chaotic behavior in their communities. Several confirmed that it was right that the elders were insisting that the people should learn and remember the Tłı̨chǫ way. No matter whose home I visited, people were talking of the attack, expressing their concerns, and explaining the proper way to care for a dog before and after its death. They explained that a dog must be tied properly, fed properly, talked to, and thought well of because dogs know what Tłı̨chǫ are thinking.[2] The elders and others in the community expressed concern that the bureaucrat's instructions had been followed. Almost everyone was very concerned that dog had been placed in the community freezer with caribou. Most said they would rather starve than eat caribou that was mixed with dog. Several—especially older people—explained, however, that if Francis had not followed government rules, he might have been charged. "You have to follow government people, they think they are the 'boss' of the land." Some—especially younger people—thought the elders should have decided what to do before putting the dog in the freezer.

The majority, however, thought that all community members should have gathered together to talk about what to do with the dog—pointing out that it is always better to talk together before taking action. They explained that the dog could have been put in a box outside—it was cold enough to stay frozen—until everyone had a say and direction had been given by the chief, whose job, they explained, is to listen to everyone and then give direction to the people. They emphasized it is also the chief's job to explain to government bureaucrats the right way for the Tłı̨chǫ.

To many, the dog incident was a clear example of why the elders were anxious about allowing the government to have more authority. Most adults wanted young people to think about possible consequences before taking action—knowing the rules set down by Yamǫǫ̀zaa. Based on what I heard, it seemed everyone in the community was told what was right—dogs are usually tied and fed and treated well; everyone knew it was right that Francis was the one to shoot the dog because he was the only single, childless male available. Everyone knew alternatives to handling the dog's body and that it was wrong to mix dog hair with caribou meat. Wrapping the dog in plastic was not sufficient.

I did not meet anyone who would eat the caribou meat. After much discussion, the little bit of meat that was left in the freezer was removed and destroyed. The freezer, which "was rotting anyway," was also destroyed, and a new community freezer built. Tension was once again dispelled, and harmony reestablished.

After this incident, I began to understand the extent to which Tłįchǫ are concerned about the chaos of modern times and resulting disharmony. They see that individuals are forgetting to discuss the right way with knowledgeable people—elders, other harvesters—and forgetting to think about a new way if the situation warrants it, as has been taught to them in the stories of Yamǫǫ̀zaa, Edzo, Mǫwhì, and Bruneau. I also realized that although most people know the right way, many think they have to follow the rules of the dominant society as directed by the government, which asserts its authority over the land.

Many Tłįchǫ rules were broken in this incident: not tying the dog, allowing the dog to escape and attack a child, mixing dog with caribou meat. Dog is not allowed in Tłįchǫ homes or near their food. Tłįchǫ will get sick from eating dog or having dog hair in their food; they are descendants of Dog, and it is Dog that gives them their particular communication skills. The breaking of taboos shows disrespect in the close relationship Tłįchǫ have with Dog. Not knowing who you are or your place within the dè will result in acting disrespectfully toward other beings. For the vast majority of Tłįchǫ, this event demonstrated general chaos and dysfunctional behavior, which for the Tłįchǫ always comes from outside the person.

Most people considered this breach of appropriate conduct as another example of young people's taking guidance from members of the dominant society, whose knowledge and way of life are different. Over the next several weeks, the story of the incident was told repeatedly, as was the Tłįchǫ origin story—the union of a woman to a "man who hunted as a dog at night."

The Origin Story

It is said, a band of people moved camp. They left an old dog behind. The camp k'àowo told his daughter to go back for the old dog. But on her return, a hunter was standing at the camp, and the dog was nowhere to be seen. She could not find the dog. She made a spruce bough tepee with the hunter, and they stayed together. They were married. He would get up early and hunt. Every morning she noticed dog prints rather than her husband's prints. She was pregnant, so sometimes she would wake up during the night. She realized that he was not beside her. She started to watch. She watched and realized that her husband could turn himself into a dog. She realized she had married Dog. She saw that he did not get up early to hunt but would leave her as soon as he thought she was sleeping. He would hunt all night.

She gave birth to three puppies. She kept them in a sack. Every time she would go to the bush to get wood, the puppies would come out of the sack and play, and as soon as their mother came back, they would go back into the sack. She never saw them as humans. However, she did notice children's footprints on the ground. She wondered if they were like their dad and could change themselves back and forth. She noticed the prints but did nothing because she loved them very much. She watched them grow. She decided to hide and to watch to see if they were turning into boys. She said she was going into the bush, and then the puppies came out. They saw her after they became boys, and they ran back. One got back in the sack and remained a dog, but she caught the other two, and they stayed human.

The Tłįchǫ, who are descendants of this family, have very strong Ɂį̀k'ǫ̀ǫ̀ because their ancestors are both animal and human. Dogs, who are able to communicate with other beings as well as between themselves, have given the Tłįchǫ the ability to have a strong voice and the ability to communicate and therefore be well organized and very thoughtful within the dè.

To bring harmony back to the community after the dog incident, adults quickly responded by repeatedly telling the story of the "woman who married the dog" in conjunction with the story of what had just occurred. First, the right words were used—telling the story. Elders especially always acknowledged that words should not be wasted or spoken flippantly because "words are sacred" and when used correctly help to make things right. Second, after listening to community members, the chief directed that the community freezer be rebuilt, which decontaminated the site and at the same time replaced an already old, decaying building. In taking these actions, harmony was reestablished in the community by doing what was right for the Tłįchǫ people rather than what was right for the government.

Followership

The tension associated both with who would oversee the traditional-governance project and with who should decide what should happen to the dog focused on the desire to reestablish harmony. In both situations, the negotiation of tension—through talk and storytelling—centered on who was the most knowledgeable and therefore who would be the best person to follow. In the first case, the Gamètì chief and band councillors were vying with Jean Wetrade and the elders for followers. Community members were thinking about who could achieve the task in a way that was right for the Tłįchǫ and their descendants. Both Chief Henry Gon and the elders' k'àowo, Jean Wetrade, were seen as being the "most knowledgeable," but by different individuals in the community. Chief Gon was seen as having the appropriate skills and knowledge because he had attended school, which gave him the basis for understanding the manner in which bureaucrats think, and he was a hunter. Chief Gon lived "both ways," as did the middle-aged men whom he wished to hire.

Jean Wetrade was considered strong-minded and had demonstrated his ability as a k'àowo to the elders and as k'àowo to Andrew Gon, who had been chief of Gamètì in the 1970s. He and Andrew had moved their families away from Behchokǫ̀, establishing their own community at Gamètì after discussing it with others, who then moved with them. He understood how Kweèt'ıı̨ ways had manifested themselves in Behchokǫ̀. He was thought of as a man who intimately understood the significance of Chief Bruneau's direction that all Tłįchǫ people should "know both ways so that each individual would be strong like two people." Jean Wetrade was considered an elder who knew the relevance of stories to maintaining an open mind and preparing oneself to think through unforeseen events.

Although during the dog incident some individuals felt they had to follow the government bureaucrats, the community as a whole would rather have discussed how to proceed, with the elders advising and with the chief making a decision and being responsible for telling the bureaucrats. In this situation, tension developed because something had gone awry in the community, causing a dog to attack a child, and because government bureaucrats considered themselves to be experts and in authority. These bureaucrats gave direction and expected community members to follow them. Tension was associated with who was "an authority" on enhancing and maintaining harmony within the dè. It was never about who was elected to be "in authority" or who administered "government policy."

Rather, most discussions of how to deal with the dog situation centered on who was capable, had the skill, and knew the right way.

Being knowledgeable is vital, yet one cannot brag about what one knows; bragging is considered a sign of self-interest and stupidity. One should not have to brag.[3] Others can see how one behaves, which indicates a person's level of ability, just as how and what one accomplishes are signs of what one knows. Actively producing is one of the few ways in which individuals can demonstrate that they are capable of maintaining respectful relations with other human and other-than-human beings. The recognized ability to do a task is tied to success. This is true in the case of Squirrel running faster than Bear, in the case of those whose ?ı̨k'ǫ̀ is the strongest and of Edzo's controlling Akaitcho's mind until Akaitcho spoke of peace, and in the following incident narrated by David Wheeler: "We found the [Bear Lake] Chief in high feather over the success of a great medicine war with his rival Old Jeremy. First Old Jeremy made medicine, but it missed the Bear Lake Chief and killed his son's wife's cousin. This made the Bear Lake Chief very angry and he made medicine, which, however, missed Jeremy and killed his squaw's brother's illegitimate daughter. After several misses Jeremy's medicine came very close and the Chief cut his foot with an axe and was laid up all winter. This gave him plenty of time to make very strong medicine and Old Jeremy caught pneumonia when he visited the houses at the post and died. Thus only one chief was left among the Bear Lake Indians" (1914, 655).

The situation in Gamètì was slightly different. The already selected leaders—the chief and the elders' k'àowo—were vying for followers to accomplish different tasks: the traditional-governance project and the self-governance/land-claim negotiation. They could not enhance their own profile; therefore, talk was necessary. Both those supporting the elders' k'àowo and those supporting the chief mentioned the other's inadequacy. Talk of this kind is not uncommon. June Helm comments on similar behavior when she says, "Over the years Vital and I worked together, two bush Indians of roughly Vital's age made the effort to tell me that Vital didn't know anything (or words to that effect). Since one of them was an absolute monolingual, he had to commandeer a bilingual bystander to register his complaint. I understood their point of view. How could a man who had spent his adult life living in Rae have all the experiences and know all the things real bush Indians know?" (1994, 76).

Several individuals of working age similarly told me that the Tłı̨chǫ researchers chosen by the elders for the traditional-governance project lacked sufficient "schooling" to do research. I listened and often sent them to Jean Wetrade, the project's k'àowo. If they did visit the k'àowo, he informed them that the researchers were chosen for their interest in the events and happenings told in stories from the past. Frank Russell (1898), who also noted this behavior in the late nineteenth century, explained it as jealousy, but I found that it acted to keep any one individual from having too much power.

Talk, combined with the telling of stories, is an important way of keeping most individuals from gaining too much power. Individuals who brag are viewed as stupid, deceitful, and lazy; knowledgeable individuals complete tasks and do not brag. It seems reasonable that any would-be leaders be seen as being successful and sharing of themselves—that is, if they want followers.

During the first several weeks of the traditional-governance project, no one bragged, but they did find fault with others who had an alternative agenda. In other words, if you cannot emphasize what you know, it is necessary to find other ways to make your point—telling stories of the past, relating observations that you experienced, talking, and discussing both the positive and the negative aspects of other individuals who are also vying for followers. As explained by the Tłįchǫ on several occasions, it is expected that people will discuss the full range of an individual's characteristics when considering whether to follow that person or not. I have heard several elders discuss the importance of knowing the strengths and weaknesses of an individual's character—as the person himself or herself should know. It is only through knowing oneself that one can know when and where to draw on the strengths of others.

I have heard such character analysis before elections; I have heard discussions about individuals who are viewed as people who like to control others and whether their skill to do the task outweighs their controlling nature. These discussions cross cultural boundaries. Andrew Gon explained this to me once when personnel from DeBeers Canada were visiting Gamèti. They had just finished a presentation that emphasized that there would be "no problems, and the animals would be monitored." "They must be lying," he said. "There are always problems. Be very suspicious of those who say everything is fine because there are always problems in life and people must be prepared for those as well. Humans are dependent on the goodwill of other beings and we must pay attention to how animals will be treated" (personal communication, comment through Sally Anne Zoe, August 1994).

In these and other situations, individuals are encouraged to think about the present by remembering the past through stories that they have heard since they were babies. As told through the stories of Yamǫǫ̀zaa, Edzo, Mǫwhì, and Bruneau, before taking action, leaders are encouraged to listen to the people that choose to follow them. Edzo listened to others who told of the Yellowknives raiding Tłįchǫ camps for furs and women, and then he decided to sit with Akaitcho, who was also a yahbahti.

Before taking action, Edzo told his followers what he planned to do. He listened to them, but only Edzo's two brothers chose to undertake the tasks necessary to control Akaitcho and his followers. Mǫwhì's and Bruneau's stories differ in that Mǫwhì was delegated the task and Bruneau was chosen through elections. But when Mǫwhì accepted the task to talk to the Treaty Commission, he listened to all those residing throughout Tłįchǫ nèèk'e and took advice from his uncle before speaking firmly with the treaty commissioner.

Each of these leaders knew and could articulate the reason for chaos or potential chaos and could formulate a solution based on what their followers said and by using their own intelligence. Yamǫǫ̀zaa understood that the chaos was caused by a lack of defined social relationships and lack of clarity on the place of different beings within the dè. Edzo understood that the chaos was caused by the fear Tłįchǫ people had of Akaitcho's band, who seemed to have forgotten their place as defined by Yamǫǫ̀zaa. Mǫwhì understood that Kweèt'ı̨ı̨ knowledge was different because it was from a different place within the dè; he understood that Kweèt'ı̨ı̨ take what they want because most do not know where they belong within the dè. Mǫwhì had heard and knew the stories of the chaotic relationships that Kweèt'ı̨ı̨ had developed with the Chipewyan and Slavey, who signed Treaty 8. Bruneau also understood that the Kweèt'ı̨ı̨ mode of thought was different; he encouraged all to learn both ways so that they would remain strong. Each of these figures had established new agreements, laws, and rules for living in harmony with other beings—human and other-than-human. Yamǫǫ̀zaa provided all beings with language, meaningful social relationships, and a place within the dè. Edzo made a peace treaty with Akaitcho, and both agreed to a number of specific rules for living in harmony and respecting the other's place. Mǫwhì signed the 1921 treaty, agreeing on how Kweèt'ı̨ı̨ and Tłįchǫ would live peacefully and on how Kweèt'ı̨ı̨ would give to as well as take from the people whose place—homeland—they were inhabiting. Finally, Bruneau provided a way for living with Kweèt'ı̨ı̨ while remaining strong within one's self.

People regularly refer to these stories. Those I have heard sometimes simply speak the personal name of one of these cultural heroes who brought peaceful relations to a chaotic life. At other times, they tell and retell all or a portion of the stories. All people are encouraged to use the stories to remember how to select whom to follow. Stories help people to think about whom to follow, why to follow him or her, and the importance of not following if a leader acts inappropriately—as in one of the Yamǫ̀ǫzaa stories, which tells of how his wife, Beaver, could no longer follow him because he forgot to behave in the manner that would maintain their relation within the dè.

Before actually beginning the traditional-governance project in the community, people used these stories to stress the appropriateness of one potential k'àowo over the other. Those who had already decided who they would follow spoke in support of their choice while "talking" about the inappropriateness of the other choice. Both elders and elected leaders used similar stories to vie for followers and to determine who would oversee the research. The tension focused on whether the traditional-governance project, using PAR, would act as a means to assist younger people to hear the stories in a variety of contexts and know how the Tłı̨chǫ governed prior to church and federal government intervention, or would the project be used to do the research that would assist government and Tłı̨chǫ negotiators to finalize an agreement. Once the followership decided which tasks needed doing and who had the skills to do those tasks,[4] two groups were formed and harmonious relationships were restored. It was the community members who decided it would take two different tasks and therefore two different groups to maintain and enhance personal autonomy while ensuring self-government within the Canadian context.

The tensions that occurred during this period meant not only that those who were "an authority" on specific tasks kept their followers, but that they did not gain excessive and destructive power. Consider the story of Raven, who stole the caribou and forgot to share. Wolf, who remembered how to share, eventually found the caribou with the help of those who had skill and abilities that he did not possess. And consider the story Alphonse Quitte told of Edzo's character as he grew older. (See also Gillespie 1970, 65, on Edzo and Akaitcho in old age.)

Edzo's burial has never been located because in his old age he became greedy . . . and took his own brother's musk-ox robe. He was a very powerful yahbahti, yet even his own brothers, who assisted him with establishing peaceful relations with Akaitcho, no longer followed him. He forgot to share. He was no longer using his power for the good of others. No one can find him. It would be good if the government gave us money to find his grave. He is important to us, just as [Sir John] Franklin is important to the Kweèt'ı̀ı̀, and the government gives money to look for Franklin's remains. They should give us money too.

For the Tłı̨chǫ, the other side of Edzo's character that eventually came to the surface does not take away from his accomplishments or his greatness; it simply shows that anyone can forget and act inappropriately. For this reason, harmony is best maintained if everyone thinks about the behavior of others. Most individuals have the ability to enhance their personal knowledge through experience and the potential to lead and to work cooperatively with others. Everyone also has the potential to become too authoritarian and controlling. Leaders can best be held in check if followers remember the stories and their responsibility to follow those who are an authority on the task at hand. All human beings can enhance cooperative working relations by knowing their own as well as others' characteristics. In other words, one must draw on the skills of others.

These stories guide listeners: those who become greedy, do not share, and forget about their followers eventually lose their authority. Tłı̨chǫ people often state, "The misuse of authority usually comes back on a person," just as they say, "The misuse of ʔı̨k'ǫ̀ǫ̀ will come back on a person," and "Bragging comes back on people."

Being Knowledgeable, Tension, and Followership

Alan Barnard argues that among foragers, people value knowledge that comes through decades of learning the skills necessary to use the knowledge of making a living, and it is these people who are followed (2002, 10). Barnard goes on to aver that this sociopolitical system works only where people have control over themselves. Different rules may come into play when outsiders are dealt with. These occurrences may create younger leaders who ignore the importance of a following. I found that during the process of struggling for the right to self-govern, the Tłı̨chǫ continue to value personal autonomy and to value those who are knowledgeable and are willing to follow them.

Here, I have considered the relationship between being knowledgeable, tension, and gaining a following by describing a situation that resulted from differences of opinion on which tasks needed doing to ensure personal autonomy and the right to self-govern among future generations of Tłı̨chǫ. I have shown that "following," "withdrawing from tension," "avoiding those with a differing point of view," "telling stories," and "talk-ing" are interrelated aspects of the same process.

Tension between generations is more problematic. The events I have described suggest that in the process of creating intelligent, responsible adults who value thinking for themselves, tension and differences are bound to occur. This conclusion does not contradict the observations of Tłįchǫ made by Sir John Richardson (1851, 17) and David Wheeler (1914, 653) concerning younger people's respectful and caring attitudes toward their elders. Rather, it demonstrates how thinking with stories and remembering the past can be used to find solutions that are correct for all concerned in a never-ending and ever-changing dè.

The tension that developed between generations within Gamètì in the early 1990s arose out of federal legislation and policy associated with the self-government and land-claim process—rules and policy brought by Kweèt'ìį from the British system. It was manifested in the Kweèt'ìį atti-tude that bureaucrats know best because they follow policy attached to already existing legislation. If Kweèt'ìį had never arrived, this particular situation and the events and happenings leading up to it would not have arisen. However, Kweèt'ìį did arrive. And as Tłįchǫ have observed other beings that dwell within the dè, they have observed Kweèt'ìį over time and discussed these observations and their interactions with Kweèt'ìį among themselves. By telling stories of Kweèt'ìį, they have remembered much of what has occurred.

Elders participate in guiding the learning of younger people, just as their parents and grandparents once showed them the way along trails and through stories. The Tłįchǫ are not "present oriented," caught in an im-mediate-return system of production, as has been argued for hunters and gatherers; rather, they are oriented to keeping their life going. The tension comes in attempting to maintain one's own as well as others' personal autonomy while working cooperatively as a viable society. Remembering is integral to the Tłįchǫ perspective and to their interactions with both human persons and other-than-human beings. Tension seems to act as a positive force that continually moves the community toward harmonious and workable relations. Richard Slobodin (1960) similarly found a general rise in tension had a positive effect among the Gwich'in.

Romie Wetrade once told me and others how he now goes out on his skidoo and sits on it while thousands of caribou migrate around him. He explained that now that he has grown sons and daughters, they do the hunting and meat preparation, and while they work for him, he visits the caribou. He continues to tell his sons and daughters—as well as their spouses and children—stories, but he no longer thinks he has to be physically present to guide them. They know enough that he can now use them in a reciprocal relationship. As individuals listen to the occurrences and happenings of the past contained in the oral narratives and gain experience through traveling trails and observing, they become knowledgeable and ready to lead through action.

CHAPTER SEVEN

Walking Stories;
Leaving Footprints

During the fall of 2003, hunters in Gamètì were recanvassing and fixing the frames of their freighter canoes. Charlie Gon and his wife's brother, Charlie Tailbone, were planning to travel through Tłı̨chǫ nèèk'e. They explained that different hunters who would be traveling with them knew different trails because they had heard the stories and had experienced them with their parents and grandparents when they were young. When asked who would be k'àowo on such a trip, they explained it would be whoever knew the trail they were traveling at any given time during the trip. The k'àowo would continually change as they traveled Tłı̨chǫ nèèk'e.

The hunters' plan was to learn from those who knew the places within each of the Tłı̨chǫ regional bands (see map 3) while providing their children and grandchildren with stories and experience so their descendants would know if there were problems within Tłı̨chǫ nèèk'e. They wanted to share the task of learning all the trails, including those that reached into regions other than their own. They thought it would take three or four summers to complete the journey, and some suggested they might stay out all year. In 2004, the trip was still being discussed. Traveling trails, walking stories, and leaving footprints enhance the Tłı̨chǫ's ability to know and understand what is around them; it is the right way for all Tłı̨chǫ to live. For me, the planning of this trip exemplified the importance to Dene of learning through observation and experience rather than through instruction.

In this chapter, I consider the process of "becoming knowledgeable" from the perspective of walking stories and leaving footprints. More specifically, I consider walking as the experience that binds narrative to the acquisition of personal knowledge. Walking, then, validates the reality of the past in the present and in so doing continually reestablishes the relation between place, story, and all the beings who use the locale. When walking, a person can become intimate with locales, where one can grow intellectually while traveling trails under the guidance of predecessors who have both followed and left footprints.

Several scholars have considered the relations between oral narratives, experience, and place. Anthropologists working with northern Dene people accept that experiential learning is associated with working and listening to those who have more skill (Goulet 1998; Jarvenpa 1998). Anthropologists agree that Dene learn through observation and experience rather than through instruction. I found that the emphasis on observation is consistent with the Tłıchǫ view that true knowledge is the outcome of personal experience, a theme that most anthropologists comment on (see, e.g., Ridington 1988; Rushforth 1992, 485–88; Scollon and Scollon 1979, 185–209; Watson and Goulet 1992, 224–27). Jean-Guy Goulet argues that Dene Tha adults quietly supervise their children in their activities (2000, 60–62). I found that although Tłıchǫ emphasize observational and experiential learning, they are not silent when guiding their children. Oral narratives are told regularly as grandparents walk and then sit with children, as women cut fish and meat to dry on racks outside or in smoking tents; stories are told in homes and offices. This mode of discourse is used to discuss individual perspectives on issues; it is how those returning to the community communicate their experience, just as elders weave these experiences with those that occurred in the past.

It is also generally accepted that Dene respect those who have traveled widely; travel is key to learning and understanding Dene cosmology (Andrews, Zoe, and Herter 1998, 312; Brody 1981; Ridington 1988). Furthermore, Dene respect those who have the ability to learn by themselves through dreams and visions, among other means (Goulet 1998; Watson and Goulet 1992).

Learning by oneself, however, does not mean doing so in isolation; rather, learning occurs during activities with and in the presence of others. Goulet (1998) shows how learning is anchored within the Dene community. Tim Ingold and Terhi Kurttila argue that among the Saami in Lapland learning involves the "generation and regeneration [of knowledge] within the contexts of people's practical engagement with significant components of the environment" (2000, 192). For the Tłıchǫ, "significant components" include humans as well as other-than-human beings, implying that learning is always situated and guided even if there are no other humans around. What I call "guided learning" for the Tłı̨chǫ entails a combination of receiving and understanding a conglomerate of past happenings and occurrences—through hearing stories—and traveling trails while carrying out tasks at particular locales. Information, then, is not to be extracted as the "content" of the story but "is the story itself"—namely, the happenings and occurrences as they are related and fit together. The stories tell of locales as they are associated with political and social endeavors. An example of such a place is Gots'ǫkàtì, where Edzo, whose descendants are Tłı̨chǫ Dene, and Akaitcho, whose descendants are Yellowknives Dene, agreed in 1829 to live in peace (Helm 1981a, 296).[1]

Places, then, are not simply spaces where people feel good when they visit them. Rather, relations with places are initiated as soon as children first hear the narratives. Tłı̨chǫ will have heard most stories many times before traveling to the sites named and experiencing them directly. Through visiting, walking, observing, and performing tasks at a locale, individuals both take something of the place with them and leave a bit of themselves. In so doing, they add their narrative to that of others while refining the deepest levels of their own perception (Casey 1996, 18). Keith Basso (1984b) emphasizes that places are used by the Western Apache Dene as indices to access stories, histories, and knowledge of the land. Place-names may convey meaning to those who know the locales and the stories connected to place (Cruikshank 1990a); however, such names can only reflect what any given person can comprehend, which is based on experience and interaction with other members of the community (Hallowell 1967, 193).

Thomas Andrews and John B. Zoe explain that, for the Tłı̨chǫ, stories reside in places along trails and that place-names serve as memory "hooks" for the stories that contain knowledge (1997, 172). Further, they explain, "places represent the physical embodiment of cultural process, which is realized through the combination of travel and story-telling" (Andrews, Zoe, and Herter 1998, 312). Building on their discussion, I consider several situations where Tłı̨chǫ of various ages follow the footprints left by their predecessors. In unraveling the relation between the story and personal knowledge gained through experience at locales and while traveling trails, I aim to show that the period between listening to stories and walking them marks an in-between phase of learning during which people who have heard information in the stories do not yet know the "truth" or reality of a narrative.

Sharing Narratives

As discussed in chapter 3, the dè is compared to one's parents because "it provides everything." The land, then, is a living entity with powers that should be shown respect if harmony is to be maintained. One way of showing respect is by paying the land, which usually entails leaving an item that one considers useful. This is done when travelers enter new bodies of water (Andrews, Zoe, and Herter 1998, 307). They also pay locales where powerful entities reside. I have never witnessed any Tłįchǫ travelers passing these places without stopping and showing respect. This often entails walking around to determine if all is as it was and tidying burials if any are in the vicinity. Individuals who have visited the place before tell the stories that dwell in the location to those who are traveling with them, and the travelers enjoy a "picnic," which usually includes feeding predecessors by putting favored food in the fire, before continuing the journey. The process allows everyone to know the place and the story a little better. These actions validate occurrences and happenings from the past while maintaining relations with the predecessors who continue to be attached to Tłįchǫ places.

I have seen Tłįchǫ elders pay the trail as they walked toward a Chipewyan sacred site where the spirit of a woman, who is willing to help those who require physical and emotional healing, resides in the waterfall. Although people leave sharp tools such as awls, needles, and knives at the falls, the Tłįchǫ elders I observed also paid the trail leading to the falls with spruce boughs. Similarly, when traveling to Scotland for the Ninth International Conference on Hunting and Gathering Societies, Georgina Chocolate from Behchokǫ̀ and Dora Nitsiza from Whatì used coins to pay the land as we left the airport terminal and train stations and before we walked around the many sites we visited. Just as when a new body of water is entered while traveling the ancestral trails, offerings are made requesting support for a safe journey while visiting any unknown place.

Elders tell narratives that guide people where to walk; no one should pass over caribou blood because that neglect shows a lack of respect and is dangerous.[2] On one afternoon in February 1999, some Tłįchǫ friends and I were driving from Whatì to Gamètì when we came to a place where caribou had been killed. Blood had been left spread across the ice road. This behavior indicated not only that the hunters had no idea how to cut up the meat in a respectful way, but also that they had not cleaned the blood from the ice road and so forced others to "step over" it. We stopped and removed the blood from the ice so that the vehicle could proceed. Everyone in the vehicle—both young and old—assumed the mess had been left either by "white hunters, who always butcher meat and who do not know any better," or by "non-Tłı̨chǫ aboriginal hunters who had not been trained well by their parents." There was much concern for the number of times these hunters had walked over the blood, showing disrespect for the caribou. All were concerned that harmonious relationships had been disrupted and wondered whether the caribou would return the next year.

Upon returning from a trip on the ice road, to the tundra, or to Scotland, or after visiting burial sites and other sacred sites, each individual shares his or her experience through stories. Elders often respond by telling stories that clarify, enhance, or add to the other stories. Listeners grow and change as they are drawn to the places, walking the footprints of others through their minds as they are drawn down the trails once again. As Basso explains, many footprints or tracks come in the form of place-names, stories, and songs telling of where past events occurred (1996, 31). Julie Cruikshank (1998) and Greg Sarris (1993) similarly note the importance of the relationship between the manner in which the storyteller relates the narration and the audience's ability to listen and understand. This is key to how people learn to think.

For the Tłı̨chǫ, predecessors' footprints are embedded in places and trails that continue to be used and traveled. Thus, the stories they think with are steeped with detailed and accurate accounts of trails and locales. These stories form the basis for building their perception of reality.

Adults tell stories to everyone, including young children, so all can grow from the place they call home, eventually traveling trails and walking locales where they can experience the stories for themselves. Robin Ridington has similarly noted that among the Dane (Dene)-zaa, children are prepared for their future experiences through the shared narrative tradition (2002, 117). Tłı̨chǫ individuals, then, regularly listen to stories, whose truth is subsequently validated through experience. Retelling the story in light of this experience, one builds on the original by incorporating one's own occurrences and happenings. Once one has gained personal knowledge, one tells one's own stories and eventually leaves one's own footprints for the future. As Ridington says of the Dane-zaa, "Each telling is an interpretive recreation rather than a recitation" (2002, 113).

It is important to note, however, that Tłı̨chǫ consider bragging about what one knows to be a demonstration of ignorance. Therefore, the stories they tell of their experiences usually focus on what one observed and encountered and with whom one was traveling. It is for others to comment on whether that person is knowledgeable. This is usually based on a person's skill in narration, but also on his or her other skills: say, success in caribou hunting, the ability to sway the attitude of government bureaucrats, the appearance of carefully prepared fish on drying racks, skill in sewing beautiful clothing, and the capacity to secure funding from territorial and federal governments.

Tłįchǫ elders encourage individuals to learn from places and to use "stories to think with" as they confront new situations. Thus, elders use stories to structure the context of how those younger than themselves perceive their experiences. As Romie Wetrade, a Tłįchǫ elder in his late seventies, said, "As for myself, I do not understand English. None at all. I do not know how to read. None at all. I do not know how to read the white man's words. . . . Even so, my elderly parents raised me and I have lived a good life because I heard their stories. My predecessors' talk is like keeping a book. I remember it. . . . I have reached this age by living on the knowledge from my predecessors. Their knowledge comes from beyond books. . . . The knowledge my predecessors possessed that has brought me thus far makes me feel as if I were sitting next to them. If I were to think about it, I am sitting under all their knowledge" (Legat and Zoe 2000, 31–32).

Andrew Gon, an elder in his mideighties, likewise explained how his predecessors had walked the land using knowledge from the past to survive. They had to know three distinct physical environments as they followed the caribou from the boreal forest to the tundra. They had to know where to camp to ensure good fishing in case the caribou migrated elsewhere, and during years when resources were limited, they had to know where their relatives may be camped—including those who lived in other regions. At the very least, this knowledge meant knowing narratives that allowed them to find trails through the complicated river systems and how to travel in the tundra where large lakes and tracts of land have to be crossed while the wind constantly blows. To emphasize the importance of knowing, Andrew said: "Our predecessors went though hard times and to this day we are still following their footprints and using their knowledge in order to survive" (Legat and Zoe 2000, 23).

In this and other statements, "their footprints" and "their knowledge" are interchangeable. "To know something" is to be able to take some form of action. Both Romie and Andrew were explaining the importance of listening to stories for the future because doing so not only acknowledges their predecessors' knowledge but also validates the truth of that knowledge so that it can be used to perform a task. The importance of maintaining and enhancing one's knowledge through action can be heard again in Madelaine Judas's statement: "I am a woman, but I did more than my share in carrying out work for my parents. Thinking it would be good for whoever lived, I did not toss away the words of my parents. . . . When a relative killed caribou, I left my footprints. . . , the prints of my snowshoes. . . . Like in the evening I would drive the dog team to get the meat; I was not afraid of any dog and the dogs would listen to me too. That is how I would load up the caribou carcasses. That is how I worked for my parents" (Dene Cultural Institute 1996, 21).

Madelaine took action, allowing herself to experience the "words" of her elders, a process that maintained the continuity of the footprints and their visibility for future generations. Being visible by means of her action allowed her to become increasingly knowledgeable and visible in the stories she would tell, allowing others to follow.

Listening to stories and following the footprints of those who are more knowledgeable allow one to think by drawing on the philosophical understanding and practical knowledge that originated in the past. This perspective encourages everyone to acknowledge that there is much to learn. It also provides people with an understanding of the importance of walking and observing—watching for the unexpected—while thinking about all that dwells within the land. As children grow to adulthood, they are taught to watch. As they walk, they are to think about what they smell, see, feel—always looking behind them to see how the trail will look on their return trip. Madelaine Chocolate remembers: "As a child, walking through the bush with my parents, I was taught to walk slowly and observe everything that was around me—including behind me. Then I went to residential school where the teachers taught me to hurry when I moved. I was then encouraged to run in races and enter in the cross-country ski races to win, and sometimes I did win. We were encouraged to go fast. It was harder to observe, understand, and remember" (personal communication, 27 November 2005).

Madelaine was encouraged to remember through being aware and through maintaining a relationship with all that was around her, and she was taught not to disconnect, which can happen if one moves too fast. This creates flexible people who carefully consider situations as they draw on all they have learned, while acknowledging that there is much more to know. They acknowledge that humans can know only a little (Ridington 1990) and therefore will always be in the process of learning. Being aware while walking and thinking with stories provides a context that allows for the acquisition of new knowledge.

Tłı̨chǫ people talk about John B. Zoe, a man in his forties who learned the stories, traveled trails, visited, and walked places. They tell of how he was offered the task of chief negotiator for Tłı̨chǫ land claims. Before he accepted, he "walked around" several southern cities. People talk approvingly about how he walked the streets, familiarizing himself with the "white character" before accepting the position, which entailed sitting across from several Kweèt'ı̨ whose homes are in southern Canada. What community members mean by this is that he learned a little bit about Kweèt'ı̨ and their habits by walking the places in which they reside. Similarly, Grand Chief Joe Rabesca never flies to a destination. He travels to places only if he can drive, canoe, or walk and thereby experience the dè. These two men are respected for knowing stories, for walking the Tłı̨chǫ nèèk'e, and for following the footprints of their predecessors.

The importance of the relationship between story, walking the land, experiencing places, and knowledge is a continual topic of discussion. Tłı̨chǫ of all ages spend a great deal of time and energy finding ways to share stories with those younger or less aware than themselves. Every autumn the Tłı̨chǫ Community Services Agency provides opportunities for teenagers and Kweèt'ı̨ teachers to travel to the tundra by canoe. I have been told that when they stop somewhere, the story of that locale is told, and they are encouraged to walk around with those who know the place. The members of the Regional Elders Committee with whom I worked requested that stories be recorded "so future generations can listen to them when they need them." They also requested that we not translate or write down their recordings; future generations should listen with those who understand the "old Tłı̨chǫ language" and the ideas and concepts the elders wish to convey through it. The elders encourage those who listen to walk the place from which every story grows—where its core dwells and from whence it spreads out through being told and retold.

These formalized storytelling sessions and trips are extensions of what takes place in people's homes every day. Adults tell "old-time stories" as well as stories of what they have seen and experienced. They share when, where, and how they experienced the stories that came from ancient times or "when the world was new." Adults throughout the Tłı̨chǫ communities encourage those younger or less experienced than themselves to visit and walk locations where they can experience the truth of stories for themselves and to share what they experience—what they saw, heard, felt and with whom they shared the experience, including other-than-human beings.

In July 2002, I was with several Tłı̨chǫ who were duck hunting. I was in a boat with Charlie Tailbone, a hunter in his late fifties, and a couple of teenage girls. The two young women were pressuring Charlie to take them to Ɂezhogǫghǫ̀, an island the elders emphasize that people should stay away from in order "not to bother those who died there." The day was beautiful. There was not a cloud in the sky, and Charlie had successfully shot several ducks. We were ready to stop for lunch. Charlie was heading for the spot where the others were already building a fire. The girls pressured Charlie, taunting him, saying that he lived in the past and believed too much in the old way and that it was all "just old legends." Finally, Charlie turned the boat toward the island, saying, "I will take you, but I will not walk on the island." As he turned toward the island, one small black thundercloud formed over the island—lightning and thunder came from the cloud in an otherwise clear blue sky. The girls quickly changed their minds, exclaiming, "OK, OK, it's true—we believe the elders." Charlie once again turned his boat and headed for where the others were preparing food and tea. We joined the others.

I listened while the older of the two girls told of our experience. She mentioned when she had first heard about the island from her grandmother, Marie Zoe. She recounted our trip up the rapids earlier that day and how she and her friend had taunted Charlie. While telling of Charlie's final willingness to take them but not to walk with them on the island, she explained how entities associated with the lake were acting. She told how calm the lake was and how the cloud, lightning, and thunder had suddenly appeared. The elders sat quietly and then simply stated that it is right to listen to the elders—it is right to follow the ancestors' footprints.

Although none of us walked on the island, the experience tied the story that originated on the island with our knowledge of why it was inappropriate to walk there. Furthermore, no one wanted to know the pain that continues to dwell on the island. Our experience brought the "truth" of the story to the present, forming a relation between the story and the locale.

By listening to and learning stories and by traveling, one realizes that sometimes you can walk only parts of a story. "Rayrock Mine, Ltd." is the official English name for the site of an abandoned uranium mine that was under production in the 1950s. The site is contaminated, and people see it as disrespected and uncared for. The locale is also called "Kwetıı̀Ɂàa," remembered through its name as where hunters used to walk to the top of the hill, sit, and feel happy as they watched for moose. In the 1950s, Kwetıı̀Ɂàa took on a new story, this one associated with uranium mining and the death of beings that traveled through or lived in the location.

When elders share oral narratives about and use the name "Kwetıı̀Ɂàa," it evokes visions of sitting on top of the hill. They use the name "Rayrock" when talking about the location of the mine, and that name brings up images of people with cancer, a yellowy powder that settled on the ground, animals floating in water with their fur coming off, and fish with spots on their livers. Rayrock is considered a place of death. Younger Tłįchǫ can know this dead place if they care to walk it, but few—if any—wish to follow their parents' and grandparents' footprints to it.

Young people can never know the reality of Kwetįį?àa or walk that place, nor can they experience or observe the changes that occurred. They will know only the story. Middle-aged people who played on the mine tailings as children vaguely remember Kwetįį?àa, but they are intimately aware of the reality of what happened there. Only the old have walked in both Kwetįį?àa and Rayrock and have personal knowledge of both. The narrative of the "two" places is told as one story or as separate stories, depending on the context. Changing the name changes the story and the images. Nevertheless, the story portrays them as separate places in the same locale. The story is always told with the intention of enabling younger people to remember: the mine managers told the young people's predecessors that uranium mining and the by-products contained in the tailings were safe; their predecessors believed the mine managers and allowed their children to walk on the tailings.

Individuals can know the stories of Kwetįį?àa and Rayrock, but they can no longer walk the story of Kwetįį?àa; they cannot know that place. Conversely, they can know the story of Rayrock, but although they can walk Rayrock and validate its story, they think it would be unwise to do so. The place-names act here as reminders. Rather than walking in this area to acquire visual cues, the people listen to the narrative. They listen and learn why one should not walk there. Not walking there, however, does not imply that they do not feel attached to the locale. They are connected because both Kwetįį?àa and Rayrock are part of Tłįchǫ nèèk'e.

Walking the Story

Observing while walking in their predecessors' footprints provides individuals with an understanding of a world that has both continuity and change. In 2001, one of the fall hunting camps was located on a sand bar on ?ewaànıt'ıtì, a lake in the barren grounds. This location was selected because caribou are known to cross the lake here if they are in the area. Before those of us who were going on the trip left for the barrens, elders who were not accompanying us told stories of this area. The stories told of hunters being lost in blizzards—some found, others never found, but whose remains are still being searched for. The stories also told of graves that have not been visited and need to be attended to and of an old-time burial that is supposed to be near Ts'ıʔehdaà, the last stand of trees on the tundra when one is traveling toward ʔek'atìtata and ʔek'atì from the south. The sand bar is also known to the women as a good place to find "stones that are just right for softening hides." Younger women were asked to find stones and bring them back.

A few days after we arrived at the camp, I was walking with Liza Jeremick'ca, Georgina Chocolate, and Dora Nitsiza. None of us had been to ʔewaànıt'ııtì, but we had heard stories of the importance of the sand bar and where to find stones for softening hides. As we walked, Dora found three of these perfectly shaped stones, and she turned to Georgina and said, "It's true, what our elders have told us. It is good to follow their footprints." We were walking on a gravelly sandbar, so no trail from the past was actually visible. I interpreted her statement to mean that her predecessors had walked on the sandbar before her and had shared their knowledge

Figure 7.1. (front to back) Elizabeth Michel, Romie Wetrade, Allice Legat, and Dora Nitsiza, resting and sharing a few stories of the area on top of an esker associated with ʔewaànıt'ııtì, 2001. The elders decided to walk to the top of the esker to see the surrounding area, including the sand bar where Dora and Liza had found stones used to soften hides. (Photograph taken with the author's camera)

through narratives so that we, too, could benefit from the resources to be found there.

A few days later several of us boated to Ts'ı̨ʔehdaà, an area that continues to be important for the Tłı̨chǫ people, in particular those living in the communities of Behchokǫ̀ and Wekweètì. All the oral narratives of Ts'ı̨ʔehdaà emphasize how safe it is to leave families there. The stories tell of the people who have camped there, of wood, of fish in the lake, and of hare and other small animals that can be snared by women, children, and older people while the trappers walk to the tundra to trap white fox in the winter. We walked around Ts'ı̨ʔehdaà. We looked at the old cabins. Some of us walked among the spruce trees. No one talked much, which surprised me because Elizabeth Michel, Jimmy Martin, and Joe Suzi Mackenzie had lived at Ts'ı̨ʔehdaà. Usually when camping at or visiting a place, these elders were happy to spend hours telling us about it. They would walk us around, explaining where to set snares, where to fish, where to find medicine. However, on this occasion they were quiet. I thought perhaps it was because Joe Suzi had been urging everyone to set up a fall camp at Ts'ı̨ʔehdaà for a decade; I thought maybe he was quiet and thoughtful about being there. Before leaving, we walked a kilometer or so to visit Georgina and Jimmy's relatives, who were buried on one of the eskers,[3] but here they were not quiet. They told us of the relationship to Georgina, spoke to the ancestor through prayer, and left gifts.

Just before leaving, we sat in the boats and motored slowly past the numerous oil barrels lying in the water around Ts'ı̨ʔehdaà. Again, no one was talking. I was struck by the fact that I did not hear anyone say, "It's true"—meaning "Ts'ı̨ʔehdaà is like we heard it would be." For several years, I had heard stories of Ts'ı̨ʔehdaà and of the trails leading to it, so I knew everyone else had heard these stories. Why weren't those who were visiting this locale for the first time saying "It's true"? Why were those who were visiting this locale after several years of absence not commenting on what Ts'ı̨ʔehdaà had to offer? Although everyone was conscious of the wind and wanted to return to camp before the waves on the lake became dangerous, the silence had to do with more than a concern for the wind. On returning to our camp on the sand bar, we sat long into the night as the elders talked about what they had observed as they walked around looking at the place. The rest of us listened. I learned that evening that the place had changed. No one could say "It's true." Elizabeth Michel, Jimmy Martin, and Joe Suzi Mackenzie, all of whom had walked with us at Ts'ı̨ʔehdaà, talked. They talked about the oil barrels that had been left in the water. They talked about the state of the berry bushes and the lack of berries. But mostly they talked about the number of trees that had disappeared and why these things may have happened.

Within the oral tradition of the Tłįchǫ, a story consists of the happenings and occurrences as they fit together. A story, then, can be part of a longer version or can lead into other occurrences. While the elders talked, their story of Ts'ı̨ʔehdaà eventually turned to Mǫwhì, who had stayed at Ts'ı̨ʔehdaà and extensively traveled the trails throughout the area. The stories of Mǫwhì himself inevitably led to talk of the Mǫwhì Trail, on which Ts'ı̨ʔehdaà is located, and of whether the federal government would agree to protect the Mǫwhì Trail under the federal and territorial Protected Areas Strategy. Tłįchǫ elders and leaders want the Mǫwhì Trail protected for several reasons, three of which are relevant here. First, they want the young people to remember the person Mǫwhì, after whom the trail acquired its name, not only because he signed Treaty 11 in 1921, but also because he knew the extent of Tłįchǫ nèèk'e. Mǫwhì is remembered as having gained his in-depth understanding through traveling trails and walking where stories originated and continue to reside. He was therefore able to tell the treaty commissioner the extent of the land mass needed for the Tłįchǫ to survive.

Second, they want Mǫwhì to be remembered for his commitment to providing young people with experience—helping them to walk the stories and follow the footprints of their predecessors while becoming knowledgeable and leaving their own footprints for others to follow. Stories would give them the ability to think and therefore the ability to survive in what the elders knew would be a continually changing world. Most of the young people who had traveled with and learned from Mǫwhì are now elders, but they continue to be socially and politically active even though they do not read, write, or speak English. Two such people are Alexie Arrowmaker, Mǫwhì's nephew, and Jimmy Martin, Mǫwhì's grandson. Both are considered individuals who are knowledgeable, and people continue to refer to them as following in the footprints of Mǫwhì. Alexie Arrowmaker advised the Tłįchǫ leadership—in particular the land negotiators— until his death in the autumn of 2005; and Jimmy Martin continued to lead the student canoe trips from Behchokǫ̀ to the tundra each September until 2003, when an injury prevented him from doing so again.

Third, they want Mǫwhì to be remembered as a person who extended his knowledge past the limits of the oral narratives he had heard as a young man and past his own political and kinship affiliations and thus into the stories of others from neighboring groups with whom he sought to establish relations. He pushed past his own knowledge to experience and know the places of others. He was the first Tłįchǫ to be chosen by people from all Tłįchǫ regions to speak for them all; he was the first to be given the task of standing up to the Canadian federal treaty commissioner because he knew through traveling trails and walking stories where the Tłįchǫ belong. The story of Mǫwhì resides on the Mǫwhì Trail—a place that incorporates the locales, stories, and trails where the footprints of Mǫwhì, his predecessors, and descendents continue to dwell.

Students follow the trails of their ancestors each year; they follow those more knowledgeable and are guided as they walk the stories that dwell along the trail. Along the Mǫwhì Trail, Tłįchǫ can experience Ts'ıʔehdaà, where trappers left their families as they traveled farther onto the tundra in the winter. Ts'ıʔehdaà has the last large stand of spruce trees before the barrens as the Mǫwhì Trail is traveled. They can experience Tsǫ̀tì, whose names originated after many Tłįchǫ were killed, gutted, and left by the lake shore. The ʔįdaàtłı similarly provides a variety of experiences. Tłįchǫ can experience the time of the sliding hill where Yamǫǫ̀zaa killed the wolverine;[4] they can experience Kǫ̀mǫ̀laa, where the Tłįchǫ took the first priest, where there had once been a cross the priest had erected, and

Figure 7.2. Fall hunting camp at Gots'ǫkàtì, 1988. Several thousand Tłįchǫ traveled by float planes and canoes to experience the peace Edzo brought to Tłįchǫ nèèk'e and the dè. (Photograph by the author)

where a new cross now stands. The people now residing in Gamètì often leave the ʔɪdaàtɪ̨lɪ and travel toward Gots'ǫkàtì, experiencing the truth of where and when Edzo made peace with Akaitcho. Human trails overlap and connect places.

It was during our time in the fall hunting camp at ʔewaànɪt'ɪɪtì that I realized that when Tłɪchǫ use the English term *place*, they mean a variety of things. *Place* can refer to a location or site along a trail or to the trail itself, including all the locales on it. *Place* also refers to the entire socioterritorial region, including the trails and locales in it, or the total extent of Tłɪchǫ nèèk'e, including all regions, trails, and locales where one expects to find Tłɪchǫ stories. People know the stories because their predecessors walked and left footprints in these places.

Combined with the discussion of Mǫwhì's Trail, a story that Robert Mackenzie told addresses the multifaceted concept of place and the importance of knowing the places of one's predecessors by knowing their stories so that one can follow their footprints. It also illustrates how walking and accomplishing tasks in a place can be understood as leaving a portion of oneself in that place while taking a bit of it with one. Robert's story, which his grandfather told him, comes from the time when the Yellow-knives Dene were raiding Tłɪchǫ camps. He said:

> One time the people were camped at Kǫk'èetì [where they were hunting caribou and musk ox] when they realized that some of Akaitcho's band were traveling close to them. They packed and left quickly. They were able to travel a trail they knew Akaitcho's band would not know— their parents and grandparents had not left their footprints around Kǫk'èetì. My grandfather said our predecessors followed the footprints of their elders and crossed the water where it was shallow enough to walk across. They were fortunate. One man traveling with them had a special relationship with Fox, and he asked Fox to help them. Although Yellowknives Dene followed them, they were unable to cross the water. They did not know the trail and did not have a story for the trail. They tried to turn back, but Fox caused them to travel in circles so they could not go back the way they came. Our predecessors were safe because they knew. Those who tried to harm them eventually starved.

Robert added:

> How can some people say a place is their land when their predecessors have not left their footprints and have not walked with their parents in

these places? They did not know that area; they had no stories to guide them. . . .

Remember the first time John B. [Zoe] led the students to Wekweètì without Jimmy Martin. John B. was traveling a trail that he had never traveled before, but Jimmy gave him a story for the trail. When John B. realized he was lost, he turned back, traveling to the place he knew was right from the story. Then he started again, paying attention to Jimmy's words. He had the story to think with. He got all those students to Wekweètì. (personal communication, 16 January 2002)

Robert emphasizes that holders of their predecessors' oral narratives do in fact use a mental map to think with as they travel the land. The Tłįchǫ people with whom I have traveled are well aware of when they are using oral narratives to think with. And although individuals' personal knowledge undergoes continuous formation as they move about in the environment (Ingold 2000, 230–31), they know that they are thinking with the totality of occurrences and events as provided in the narratives, which they have heard numerous times and on a regular basis.

Leaving Footprints

Just as Robert Mackenzie pointed out in his narrative, the Yellowknives Dene did not have a relationship with the area because even in his grandfather's time they did not know it. They literally did not have stories with which to follow their predecessors' footprints. But the Tłįchǫ of his grandfather's generation did have stories, including those from the time when the world was new, some of which are attached to locations and others are not—stories that English speakers would refer to as "myths." People experience the perspective provided in stories through everyday relations with each other and with other beings, and so the elders encourage their juniors to use these very old stories to think with. Most Dene elders stress the importance of understanding the difference between someone who claims he or she knows something—including a place—and those who have the experience and are perceived by others as actually knowing something. It is only through having taken action—usually in the form of tasks such as hunting, trapping, gathering plants, tidying burial sites, and building an ice road—that those who have gone before are considered to have left their footprints for others to follow. This point became particularly clear in 1995 when the Tłįchǫ were discussing the environmental-management plans presented by BHP, which wanted to develop a diamond mine. In reference to both this plan and the intense prospecting activity associated with staking mineral claims that had in many cases taken place in Tłı̨chǫ communities without regard to how close the mineral claim was to Tłı̨chǫ homes, Romie Wetrade said:

> [Our ancestors'] footprints show on the ground. What about these people from down south? There are no footprints of theirs or their trails around this area, but still they are talking about the land. They're saying they are going to look for diamonds, they're going to look for gas. There's no footprints of theirs, but still they explore beside us. . . . They don't have any trails; they haven't left their footprints, but that's what they are assuming, that they have worked on the land. They are telling the people "this is how I worked on the land and this is how the land looks like." All the Tłı̨chǫ have been all over the land . . . and have traveled way beyond the map, . . . but still it seems like they are prowling through our houses. . . . Around our cabin area they find diamonds, they find gas. They find everything while there's no one at the cabin, and it seems like that's what they are doing to our ancestors' home. They break in and look around everywhere on our land. . . . They have never been there, but they are still looking . . . where our ancestors used to travel[;] they are prowling through our property. (Dene Cultural Institute 1996, 10)

Romie's use of the term *footprints* describes an action taken, an action that is dependent on knowing how to live and leave information for others to follow, thus emphasizing the continual use of both the trails that are visible and the story in which the footprints bind person to place. The narrative provides details of the events as they originally occurred and describes the land, including other beings—animals, plants, land forms—that also inhabit and use the locale. The narrative, then, both recounts ongoing relations with those who walked a place previously and circumscribes the walking of the story for oneself. It tells the life history of places. Without walking and leaving footprints, one can only listen to and repeat the narratives of others who have walked the story.

Following the story that comes from others who have left footprints is often not enough; it depends on with whom one walks. When following the footprints of one's predecessors, one ideally walks with someone who has already walked there before and is considered to know something about the place and the event(s) that occurred there.[5] This is part of becoming ever more knowledgeable. I can best explain this relationship by briefly describing a discussion among twenty-four Tłı̨chǫ elders and active harvesters who continue to obtain most of their resources directly or indirectly from the land. Their discussion was in response to the request from the federal government that traditional knowledge be used along with scientific knowledge in an environmental-monitoring program. The monitoring program was to be associated with the ʔek'atì area,[6] where the BHP mining company was in operation and Diavik was in the process of construction. Hunters, fishers, trappers, and gatherers were concerned that decisions were being made based only on data collected from plane-based surveys and satellite tracking of several animals, including caribou—views, they quietly but firmly explained, that provided only limited understanding of the place. They were particularly concerned about the "fine yellow substance" that lay on the plants and that reminded them of the powder attached to Rayrock Mine. They knew that the substance could not be observed unless one was walking—as many of them had done while hunting near the mines. Given their concerns, they agreed to discuss how they could contribute to the environmental-monitoring process.

They devised a monitoring program based on walking and learning from those with more experience, while drawing on the skills of everyone. Three generations would be involved. The middle-aged would both learn from the elders and walk with them and tell stories of their observations. Those younger would hear the narratives providing them with information that would enable them to walk the land in their predecessors' footprints. They could use the knowledge from the past so they would know what was changing and what was staying the same. Charlie Tailbone, a hunter and trapper, said, "I know places from my father; other men my age know places I have only heard stories about. If we are to go to other regions to observe the land, the elders and hunters, who know the place, will have to walk with us so we can know—so we can pass the knowledge on to those of the next generation" (personal communication, May 2002).[7]

These men and women are acutely aware that it is their responsibility to pass their predecessors' knowledge on so that Tłı̨chǫ in the future can monitor and make decisions about areas where their predecessors dwell and continue to walk. Those still involved with land-based procurement would guide the learning of high school students by sharing their own knowledge through oral narratives and by walking the area of ʔek'atì with them, discussing the taste, look, and smell of fish and plants, the condition of caribou, and other such considerations. The students, too, would have a task. They would take notes and pictures, while others would contribute by writing reports for the bureaucrats. Knowledge would be continually

Figure 7.3. Pierre Mantla Sr. and his grandson Elvis Apples taking an initial walk around Nįdzįįkaà on the lake Semįtì, 1998. Pierre was pointing out the intricacies of the place. (Photograph by the author)

passed though generations in narrative form while walking so that each successive generation can become knowledgeable of the intricate details of the place known as ?ek'atì.

Although this plan has yet to materialize, it shows the continuing importance of sharing skills between all generations, while guiding the learning of others through sharing stories and walking places where predecessors have left their footprints. It also demonstrates the importance to the Tłįchǫ of regularly updating occurrences and happenings through experience—by walking the story.

Traveling Trails—Experiencing Place

Stories may reside in locales, but they grow out from where the original event occurred, just as individuals grow out from their home—the place where they began. Storytellers usually incorporate the events leading up to the situation and those occurring after, just as two young women did after they experienced the story of ʔezhogǫghǫ̀, and just as the elders did when they were visiting a Chipewyan sacred site and paid the trail with spruce boughs, acknowledging its relation with the "Lady in the Falls." They paid both the trail and the spot where the lady dwells.

Although many trails are well worn, footprints are not always visible on the ground, nor can material remains from human activity always be seen (Andrews, Zoe, and Herter 1998, 306). One's predecessors' footprints are not always visible on the bedrock and the muskeg where snow cover lasts at least seven months or on the ice that gives way to complicated river and lake routes. "Footprints," then, are not necessarily the actual impressions of a track or trail made by the movement of human feet. Many footprints and trails are accessible only through stories that tell of what has gone before so that one can grow into the present and think about what is the same and what has changed.

I have shown that Tłı̨chǫ individuals are encouraged to "walk the land" so that they can experience and validate occurrences and events in the stories that reside in and grow from places. Through listening to narratives and walking with one's predecessors, the process of guided learning is continuous. It provides individuals with the understanding necessary to keep life going and to maintain harmonious relations by showing respect to all entities that dwell within the land. Furthermore, the Tłı̨chǫ understand that one always has more to learn, more stories to experience, and therefore more places to walk. They learn that the world is in constant flux and that they must remain flexible and willing to think about new and unexpected situations. Their movements, then, are those of a wayfarer who should be at once knowledgeable, task oriented, and attentive to relations with other beings and entities in the environment through which they pass.

Walking is an action that implies not being cut off, as one is in an airplane or when one is too busy or going too fast or not paying attention to one's surroundings. Instead, walking entails carefully considering one's surroundings while thinking with the multitude of stories that one has heard. Following footprints is similarly about gaining knowledge through action and the ability to use that knowledge. Individuals who walk places within the dè are respected because they have experience, the interpretation of which is based on social interaction.

Personal knowledge comes when the story and one's experience converge in a narration. Although the focus of the story remains the same, it grows in ways that depend on with whom the story is shared and within what context and who goes on to retell it. In the telling, the stories reach out to other individuals, drawing them back down the trail, back to the places where individuals can experience the story for themselves. Thus, individuals grow outward at the same time as they become rooted within several locales of Tłįchǫ nèèk'e. Tłįchǫ are encouraged to grow through the knowledge that their parents and grandparents (and others) have offered them. In other words, being knowledgeable is the culmination of listening to stories and following footprints. This provides the foundation for leaving one's own footprints for future generations.

To return to a comment I made near the beginning of this chapter, walking stories and leaving footprints bind experience and narrative. The period between listening to and walking stories is the phase "in between," where people who have heard stories do not yet know the "truth" or reality of a narrative.

CHAPTER EIGHT

The Centrality of Knowledge

While working in Tłįchǫ communities, I often walked between homes and locations on well-worn paths. On arrival, I would listen to oral narratives being told near fires from which warm tea and coffee were served, food cooked, and meat or fish were being dried. At times, women smoked hides. As I sat listening to individuals tell of their recent experiences, the most senior elders would listen and then weave these events into occurrences of the past. I gradually came to appreciate the importance of verifying happenings within the dè, where individuals are encouraged to observe activities both when interacting with the unpredictable and while doing the routine. As I followed Tłįchǫ friends and colleagues along the trails—both mental and physical—they continually verified their own personal truths as well as what they had heard from others. As I walked stories through Tłįchǫ nèèk'e and through the academic literature found in libraries and archives, I was taken on new paths, where I experienced my own truth in relation to the anthropological question of what it means to be knowledgeable if you say you are "from the land."

In addressing the meaning of "becoming and being knowledgeable" among the Tłįchǫ, I considered several questions: What does it mean to be from the land? How does one become knowledgeable? How does one learn to see from a particular perspective? Who credits those who are knowledgeable? What responsibilities do those who are credited with being knowledgeable have toward others? How do ideas of what it means to be knowledgeable influence social organization within the community and the region? How is the past remembered?

An understanding of becoming and being knowledgeable among the Tłı̨chǫ has to take into account several dynamics. To become and be knowledgeable is a lifelong process that begins with gaining a perspective from oral narratives that originate within the dè. Key elements of the Tłı̨chǫ perspective include such things as knowing one's place and the place of others, interacting and maintaining harmonious relationships, and having and sharing knowledge.

The Tłı̨chǫ perspective is learned while listening to stories and reinforced through experience, providing personal knowledge and truths. Individuals can expect to have experiences without stories and still gain personal truth when those who have more knowledge weave the experience together with stories from the past. Stories are used to think with. The interplay between stories, knowledge, and truth through experience never ends. Human beings are never completely knowing; rather, they are in the never-ending process of becoming knowledgeable through experiencing life.

Figure 8.1. Rita Blackduck, Belinda Wetrade (child), Marie Zoe, Mònı Tsatchia, and Madelaine Drybone, 1993. Rita had asked Madelaine (88 years old) and Marie (90 years old) a question. They explained to her that they needed to go to someone older who had experienced the story. We all traveled to Wekweètì to visit Mònı, who at that time was said to be about 106 years old. She shared her story with Rita. (Photograph by the author)

The past is intimately woven to occurrences in the present to be verified in the future. Stories from the past are continually pulled through to the present as they are experienced and threaded to the future by being shared with descendants. The points of entry and exit are the same. All happenings and events are continuously being connected and reconnected. Knowledgeable individuals know Tłįchǫ temporal sequencing; they know occurrences that originated in the past continue in the present and future.

To consider what it means to be knowledgeable, we need to think about social relations and organization. Individuals are considered by others to be knowledgeable when they have skills and competence and can think for themselves while considering ways to contribute to their society as a whole. Some knowledgeable individuals are also seen to have intelligence or access to ʔįk'ǫ̀. Individuals need to use and enhance their knowledge and intelligence while interacting with human and other-than-human beings, or their ability will be lost.

Members of a community recognize knowledge and intelligence in others through what they have by doing tasks while dwelling within the dè, how they share, if they are willing to use and to be used, how they speak about experiences in their life, and if they know when and where stories originated. Everyone knows "a little bit," but no one is all knowing; for some tasks, it is best to be a follower. It is the responsibility of followers to know who is the authority on any given task. Followers base their decisions on their own experience as well as on the known competence of others. Both potential leaders and followers can experience considerable tension as they decide what tasks need to be done and who should be followed.

Personal integrity and the ability to think independently will deem any person knowledgeable and intelligent. If, however, the person lacks these qualities, he or she will be deemed incapable. All but a few humans are capable of being "an authority" on a given task. Individuals have a responsibility to follow the "right person" when undertaking a task that entails a group. Elders are often reluctant to follow persons younger than themselves, and tension may occur until the elders are convinced they are following a competent individual. Tension may also occur between individuals with similar degrees of knowledge or intelligence until followers identify what tasks need to be done and which individuals have the appropriate skills to accomplish them.

An important aspect of maintaining and achieving harmony is the negotiation of tension in social relations, which rarely allows any individual to become overly authoritarian. Those who are followed over extended periods of time are individuals who continue to be viewed as "authorities" on tasks that need doing and as individuals who care for others and are willing to share their skills and resources when required. Individuals who are viewed as wielding excessive power over others are usually avoided, whereas those who show respect and care for others and who provide direction to them are followed. The system is thus designed to limit authority over others.

Being knowledgeable affects other social relations besides the one in which followers choose leaders. All beings dwell within the dè, gaining competence, skill, and know-how as they travel trails and experience places; they follow and learn from those who know more. The ability that adults have is often credited to their elders, who guided their learning. Elders pass the oral narratives that carry their knowledge to those people who work alongside them and are therefore closest to them—usually members of their family. But narratives are told in a variety of situations for all to hear if they choose to listen. In the telling, they are speaking to future descendants as well as to the present company.

The Tłįchǫ perspective includes knowing how to maintain relations with both humans and other-than-human beings. Tłįchǫ stories and behavior distinguish between humans and other-than-human beings and show that other-than-human beings are considered the more intelligent. Because humans have limited access to ʔįk'ǫǫ̀, the onus is on them to learn about all entities through observing and experiencing. If one gains too much knowledge by becoming another being, however, one risks seeing only from the place where that being belongs and thus losing one's own perspective and spirit.

Individuals and groupings of humans and other-than-human beings rely on the place where they belong to learn how to think with stories so that they can become knowledgeable as they experience life within both their own place and the places of others. All beings have their own place and their own trails within the dè. There are no empty spaces; human and other-than-human beings perceive the dè from the place where they belong. The place from which they see gives them their unique knowledge and perspective. For example, Tłįchǫ nèèk'e within the dè is the basis of the Tłįchǫ Dene knowledge. At the points where places and trails meet, actions and relationships among human and other-than-human beings create and re-create taskscapes through space and time.

Individual persons carry with them oral narratives that travel along trails that eventually reach into the minds of their descendants. The basis of Tłįchǫ knowledge and the ability to think depend on remembering the oral narratives that prepare people for the present and future; they also depend on understanding the observations and experiences that occur in locations within their place as well as within the places of others.

The Tłįchǫ demonstrate respect for the dè and for all that dwell within it by observing, knowing, and sharing. They share observations during daily gatherings as well as during larger events that occur less frequently. One remembers others' observations and experiences through oral narratives so they can be drawn on when needed to think with. Observing for oneself while remembering what others have said allows one to verify observations made in the past.

The relationship between memory, time, temporality, and tasks is key to understanding a society's ideals associated with being knowledgeable, ways of knowing, and what knowledge constitutes. Fredrik Barth (2002) has challenged anthropologists to bring to bear a framework that stresses the centrality of knowledge. He argues that systems of knowledge have three aspects that can be distinguished analytically, even though they are interconnected. First, such systems contain a perspective of the world. Second, this perspective is communicated in at least one medium as a series of words, symbols, gestures, and actions. Third, traditions of knowledge are employed and transmitted within institutionalized social relations. I found that all three aspects are grounded in a fourth: the very process of knowledge formation or of becoming knowledgeable. This process provides the matrix in which we can understand how knowledge is acquired and shared, the particular perspectives it offers, and the social and institutional dynamics of its deployment.

My time among the Tłįchǫ has led to my questioning several anthropological issues associated with cultural change. Most of these issues relate to changing concepts. Listening to the elders and their stories clearly emphasizes that the term *dè* means much more than the English term *land* can convey, yet *dè* is currently translated as "land." "Tłįchǫ lands" is a concept defined in the Tłįchǫ Agreement, but "Tłįchǫ Land" is significantly smaller than "Tłįchǫ nèèk'e" (see map 3). *Wek'èezhìi*, the term for yet another concept found in the agreement, means "within here" and is used in the names of two co-management boards—"Wek'èezhìi Land and Water Board" and "Wek'èezhìi Renewable Resources Board." Both boards are mandated through the Tłįchǫ Agreement to make recommendations that will impact the dè. Wek'èezhìi seems a contradiction to the very ideology of Tłįchǫ perspective on thinking and understanding. For the Tłįchǫ with whom I work, becoming knowledgeable and understanding the dè are about reaching outward while learning more, not about limiting their thinking and understanding to a bounded area. Consistent with ideas of "land"

and "boundaries" in the agreement, the education curriculum conceptualizes these terms from a perspective accepted by the dominant society.

How, then, will the concept of "dè" change and become narrow with the continual use and reinforcement of Western concepts of land? Will the boundedness that is now associated with Tłįchǫ lands and the "wek'èezhìi" area affect ideas of belonging to a place? If, indeed, ideas of place change, will this change affect ideas of what it means to be knowledgeable? How will a concept—such as "wek'èezhìi"—that encourages people to think inward rather than outward impact on the importance of being open-minded, while experiencing and building on a personal and collective knowledge base? Will it impact personal autonomy and the process of selecting leaders who are "an authority" rather than "in authority"? Tłįchǫ will conceivably incorporate their perspective into new processes. The question, though, is, How will ideas of interconnectedness and belonging to place be maintained and potentially enhanced?

Given that grandparents and trails that connect stories and place are key to becoming knowledgeable, I am curious as to what impact daycare centers initiated and established throughout the mid- to late 1990s will have on the Tłįchǫ children. Rather than spending time with grandparents and other elders who guide their learning through telling them stories, children will be trained from the perspective of the dominant society. How will the Tłįchǫ use this institution to instill their perspective? Will canoe trips with elders in addition to discussions and storytelling at home be sufficient to maintain in the children the Tłįchǫ way of perceiving surroundings and the ability to continue thinking with stories?

Prior to the establishment of the daycare centers, land-claims legislation, and the current massive development projects, religious and government residential (boarding) schools separated children from the places where they belonged. We know the damage of residential schools to the knowledge system and to personal autonomy. How will the sense of place and ideas of how to become and be knowledgeable be affected as Tłįchǫ individuals working in mines learn knowledge associated with the mining industry? What will happen to the spirit that depends on the acquisition of knowledge through the place where Tłįchǫ belong while they are traveling outside Tłįchǫ nèèk'e to work? How will the loss of the Tłįchǫ system of acquiring knowledge impact the community's social relations?

At what point does a community take on the knowledge system and institutions of other societies? Is the point of cultural construction equal to the initial stage of using concepts from the dominant society? Will such a community start thinking only from a Cartesian perspective as they fully incorporate outside institutions as their own? Or will they maintain their perspective of the dè—the dwelling perspective as defined by Tim Ingold? In the case of the Tłįchǫ, will their own knowledge system continue to play a central role in establishing social and political relations in spite of all outside pressures?

It is interesting to note that John Mason (1946)—who was interested in documenting cultural traits in accordance with the Boasian approach and, like so many anthropologists during the early part of the twentieth century, wanted to pursue a salvage ethnography because they believed that the eventual loss of aboriginal culture was inevitable—probably stayed in the vicinity of Hàèlı̨ during the summer of 1914, where an "old village" was located. He worked almost exclusively with an old Slavey whom he referred to as a "medicine man." Mason documented information on leadership, band, and kin organization and hunting. When publishing his material thirty years later, he thought that with the intensification of colonialism and the associated extension of the railway, air travel, and the discovery of oil and radium, the Tłįchǫ had probably changed a great deal (1946, 3). In reading Mason's ethnography, however, I found many similarities between what he noted about the Tłįchǫ in the first decade of the 1900s and what I noticed and experienced in the 1990s, such as the emphasis on personal autonomy and the respect for and treatment of all that is part of the dè. Again I ask, what happens to knowledge systems deeply entrenched in dwelling as part of the dè?

Answers to this question and others concerning anthropological issues associated with cultural change are difficult to determine; as the elders have pointed out to me and others, we cannot know the future. But the elders also point out that the present and the past can inform the future. And in the present, I have shared—based on my perspective and experiences in listening, observing, walking—something of what I understand of "what it means to be knowledgeable if dwelling as part of dè." First, the past is continually pulled through to the present by the experiencing of truths that originated in the past and is threaded to the future by the sharing of stories with young people. It is like crocheting: all is continually connected because the points of entry and exit are the same. Second, human individuals are never completely knowing; rather, they are constantly becoming knowledgeable through experiencing life. This situation creates tension because personal autonomy is based on validating stories that are known. Third, all beings take different trails, each utilizing different places within the dè. By traveling their own trails and experiencing their own places, the knowledge gained by each group of beings and any entity differs from that of others. Fourth, all beings—humans and other-than-human beings—actively participate in a world of relations. Each being has a different perspective based on the place that being occupies. Tłįchǫ are encouraged to learn the perspectives of others through observation, interaction, dreams, and visions. The perspectives and knowledge of other beings need to be understood if Tłįchǫ are to have meaningful relations with them. And fifth, the understanding of knowing and being or of how to dwell continues to be taught—along with associated modes of thought and discourse—through telling stories and traveling places while observing all there is.

Figure 8.2. Drumming and drum dances in Behchokǫ̀, held on February 8, 2005, shortly after the third reading of Bill C-14, An Act to give effect to a land-claims and self-government agreement among the Tłįchǫ, the Government of the Northwest Territories, and the Government of Canada. (Photograph from Tessa Macintosh Photography)

Notes

Chapter 1

1. A similar translation appears in Chocolate et al. 2000, 2–6.

2. In the literature, also spelled "Yahmozah" and "Yamòzhah" or "Yamoria" if the author is referring to a Slavey story.

Chapter 2

1. Many people have come to use the term *whaèhdǫ̀* for any time period prior to the present, so I do the same.

2. David Smith makes similar observations regarding the Chipewyan (1998, 415–17), as do others who have worked with northern Dene, Cruikshank being most explicit in *Life Lived Like a Story* (1990b).

3. I have heard several different Tłı̨chǫ individuals—all older than thirty—use the word *intelligence* or *intelligent* to replace *ʔı̨k'ǫ̀* when speaking English. For example, "She is very intelligent; talk to her about finding your ring," or "She has a lot of intelligence; she must use it in the spring, or it will come back on her."

4. In their article "On Yamòzhah's Trail: Dogrib Sacred Sites and the Anthropology of Travel," Thomas Andrews, John B. Zoe, and Aaron Herter (1998) consider the archaeological and physiographic features of these places.

5. Yvon Csonka (1999) shows that many Chipewyan and Caribou Inuit had close relations with each other and formed partnerships between families, temporarily camping side by side, socializing and feasting together. Likewise, the Kitikmeot Inuit and Tłı̨chǫ often camped side by side, socializing and traveling together.

6. Although the Mǫwhìtłı̀ was submitted for consideration as a protected site, it has not as yet been included in the NWT Protected Areas Strategy reports. In the literature, "Mǫwhì" is spelled "Mowhi" and "Monwhi," and he is often referred to as "Murphy." I use the first spelling because that is the way the name appears in the Tłı̨chǫ Agreement.

7. *Goʔeh* is the term for both uncle and father-in-law.

8. See Blondin 1996 for a Sahtu Dene elder's perspective of ʔįk'ǫ̀ or "medicine power."

Chapter 3

1. ʔedèezhìì is in the process of becoming a protected area supported by both the Dehcho Dene and the Tłįchǫ. Its official name is now "Edéhzhíe," as it is known in South Slavey, the language of the Dehcho Dene.

2. In 2010 and 2011, the annual gathering was held in July rather than August.

3. Mason (1946, 16) in the early 1900s and Ryan (1995, 25) in the late 1980s stated that bears were hunted and snared during the berry season. Ryan described the rules associated with respecting the bear after it has been killed (1995, 31).

4. In the not so distant past, this season was the time when people were most likely to starve if during the winter caribou had been difficult to find and if the Tłįchǫ did not have sufficient food to tide them over because they were waiting for the return of the migratory birds; it is also the time when the ice breakup on the lakes makes it virtually impossible to put their fishing nets to the water.

5. Assemblies have a new structure, as defined in the Tłįchǫ Constitution. Assembly members must meet at least five times per year.

6. The homes in which I always saw visitors included those of Andrew Gon, Jean and Rosalie Wetrade, Romie Wetrade, Louis and Therese Zoe, and Joe and Rosa Mantla in Gamètì; Louis Whane and Alexie Arrowmaker in Wekweètì; Albert Wedawin in Whatì; Jimmy Martin, Moise Martin, Johnny Eyakfwo, Nick Black, and Joe Suzi Mackenzie in Behchokǫ̀. Louis Whane continued to be an active hunter until he was diagnosed with throat cancer in 2004. Alexie Arrowmaker, who was trained by Mǫwhì, has always been active in politics as well as hunting. Alexie's son Joseph was raised to be a harvester (hunter, trapper, fisher) by Louis Whane. Chief Charlie Nitsiza's son was similarly raised by his maternal grandfather, Jean Wetrade, to be a harvester. Both Joseph and Tony have difficulty hearing, yet are known for their knowledge of the dè, their skill as trappers, fishers, and hunters, and their willingness to share fish, caribou, and moose. Their abilities are due to their observational skills.

7. *Dǫ* is translated as "person, human, man, people" (Dogrib Divisional Board of Education 1996, 20).

Chapter 4

1. Tłįchǫ know the Coppermine River as "Deèzàatìdeè."

2. Old Fort Rae is known to the Tłįchǫ as "Nįhshìì."

3. They call themselves "Yellowknives," so I do the same.

4. Fort Enterprise is known to the Tłįchǫ as "Mǫ̀lakǫ̀k'è"; and Fort Franklin is now officially "Délįne," the traditional Slavey place-name.

5. Ryan says: "As people began to age, the elders were treated with respect and caring. No longer able to go on the traplines or to walk long distances, elders began to enjoy the benefits of having raised many children who now brought them meat and fish, fresh boughs, and wood" (1995, 48).

6. For an overview of the Hare Dene (North Slavey), see Hultkrantz 1972 and Savishinsky 1994.

7. Tuberculosis and diabetes continue to be prominent in Dene communities.

8. Thirty-five years later the caribou are once again in a low cycle. Since the caribou summit in Inuvik in January 2007, the government has encouraged restriction on hunting. On 23 February 2007, the Tłı̨chǫ grand chief, George Mackenzie, announced on CBC Radio that the Tłı̨chǫ would not restrict caribou hunting. On January 13, 2011, the GNWT and Tłı̨chǫ Government jointly advised the Wek'èezhìı that Tłı̨chǫ citizens could harvest 150 Bathurst caribou, and other Aboriginal people with rights to hunt in Moǫwhì Gogha Dè Nı̨ı̨tłèè could harveswt 150 animals (see www.wrrb.ca).

9. In 2009, Behchokǫ̀ once again voted to be a dry community.

10. This Order-in-Council was separate from those associated with the Mackenzie Valley oil-development regulations put in place in response to the Berger report.

11. See Selleck and Thompson 1997 for a discussion of the politics of mining and striking associated with this period of Yellowknife's history.

Chapter 5

1. George Blondin was a Slavey elder who married a Tłı̨chǫ woman and lived in Behchokǫ̀, writing and publishing several books (Blondin 1990, 1996, 1999) until his death on 12 October 2008.

Chapter 6

1. Jane Christian and Peter Gardner similarly found that the chief among the northern Slavey was supposed to represent the people to the government and to explain to his community the federal and territorial governments' positions on issues (1977, 91).

2. Henry Sharp, who worked among the Chipewyan, found that whether individual dogs are valued for their performance as part of a dog team or not, their inability to survive on their own demonstrates the absence of "power/knowledge" in them (2001, 88). They are not therefore respected in the same way wild animals are.

3. Christian and Gardner found that among the Slavey Dene electoral speeches are considered bragging (1977, 92).

4. See also Scott Rushforth's discussion of primary knowledge, authority, and productive tasks (1994, 337).

Chapter 7

1. See Helm and Gillespie 1981 for an explanation of the fighting between these two Dene groups.

2. See Helm 2000, 275–77, for a more in-depth discussion of the danger of blood and the need to handle it carefully.

3. Most burials are located in high areas with good drainage. In the tundra, eskers

are ideal because they consist of gravel left by retreating glaciers. Furthermore, both human and caribou beings use the eskers to walk on because they are higher and dryer than the surrounding muskeg and thus provide both relief from mosquitoes and a long-range view.

4. Romie Wetrade asked me not to use the name for this place but encouraged me to tell my story, because I had walked and experienced the place.

5. In her article on "walking and talking" among the Saulteaux, Linda Akan (1999) discusses the importance of not leaving young people alone with their thoughts. Saulteaux elders consider it their responsibility to live in a way that reflects the discourse they share with young people.

6. ?ek'atì is known as a place that always has lots of fish, and the caribou, more often than not, travel through the area in the spring and fall. ?ek'atì has been used by people from all Tłıchǫ regional bands, especially in times when resources were scarce in other areas. It is said to be "like a freezer."

7. Stephen Ellis (2002) similarly found oral histories, knowledge, and experience to be key to traditional monitoring methods among the Chipewyan.

Glossary of Tłįchǫ Terms and Place-Names

An approximation of the word *Tłįchǫ* in English orthography would be *Klinchon*. All place-names and terms listed here follow the pronunciation as directed by the *Tłįchǫ* Regional Elders Committee. Unless otherwise stated, the place-names are listed in Dogrib Treaty 11 Council 2002, distributed by the West Kitikmeot Slave Study Society; and other terms are listed in the *Tłįchǫ* dictionary found on the *Tłįchǫ* Web site at http://www.tlicho.ling.uvic.ca.

?edaàtsotì "Lake of Big Crossing." An important caribou crossing that is known in English as "Artillery Lake."

?edèezhìì "Horn Mountain." Officially known as "Horn Plateau"; Slavey name is "Edéhzhíe." As of March 2006, a candidate as a protected area under the NWT Protected Area Strategy; in that literature, referred to under Slavey name.

?ek'aàwıdeè An important male "trading boss" who represented trappers of several local bands within his own region in the late nineteenth century. He was given the authority to trade because his knowledge of the trading system and of Kweèt'ıì was seen to be extensive. Mǫwhì was being trained to be a k'aàwı by his uncle, the renowned ?ek'aàwıdeè.

?ek'adìì "Island of ?ek'atì." An important caribou water crossing, which is now the location of a pit mine belonging to Diavik Diamond Mines, Inc.

?ek'atì "Fat Lake." Officially known as "Lac de Gras."

ʔek'atìtata   Tata is a large grassy area found in the tundra. It is usually surrounded by two or more lakes and is a favored spot for caribou. Area south of ʔek'atì.

ʔewaànıt'ııtì   "'Lake of a Stretch of Sand.'" Officially known as "Courageous Lake."

ʔezǫdzìtì   "Spirit Lake." Officially known as "Rivière Grandin."

ʔıdaàtı̨lı   "Up Ahead Trail." Traditionally an important travel route between Sahtì and Tıdeè because all trails are connected to it.

ʔı̨hdaak'ètì   "Jackfish Lake." Officially known as "Marian Lake."

ʔı̨k'ǫǫ̀   Often referred to as "medicine power" in the literature and during official translating events; however, when middle-aged Tłı̨chǫ are speaking English, they often use the term *intelligence*.

ʔı̨ts'èetì   "Moose Lake." Officially known as "Hottah Lake."

ʔǫhtsı̨k'e   "On Packsack." Known always to have fish and caribou in the area. Located at the headwaters of the Deèzàatìdeè (Coppermine River).

Beʔaıtì   Officially known as "Winter Lake."

Behchokǫ̀   "Place of Mbehcho." Officially changed from "Rae-Edzo" on 4 August 2005.

dè   Concept includes everything that is associated with "land, ground, dirt, earth" and with whom Tłı̨chǫ have a relationship that is responsive to their attention, action, and behavior.

Deèzàatì   Officially known as "Point Lake."

Deèzàatìdeè   Officially known as "Coppermine River."

dǫ   Term is usually translated as "person, human, man, people."

Gamètì   "Gamè's Lake." Officially changed from "Rae Lakes" on 4 August 2005. Northwest Territories Official Community Names (2006) translates the name as "rabbit-net lake," but elders explain "Gamè" as a person's name. The list is available at http://pwnhc.learnnet.nt.ca/programs/downloads/OfficialCommunityNames.pdf.

Gots'ǫkàtì   "Cloudberry Lake." Officially known as "Mesa Lake"; the place where Edzo and Akaitcho made peace in the early 1800s.

Hàèlı̨ı̨   "Outflow." Mouth of the Marian River. An old village is located here, where families have cabins.

hozìi   Translated as "barren ground or tundra," but the concept is more closely linked to "beneath winter."

K'aàtì   "Wait! Lake." Officially known as "Indin Lake."

k'aàwı   A Tłı̨chǫ trading boss. Defined in *Tłı̨chǫ Yatıì Enı̨htł'e: A Dogrib Dictionary* (Dogrib Divisional Board of Education 1996) as "store clerk, middleman between trader and people." It has also come to mean "king in cards" and "wealthy person."

k'àowo A boss, leader, ruler, foreman. There currently are community, hunting, camp, and hunting k'àowo as well as highway-construction k'àowo and forestry k'àowo. The Tłı̨chǫ dictionary indicates that the term is also used when referring to the Lord.

k'àowodeè A leader whose following is larger than a local band and whose knowledge is extensive. Mǫwhì, who signed Treaty 11, is referred to as a k'àowodeè. Refers to an important or great leader who is both knowledgeable and has the capacity to care for others and oversee tasks that affect regional groups of people.

K'ı̨ahkw'àı̨kaà "Dried Birch Bark Narrows." Place named for the abundance of birch trees there.

Kǫk'èetì "Empty Campsite Lake." The word *kǫk'è* refers to an empty campsite. Officially known as "Contwoyto Lake."

Kǫmǫ̀laa "There Are Houses Around." The name refers to the graves there and is the abbreviated form of *kǫ mǫ̀ whelaa,* an old term for gravesites used because of the fences surrounding them. The elders say that before their time there was a cross there and that it is the place where the Tłı̨chǫ first met a priest.

Kweedoò "Rock Blood." A small, steep hill where Yamǫ̀ǫzaa's grandfather was killed.

Kweèt'ı̨ı̨ The word for a person of English-speaking descent and translated quickly as "white people."

Kwetı̨ı̨ʔàa "Rock Extends into the Water." Officially known as "Rayrock Mine Ltd." An abandoned uranium mine from the mid-1950s. Kwetı̨ı̨ʔàa was formerly a favored hunting lookout.

Łutselk'e A Chipewyan community named "Place of Łútsël" (referring to a small type of fish). Official name changed from "Snowdrift" on 1 July 1992.

masì Can mean to "be thankful" or to "be well" and is also used as an expression for greeting people as well as for saying good-bye.

Mǫ̀la Refers to individuals with French background and used to refer to Métis. In discussions of the term, Tłı̨chǫ will often explain that the Sahtu Dene use the term for "white people" in general.

Mǫ̀lakǫk'è "Frenchman's Empty Camp." Sir John Franklin had cabins here. Officially known as "Fort Enterprise."

Mǫwhì Gogha Dè Nı̨ı̨tł'èè The territory acquired by Tłı̨chǫ as described by Mǫwhì to the Treaty Commission in 1921.

Mǫwhìtłı Mǫwhì's Trail.

Nàdenìɂàatì Officially known as "Exeter Lake." This is one of the areas where foxes were trapped on the tundra.

nàowo Translated as "laws, rules, agreements, knowledge, principles, and way of life." When the possessive form is used, it is spelled *nàowoò*, as in *gonàowoò*, "our laws" or "our knowledge."

Nıdzııkaà "(Something) Narrows." Old village located here.

Nıhshìı "(Something) Mountain." Elders were not sure of what the first part of this word means. It is the location of (Old) Fort Rae; original location of Hudson's Bay Trading Post.

Sahtì "Bear Lake." Officially known as "Great Bear Lake."

Semìtì "(Something) Net Lake." Officially known as "Faber Lake."

Tıdeè "Great Lake." Officially known as "Great Slave Lake."

Tłıchǫ nèèk'e "The place where you expect to find Tłıchǫ within the dè." This term comes up again and again when elders explain the place they call home.

Ts'eèhgootì "Forked Lake." Officially known as "Aylmer Lake."

Ts'ıɂehdaà "Living White Spruce Tree." Significant location because it is where women, children, and elders were left while trappers went on the tundra in past winters.

Tułıt'a "Where the Water Meets." The name is Slavey. Officially changed from "Fort Norman" on 1 January 1996. English spelling "Tulita."

Wekweètì "Lake of His Rock." Officially known as "Roundrock Lake." The Tłıchǫ place-name identifies a long lake whose southerly and northerly ends are given the two names in English: "Roundrock Lake" and "Winter Lake." The community of Wekweètì was previously called "Snare Lake." The official name changed to "Wekweètì" on 4 August 2005. Officially "Wekweti" for a short period prior to 2005.

Wetł'aezǫtì "Spirit Lake." Officially known as "Rebesca Lake." Many spirits reside here. Boats avoid the area by traveling along either the southwest or north shore. Spirits are associated with whirlpools and northern lights.

Whatì "Marten Lake."

Yabàahtì "Lake of the Edge of the Sky." Officially known as "Yamba Lake."

yahbahti A regional leader with powerful ɂık'ǫò. Edzo is discussed as the last Tłı̨chǫ yahbahti. Like any person, they are capable of both positive and negative acts depending on how they use their ʔı̨k'ǫ̀. Yahbahti usually had k'àowo assist them.

Yamǫ̀ǫzaa Along with his brother, Yamǫǫ̀gaà, is acknowledged for teaching the laws governing the placement and relationships of all human beings and other-than-human beings in the world.

References

Abel, Kerry. 1993. *Drum Songs: Glimpses of Dene History*. Montreal: McGill-Queen's University Press.

Akan, Linda. 1999. "Pimosatamowin Sikaw Kakeequaywin: Walking and Talking." *Canadian Journal of Native Education* 23 (1): 16–39.

Andrews, Thomas D. 1990. *Yamoria's Arrows: Stories, Place Names, and the Land in Dene Oral Tradition*. Yellowknife, Canada: Northern Parks Establishment Office.

———. 2004. "'The Land Is Like a Book': Cultural Landscape Management in the Northwest Territories, Canada." In *Northern Ethnographic Landscapes: Perspectives from Circumpolar Nations*, edited by Igor Krupnik, Rachel Mason, and Tonia Horton, 301–22. Washington, DC: Arctic Studies Center, National Museum of Natural History, Smithsonian Institution in collaboration with the National Park Service.

Andrews, Thomas D., and John B. Zoe. 1997. "The *Idaà* Trail: Archaeology and the Dogrib Cultural Landscape, Northwest Territories, Canada." In *At a Crossroads: Archaeology and First Peoples in Canada*, edited by George P. Nicholas and Thomas D. Andrews, 160–77. Burnaby, Canada: Archaeology Press, Simon Fraser University.

Andrews, Thomas D., John B. Zoe, and Aaron Herter. 1998. "On Yamòzhah's Trail: Dogrib Sacred Sites and the Anthropology of Travel." In *Sacred Lands: Aboriginal World Views, Claims, and Conflicts*, edited by Jill Oakes, Rick Riewe, Kathi Kinew, and Elaine Maloney, 305–20. Edmonton: Canadian Circumpolar Institute.

Asch, Michael I. 1984. *Home and Native Land*. Scarborough: Nelson Canada.

———. 1988. *Kinship and the Drum Dance in a Northern Dene Community*. Edmonton, Canada: Boreal Institute for Northern Studies.

———. ed. 1997. *Aboriginal and Treaty Rights in Canada: Essays on Law, Equality, and Respect for Differences*. Vancouver: University of British Columbia Press.

Asch, Michael I., Thomas D. Andrews, and Sheree Smith. 1986. "The Dene Mapping Project on Land Use and Occupancy: An Introduction." In *Anthropology in Praxis*, edited by Philip Spaulding, 36–43. Calgary: University of Calgary Press.

Asch, Michael I., and Norman Zlotkin. 1997. "Affirming Aboriginal Title: A New Basis for Comprehensive Claims Negotiations." In *Aboriginal and Treaty Rights in*

Canada: Essays on Law, Equality, and Respect for Differences, edited by Michael Asch, 208–29. Vancouver: University of British Columbia Press.

Atwood, Margaret E. 1995. Strange Things: The Malevolent North in Canadian Literature. Oxford: Clarendon Press.

Barnaby, Joanne. 2004. "Epilogue." In As Long as This Land Shall Last: A History of Treaty 8 and Treaty 11, 1870–1939, 2nd ed., written and compiled by René Fumoleau, 522–35. Calgary: University of Calgary Press.

Barnard, Alan. 2002. "The Foraging Mode of Thought." In Self- and Other-Images of Hunter-Gatherers: Papers Presented at the Eighth International Conference on Hunting and Gathering Societies (CHAGS8), National Museum of Ethnology, Osaka, October 1998, edited by Henry Stewart, Alan Barnard, and Keiichi Omura, 5–24. Osaka, Japan: National Museum of Ethnology.

Barth, Fredrik. 2002. "An Anthropology of Knowledge." Current Anthropology 43 (1): 1–18.

Basso, Keith H. 1979. Portraits of "the Whiteman": Linguistic Play and Cultural Symbols among the Western Apache. Cambridge: Cambridge University Press.

——. 1984a. "Stalking with Stories: Names, Places, and Moral Narratives among the Western Apache." In Text, Play, and Story: The Construction and Reconstruction of Self and Society, edited by Edward Bruner, 19–55. Washington, DC: American Ethnological Society.

——. 1984b. "Western Apache Place-Name Hierarchies." In Naming Systems, edited by Elisabeth Tooker, 78–94. Washington, DC: American Ethnological Society.

——. 1988. "Speaking with Names: Language and Landscape among the Western Apache." Cultural Anthropology 3:99–130.

——. 1996. Wisdom Sits in Places: Landscape and Language among the Western Apache. Albuquerque: University of New Mexico Press.

Berger, Thomas R. 1977. Northern Frontier, Northern Homeland: The Report of the Mackenzie Valley Pipeline Inquiry. Toronto: James Lorimer.

Berkes, Fikret. 2000. "Rediscovery of Traditional Ecological Knowledge as Adaptive Management." Ecological Applications 10 (5): 1251–62.

Blondin, George. 1990. When the World Was New: Stories of the Sahtú Dene. Yellowknife, Canada: Outcrop.

——. 1996. Medicine Power. Hay River, Canada: Dene Cultural Institute.

——. 1999. Yamoria the Lawmaker: Stories of the Dene. Edmonton, Canada: NuWest Press.

Breynat, Bishop Gabriel. 2004. "Appendix XI: Canada's Blackest Blot." In As Long as This Land Shall Last: A History of Treaty 8 and Treaty 11, 1870–1939, 2nd ed., written and compiled by Rene Fumoleau, 494–507. Calgary: University of Calgary Press and the Arctic Institute of North America.

Brody, Hugh. 1981. Maps and Dreams. Vancouver: Douglas & McIntyre Ltd.

Casey, Edward. 1996. "How to Get from Space to Place in a Fairly Short Stretch of Time: Phenomenological Prolegomena." In Senses of Place, edited by Steven Feld and Keith Basso, 13–52. Santa Fe: School of American Research Press.

Chocolate, Georgina, Allice Legat, Gabrielle Mackenzie-Scott, Dawn Sprecher, and Sally A. Zoe. 2000. A Tåîchô Perspective on Biodiversity. Yellowknife, Canada: BHP Diamonds.

Christian, Jane, and Peter M. Gardner. 1977. The Individual in Northern Dene Thought and Communication: A Study in Sharing and Diversity. Ottawa: National Museum of Man.

Coulthard, Glen S. 2003. "Facing the Challenge of Freedom: Dene Nationalism and the Politics of Cultural Recognition." Master's thesis, University of Victoria.

Croll, Elisabeth, and David Parkin. 1992. "Cultural Understandings of the Environment." In *Bush Base, Forest Farm: Culture, Environment, and Development,* edited by Elisabeth Croll and David Parkin, 11–36. London: Routledge.

Cruikshank, Julie. 1983. *The Stolen Woman: Female Journeys in Tagish and Tutchone Narrative.* Ottawa: National Museum of Canada.

——. 1989. "Oral Traditions and Written Accounts: An Incident from the Klondike Gold Rush." *Culture* 9 (2): 25–34.

——. 1990a. "Getting the Words Right: Perspectives on Naming and Places in Athapaskan Oral History." *Arctic Anthropology* 27:52–65.

——. 1990b. *Live Lived Like a Story: Life Stories of Three Yukon Native Elders.* Lincoln: University of Nebraska Press.

——. 1998. *The Social Life of Stories: Narrative and Knowledge in the Yukon Territories.* Vancouver: University of British Columbia Press.

——. 2001. "Glaciers and Climate Change: Perspectives from Oral Tradition." *Arctic* 54 (4): 377–93.

Csonka, Yvon. 1999. "A Stereotype Further Dispelled: Inuit–Dene Relations West of Hudson Bay, 1920–1956." *Inuit Studies* 23 (1–2): 117–44.

Darnell, Regna. 1974. "Correlates of Cree Narrative Performance." In *Explorations in the Ethnography of Speaking,* edited by Richard Bauman and Joel Sherzer, 315–36. Cambridge: Cambridge University Press.

De Laguna, Frederica. 1995. *Tales from the Dena: Indian Stories from the Tanana, Koyukuk, & Yukon Rivers.* Seattle: University of Washington Press.

DeLancey, Debbie. 1984. "Research in Northern and Remote Areas—the Native Experience." *Research in Remote Areas* 4:1–11.

——. 1985. "Trapping and the Aboriginal Economy." *Information North* (Winter): 5–12.

Dene Cultural Institute. 1996. *We Know and Love Tłįchǫ Ndè: Comments and Concerns from the Dechįlaat'įį Elders to the Environment Assessment Review Panel.* Behchokǫ̀, Canada: Dogrib Treaty 11 Council.

Dene Nation. 1977. "Dene Declaration." In *Dene Nation: The Colony Within,* edited by Mel Watkins, 2–4. Toronto: University of Toronto Press.

——. 1984. *Denendeh: A Dene Celebration.* Yellowknife, Canada: Dene Nation.

Dickerson, Mark O. 1992. *Whose North? Political Change, Political Development, and Self-Government in the Northwest Territories.* Vancouver: University of British Columbia Press and Arctic Institute of North America.

Dilley, Roy. 1999. *The Problem of Context.* Oxford: Berghahn Books.

Dogrib Divisional Board of Education. 1996. *Tłįchǫ Yatìì Enįhtł'e: A Dogrib Dictionary.* Rae-Edzo, Canada: Dogrib Divisional Board of Education.

Dogrib Treaty 11 Council. 2002. *Dogrib Knowledge on Placenames, Caribou, and Habitat.* Yellowknife, Canada: West Kitikmeot Slave Study Society. The reports are available at http://www.enr.gov.nt.ca/_live/pages/wpPages/WKSS.

Ellis, Stephen. 2002. *Traditional Knowledge in the Kache Tué Study Region: Phase Three—Towards a Comprehensive Environmental Monitoring Program in the Kakinene Region.* Yellowknife, Canada: West Kitikmeot Slave Study Society.

"Empire Builders." 1920. *The Beaver: A Journal of Progress* 1 (October): 20.

Franklin, Sir John. 1823. *Narrative of a Journey to the Shores of the Polar Sea, in the Years 1819, 20, 21, and 22.* London: John Murray.

———. 1828. *Narrative of a Second Expedition to the Shores of the Polar Sea, in the Years 1825, 1826, and 1827*. London: John Murray.

Freire, Paulo. 1972. *Pedagogy of the Oppressed*. New York: Penguin Books.

Fumoleau, René. 2004. *As Long as This Land Shall Last: A History of Treaty 8 and Treat 11*. Calgary: University of Calgary Press and Arctic Institute of North America.

Gamble, Donald J. 1986. "Crushing of Cultures: Western Applied Science in Northern Societies." *Arctic* 36 (1): 20–23.

Gardner, Peter M. n.d. "Rethinking Foragers' Handling of Environmental and Subsistence Knowledge." Available at http://www.abdn.ac.uk/chags9/1gardner1.htm.

Gillespie, Beryl G. 1970. "Yellowknives: Quo Iverunt?" In *Proceedings of the 1970 Annual Spring Meeting of the American Ethnological Society*, 61–70. [Arlington, VA: American Ethnological Society, 1970.] Copy in Dr. Joan Ryan's files.

———. 1981. "Yellowknife." In *Subarctic*, vol. 6 of *Handbook of North American Indians*, edited by June Helm, 285–320. Washington, DC: Smithsonian Institution.

Goulet, Jean-Guy A. 1982. "Religious Dualism among Athapaskan Catholics." *Canadian Journal of Anthropology* 3 (1): 1–18.

———. 1998. *Ways of Knowing: Experience, Knowledge, and Power among the Dene Tha*. Vancouver: University of British Columbia Press.

———. 2000. "Visions of Conflict, Conflicts of Vision among Contemporary Dene Tha." In *Hunters and Gatherers in the Modern World: Conflict, Resistance, and Self-Determination*, edited by Peter P. Schweitzer, Megan Biesele, and Robert K. Hitchcock, 55–76. New York: Berghahn Books.

Hallowell, A. I. 1960. "Ojibwa Ontology, Behaviour, and Worldview." In *Culture in History: Essays in Honor of Paul Radin*, edited by Stanley Diamond, 19–52. New York: Columbia University Press.

———. 1967. *Culture and Experience*. New York: Schocken Books.

Hanks, Christopher C. 1996. *The 1825–26 Wintering Place of Sir John Franklin's Second Expedition: A Dene Perspective*. Ottawa: Historic Sites and Monuments Board of Canada.

———. 1997. "Ancient Knowledge of Ancient Sites: Tracing Dene Identity from the Late Pleistocene and Holocene." In *At a Crossroads: Archaeology and First Peoples in Canada*, edited by George P. Nicholas and Thomas D. Andrews, 178–89. Burnaby, Canada: Archaeology Press.

Hanks, Christopher C., and David L. Pokotylo. 1989. "The Mackenzie Basin: An Alternative Approach to Dene and Metis Archaeology." *Arctic* 42 (2): 139–47.

Hanks, Christopher C., and Barbara Winters. 1983. "Dene Names as an Organizing Principle in Ethno-Archaeological Research." *Muskox* 33:49–55.

———. 1986. "Local Knowledge and Ethno-Archaeology: An Approach to Dene Settlement Systems." *Current Anthropology* 27 (3): 272–75.

Hearne, Samuel. 1795. *A Journey from Prince of Wales's Fort in Hudson's Bay, to the Northern Ocean: Undertaken by Order of the Hudson's Bay Company, for the Discovery of Copper Mines, a North West Passage. In the Years 1769, 1770, 1771, and 1772*. London: A. Strahan and T. Cadell.

Helm, June. 1961. *The Lynx Point People: The Dynamics of a Northern Athapaskan Band*. Ottawa: Queen's Printer.

———. 1965. "Bilaterality in the Socio-Territorial Organization of the Arctic Drainage Dene." *Ethnology: An International Journal of Cultural and Social Anthropology* 4:361–85.

———. 1968. "The Nature of Dogrib Socioterritorial Groups." In *Man the Hunter*, edited by Richard B. Lee and Irvin DeVore, 118–25. Chicago: Aldine.

———. 1979. "Long-Term Research among the Dogrib and Other Dene." In *Long-Term Field Research in Social Anthropology*, edited by George M. Foster, Thayer Scudder, Elizabeth Colson, and Robert V. Kemper, 145–63. New York: Academic Press.

———. 1981a. "Dogrib." In *Subarctic*, vol. 6 of *Handbook of North American Indians*, edited by June Helm, 291–309. Washington, DC: Smithsonian Institution.

———. 1981b. "Indian Dependency and Indian Self-Determination: Problems and Paradoxes in Canada's Northwest Territories." In *Political Organization of Native North Americans*, edited by Ernest L. Schusky, 215–42. Washington, DC: Smithsonian Institution.

———. 1994. *Prophecy and Power among the Dogrib Indians*. Lincoln: University of Nebraska Press.

———. 2000. *The People of Denendeh: Ethnohistory of the Indians of Canada's Northwest Territories*. Montreal: McGill-Queen's University Press.

Helm, June, and David Damas. 1963. "The Contact-Traditional All-Native Community of the Canadian North: The Upper Mackenzie 'Bush' Athapaskans and the Igluligmiut." *Anthropologica* 5 (1): 9–21.

Helm, June, and Beryl Gillespie. 1981. "Dogrib Oral Tradition as History: War and Peace in the 1820's." *Journal of Anthropological Research* 37 (1): 8–27.

Helm, June, and Nancy O. Lurie. 1961. *The Subsistence Economy of the Dogrib Indians of Lac La Martre in the Mackenzie District of the Northwest Territories*. Ottawa: Department of Northern Affairs and National Resources.

Hendry, Joy. 2000. *The Orient Strikes Back: A Global View of Cultural Display*. Oxford: Berg.

Henriksen, Georg. 1973. *Hunters in the Barrens: The Naskapi on the Edge of the White Man's World*. St. John's, Canada: Memorial University of Newfoundland.

Hultkrantz, Ake. 1972. "The Hare Indians: Notes on Their Traditional Culture and Religion Past and Present." *Ethnos* 1 (4): 113–52.

Indian and Northern Affairs Canada. 2006. "Agreements." 20 November. Available at http://www.ainc-inac.gc.ca/pr/agr/index_e.html#ComprehensiveClaimsAgreement.

Ingold, Tim. 2000. *The Perception of the Environment: Essays in Livelihood, Dwelling, and Skill*. London: Routledge.

———. 2005. "Time, Memory, and Property." In *Property and Equality: Ritualisation, Sharing, Egalitarianism*, edited by Thomas Widlok and Wolde G. Tadesse, 165–75. Oxford: Berghahn Books.

Ingold, Tim, and Terhi Kurttila. 2000. "Perceiving the Environment in Finnish Lapland." *Body & Society* 6 (3–4): 183–96.

Janes, Robert R. 1983. *Archaeological Ethnography among Mackenzie Basin Dene, Canada*. Arctic Institute of North America Technical Paper no. 28. Calgary: Arctic Institute of North America.

———. 1991. *Preserving Diversity: Ethno-Archaeological Perspectives on Culture Change in the Western Canadian Subarctic*. New York: Garland.

Jarvenpa, Robert. 1998. *Northern Passage: Ethnography and Apprenticeship among the Subarctic Dene*. Prospect Heights, IL: Waveland Press.

Johnson, Martha. 1992. "Documenting Dene Traditional Environmental Knowledge." *Akwe: Kon Journal* 9 (2): 72–79.

Johnson, Martha, and Robert A. Ruttan. 1993. *Traditional Dene Environmental Knowledge*. Hay River, Canada: Dene Cultural Institute.

Krech, Shepard, III. 1984. "The Trade of the Slavey and Dogrib at Fort Simpson in the Early Nineteenth Century." In *The Subarctic Fur Trade*, edited by Shepard Krech III, 99–146. Vancouver: University of British Columbia Press.

Kritsch, Ingrid D., and Alestine M. Andre. 1997. "Gwich'in Traditional Knowledge and Heritage Studies in the Gwich'in Settlement Area." In *At a Crossroads: Archaeology and First People in Canada*, edited by George P. Nicholas and Thomas D. Andrews, 125–44. Burnaby, Canada: Archaeology Press.

Lave, Jean. 1990. "The Culture of Acquisition and the Practice of Understanding." In *Cultural Psychology: Essays on Comparative Human Development*, edited by James W. Stigler, Richard A. Shweder, and Gilbert Herdt, 309–27. Cambridge: Cambridge University Press.

Lave, Jean, and Etienne Wenger. 1991. *Situated Learning: Legitimate Peripheral Participation*. Cambridge: Cambridge University Press.

Legat, Allice, Madelaine Chocolate, Celina Football, and Sally A. Zoe. 1995. "Traditional Methods Used by the Dogrib to Harvest Caribou." Unpublished manuscript.

Legat, Allice, Joan Ryan, Madelaine Chocolate, Marie A. Rabesca, and Sally A. Zoe, comps. 1997. *"The Trees All Changed to Wood": A Report Prepared by Dogrib Renewable Resources Committee, Dogrib Treaty 11 Council for the Arctic Environmental Strategy, DIAND*. Yellowknife, Canada: Arctic Environmental Strategy, Department of Indian Affairs and Northern Development.

Legat, Allice, and Sally A. Zoe. 2000. "Tłįchǫ Traditional Governance, Gamètì NWT." Unpublished manuscript.

Lurie, Nancy O. 2000. "Effects of the Highway, Rae 1967." In *The People of the Denendeh: Ethnohistory of the Indians of Canada's Northwest Territories*, compiled by June Helm, 95–100. Montreal: McGill-Queen's University Press.

Mackenzie, Sir Alexander. 1970. *The Journals and Letters of Sir Alexander Mackenzie*. Edited by W. K. Lamb. Cambridge: University of Cambridge Press.

Mackenzie-Scott, Gabrielle. 2001. "Mining and Caribou Distribution within the Monfwi Territory: A Historical Look." In *Caribou Migration and the State of Their Habitat*, by Allice Legat, Georgina Chocolate, Bobby Gon, Sally A. Zoe, and Madelaine Chocolate, appendix V. Yellowknife, Canada: West Kitikmeot Slave Study Society.

MacNeish, June H. 1956. "Leadership among the Northeastern Athabascans." *Anthropologica* 2:131–63.

Mason, John A. 1946. *Notes on the Indians of the Great Slave Lake Area*. New Haven, CT: Yale University Press.

McDonnell, Roger. 1984. "Symbolic Orientations and Systematic Turmoil: Centering on the Kaska Symbol of *Dene*." *Canadian Journal of Anthropology* 4:39–56.

McTaggart, Robin, ed. 1997. *Participatory Action Research: International Contexts and Consequences*. Albany: State University of New York Press.

Moore, Pat, and Angela Wheelock. 1990a. "Introduction to the Dene Prophets." In *Wolverine Myths and Visions: Dene Traditions from Northern Alberta*, edited by Pat Moore and Angela Wheelock, 59–62. Edmonton, Canada: University of Alberta Press.

Moore, Pat, and Angela Wheelock, eds. 1990b. *Wolverine Myths and Visions: Dene Traditions from Northern Alberta*. Edmonton, Canada: University of Alberta Press.

Nelson, Richard K. 1983. *Make Prayers to the Raven: A Koyukon View of the Northern Forest*. Chicago: University of Chicago Press.

Nicholas, George P., and Thomas D. Andrews, eds. 1997. *At a Crossroads: Archaeology and First Peoples in Canada*. Burnaby, Canada: Archaeology Press.

Parks Canada. 2004. "Prince of Wales Fort National Historic Site of Canada." 10 August. Available at http://www.pc.gc.ca/lhn-nhs/mb/prince/natcul/natcul1_e.asp.

Payne, Michael. 1979. "'The Healthiest Part in the Known World': Prince of Wales's Fort as Fur Trade Post and Community in the Eighteenth Century." *MHS Transactions Series* 3 (35): 1978–79. Available at http:www.mhs.mb.ca/docs/transactions/3/princeofwalesfort.shtml.

Petitot, Emile. 1976. *The Book of Dene: Containing the Traditions and Beliefs of Chipewyan, Dogrib, Slavey, and Loucheux Peoples*. Yellowknife, Canada: Department of Education, Government of the Northwest Territories.

Richardson, Sir John. 1851. *Arctic Searching Expedition: A Journal of a Boat-Voyage Through Rupert's Land and the Arctic Sea, in Search of the Discovery Ships under Command of Sir John Franklin*. London: Longman, Brown, Green, and Longmans.

Ridington, Robin. 1988. *Trail to Heaven: Knowledge and Narrative in a Northern Native Community*. Iowa City: University of Iowa Press.

———. 1990. *Little Bit Know Something: Stories in a Language of Anthropology*. Iowa City: University of Iowa Press.

———. 2002. "When You Sing It Now, Just Like New: Re-Creation in Native American Narrative Tradition." In *Self- and Other-Images of Hunter-Gatherers: Papers Presented at the Eighth International Conference on Hunting and Gathering Societies (CHAGS8), National Museum of Ethnology, Osaka, October 1998*, edited by Henry Steward, Alan Barnard, and Keiichi Omura, 113–31. Osaka, Japan: National Museum of Ethnology.

Rosaldo, Renato. 1980. *Ilongot Headhunting, 1833–1974*. Stanford, CA: Stanford University Press.

Rushforth, Scott. 1992. "The Legitimation of Beliefs in a Hunter-Gatherer Society: Bearlake Athapaskan Knowledge and Authority." *American Ethnologist* 19 (3): 483–500.

———. 1994. "Political Resistance in a Contemporary Hunter-Gatherer Society: More about Bearlake Athapaskan Knowledge and Authority." *American Ethnologist* 21 (2): 335–52.

Russell, Frank. 1898. *Explorations in the Far North: Being the Report of an Expedition under the Auspices of the University of Iowa during the Years of 1892, '93, and '94*. Iowa City: University of Iowa Press.

Ryan, Joan. 1995. *Doing Things the Right Way*. Calgary: University of Calgary Press.

Ryan, Joan, and Martha Johnson. 1994. *Traditional Dene Medicine*. Hay River, Canada: Dene Cultural Institute.

Ryan, Joan, and Michael Robinson. 1990. "Implementing Participatory Action Research in the Canadian North: A Case Study of the Gwich'in Language and Cultural Project." *Culture* 10 (2): 57–71.

Sandlos, John. 2003. "Landscaping Desire: Poetics, Politics in the Early Biological Surveys of the Canadian North." *Space & Culture* 6 (4): 394–414.

Sarris, Greg. 1993. *Keeping Slug Woman Alive*. Berkeley and Los Angeles: University of California Press.

Savishinsky, Joel S. 1994. *The Trail of the Hare: Environment and Stress in a Sub-Arctic Community.* 2nd ed. Langhorne, PA: Gordon and Breach Science.

Savoie, Donat, ed. 2001. *Land Occupancy by the Amerindians of the Canadian Northwest in the 19th Century, as Reported by Émile Petitot.* Ottawa: CCI Press.

Scollon, Ronald, and Suzanne B. Scollon. 1979. *Linguistic Convergence: Ethnography of Speaking at Fort Chipewyan, Alberta.* New York: Academic Press.

Scott, Patrick. 2007. *Stories Told: Stories and Images of the Berger Inquiry.* Yellowknife, Canada: Edzo Institute.

Selleck, Lee, and Francis Thompson. 1997. *Dying for Gold: The True Story of the Giant Mine Murders.* Toronto: Harper Collins.

Sharp, Henry S. 2001. *Loon: Memory, Meaning, and Reality in a Northern Dene Community.* Lincoln: University of Nebraska Press.

Slobodin, Richard. 1960. "Some Social Functions of Kutchin Anxiety." *American Anthropologist* 62 (1): 122–33.

———. 1962. *Band Organization of the Peel River Kitchen.* Ottawa: Department of Northern Affairs and National Resources.

———. 1969. "Leadership and Participation in a Kutchin Trapping Party." In *Contributions to Anthropology: Band Societies,* edited by David Damas, 56–92. Ottawa: National Museums of Canada.

Smith, David M. 1973. *Inkonze: Magico-Religious Beliefs of Contract-Traditional Chipewyan Trading at Fort Resolution, NWT, Canada.* Ottawa: National Museums of Canada.

———. 1982. *Moose-Deer Island House People: A History of the Native People of Fort Resolution.* Ottawa: National Museums of Canada.

———. 1992. "The Dynamics of a Dene Struggle for Self-Determination." *Anthropologica* 34:21–49.

———. 1998. "An Athapaskan Way of Knowing: Chipewyan Ontology." *American Ethnologist* 25 (3): 412–32.

Smith, James G. E. 1976. "Local Band Organization of the Caribou Eater Chipewyan in the Eighteenth and Early Nineteenth Centuries." *Western Canadian Journal of Anthropology* 6 (1): 72–90.

Steward, Julian. 1955. *Theory of Culture Change: The Methodology of Multilinear Evolution.* Urbana: University of Illinois Press.

Tanner, Adrian. 1979. *Bringing Home Animals: Religious Ideology and Mode of Production of the Mistassini Cree Hunters.* St. John's, Canada: Memorial University Institute of Social and Economic Research.

Tax, Sol. 1988. "Pride and Puzzlement: A Retro-Introspective Record of 60 Years of Anthropology." *Annual Review of Anthropology* 17:1–22.

Tedlock, Dennis. 1983. "The Spoken Word and the Work of Interpretation in American Indian Religion." In *The Spoken Word and the Work of Interpretation,* 233–46. Philadelphia: University of Pennsylvania Press.

Tilly, Christopher. 1994. *A Phenomenology of Landscape: Places, Paths, and Monuments.* Oxford: Berg.

Tracy, B. L., and G. H. Kramer. 2000. "A Method for Estimating Caribou Consumption by Northern Canadians." *Arctic* 53 (1): 42–52.

Usher, Peter J. 1971. *Fur Trade Posts of the Northwest Territories, 1870–1970.* Ottawa: Northern Science Research Group, Department of Indian Affairs and Northern Development.

Vansina, Jan. 2006. *Oral Tradition: A Study in Historical Methodology*. London: Aldine Transactions.

Watson, Graham, and Jean Goulet. 1992. "Gold in, Gold out: The Objectification of Dene Tha Accounts of Dreams and Visions." *Journal of Anthropological Research* 48:215–30.

Wheeler, David E. 1914. "The Elusive Musk-Ox and the Delusive Dog-Rib." Unpublished manuscript.

Wishart, Robert, and Michael Asch. n.d. "Writing Against the Grain of Materialist Orthodoxy: Richard Slobodin and the Teetl'It Gwich'in." Unpublished paper.

Zoe, John B., and Zabey Nevitt. 1998. *Opening Trails Project*. Rae-Edzo, Canada: Dogrib Division Board of Education.

Index

223

About the Author

Allice Legat is a practicing anthropologist with an interest in knowledge and culture. She has done fieldwork in Afghanistan, northern British Columbia, and Nunavut, but in 2003 the Tłįchǫ of the Northwest Territories held her heart. She continues to participate in research projects conceived by Tłįchǫ today. This book draws on her scholarship and work with the Tłįchǫ—in their home communities, in the bush, and on the tundra. Her writing makes a case for not separating intellectual from emotional, physical, and spiritual experiences. She completed her BA in archaeology in 1978 and her MA in anthropology in 1982, both at the University of Calgary; and she completed her PhD at the University of Aberdeen, Scotland, in 2007. She has coauthored many reports and papers with Tłįchǫ researchers; her most recent paper is part of the collection *Ways of Walking: Ethnography and Practice on Foot*, edited by Tim Ingold and Jo Lee Vergunst (2008).

Legat is currently interested in how the past informs present decision making and what it means to be knowledgeable, especially in an environment of industrial development and climate change. She is also interested in how practice anthropology can inform theoretical understandings in the social sciences. She has held senior management positions with nonprofit organizations and with the territorial government and as an environmental anthropologist with a renewable-resource board. She continues to assist the Tłįchǫ knowledge research division, Tłįchǫ Government. She is currently an Honorary Research Fellow with the Anthropology Department at the University of Aberdeen and has recently been appointed the Roberta Bondar Fellowship, Trent University. Yellowknife, Northwest Territories, has been her home since 1986.